A
KING
AMONG
MINISTERS

A
KING
AMONG
MINISTERS

Fifty Years in
Parliament Recalled

TOM KING

UNICORN

First published by Unicorn
an imprint of the Unicorn Publishing Group LLP, 2020
5 Newburgh Street
London W1F 7RG

www.unicornpublishing.org

Every effort has been made to trace copyright holders and to obtain their
permission for the use of copyrighted material. The publisher apologises for any
errors or omissions and would be grateful to be notified of any corrections that
should be incorporated in future reprints or editions of this book.

© Tom King, 2020

10 9 8 7 6 5 4 3 2 1

ISBN 978-1-913491-14-7

Cover design Unicorn Publishing Group
Typeset by Vivian@Bookscribe

All photographs from the author's collection unless stated otherwise.

Printed and bound by Gomer Press, Llandysul, Ceredigion

CONTENTS

INTRODUCTION

I never really intended this book to see the light of day for a wider public. I had it in mind originally as a memoir for my grandchildren, all born after I left office, and, up to now, blissfully unaware of this tangled web! However, as I remembered many of the remarkable events in which I was involved, I realised that they could well be of interest to a much wider audience and recognised how relevant some of the lessons learnt from them are to the challenges of today.

This memoir is certainly not a complete account of every step of the way, but rather the highlights of a fairly busy life, even before my arrival in Parliament, of which this happens now to be my fiftieth anniversary.

Some excellent schooling, which started under the threatening shadow of a German invasion in World War II, an adequate classical education, and a surfeit of sport led to a national service spent in part commanding, at the age of nineteen, a company on active service against the Mau Mau in the Kenyan forests. Then came Cambridge, and further African adventures.

This was an unusual preparation for a career in the printing industry and, as a young general manager of a large printing factory, I had an early immersion in difficult trade union relations, which were elsewhere doing such damage to the British economy at that time.

It was the relevance of that industrial experience that led friends and colleagues to encourage me to stand for Parliament, and after an early front-bench apprenticeship in opposition, I was ready for the major challenge of government, in which I served for Margaret Thatcher's full term as Prime Minister and briefly also with John Major. I then decided to take a break, only to be invited back shortly afterwards to be the founder Chairman of the Intelligence and Security Committee, and later founder Chairman of Excel London, the exhibition centre.

I was proud to be part of a government under Margaret Thatcher that did much to restore Britain's pride and regain respect in the eyes of the world. Of the five different offices I held in the Cabinet, the first two, Environment and Transport, were necessarily brief, but the next ones were longer – two years at Employment, culminating in the successful introduction of the requirement for secret ballots before strikes; four years in Northern Ireland, including seeing through the contentious Anglo-Irish Agreement, in which the acceptance of the principle of consent became a key ingredient in the start of the peace process, all against a background of some particularly nasty terrorist incidents; then three years in Defence, a most remarkable three years in the life of the Ministry of Defence, with the collapse of the Soviet Union and the tearing down of the Iron Curtain, followed shortly thereafter by the first Gulf War, involving the biggest deployment of British troops and heavy armour since World War II. This spectacularly successful war achieved its objectives in a remarkably short time and with minimal casualties, a model that should have provided a blueprint for any subsequent engagements, but which has sadly been ignored in both Afghanistan and Iraq to this day.

I was fortunate to be active in an exceptional period of years, with close involvement not just with Margaret Thatcher, but also with a raft of fascinating figures round the world, including an unplanned private meeting with Saddam Hussein in Baghdad, some years before the Gulf War; being hosted in Moscow by the Defence Minister, Marshal Yazov, later a leader of the conspiracy against President Gorbachev; working with Dick Cheney and 'Stormin' Norman' Schwarzkopf; Charlie Haughey and Ian Paisley; François Mitterand and Helmut Kohl; George Bush and Teddy Kennedy; King Fahd of Saudi Arabia, Iain Macleod, Alan Clark and Boris Johnson – and the crowning achievement of going viral on YouTube with my old friend Jean Trumpington, with her famous two-finger salute!

As I said, this is not an exhaustive account of every phase of an eventful life but rather seeks to present the main features and to include as well some of the lighter-hearted moments, which I hope will make for not only interesting but enjoyable reading as well.

1 FAMILY AND EARLY YEARS

In describing the history of my family, my researches have shown how ignorant I have been of it, and it has been a real pleasure to discover it now. Starting on my father's side, my great-grandfather Tom King farmed at Chadshunt in Warwickshire. It must have been quite a considerable farm, because at the time of the Great Exhibition in London, in 1851, he took a fifty-strong party of his employees and their families to visit it. He sent my grandfather, also Tom King, to Mercombe House School at Overbury in Worcestershire, a house once owned by his uncle. This was later bought by Alfred Robinson, who changed the name to Kemerton Castle, and with the wonders of Google you can see that it was quite a substantial house – which further suggested that the King family was rather better established than I ever knew. It was at the school, when he was sixteen, that Tom King met Alfred Robinson, whose father owned the paper mill at Overbury. Alfred offered Tom a job in the paper business that he and his elder brother, Elisha Smith Robinson, had started in Bristol. Tom King accepted the offer and at the age of sixteen went to Bristol to join E.S. and A. Robinson. He worked there all his life, starting in the general office in the Redcliffe Street building; he then became a sales representative and subsequently, in 1898, a director. In 1917 he became managing director and retired in 1929.

An excerpt from the Board minutes of E.S. and A. Robinson Ltd dated 28 October 1929 states:

> In accepting the resignation of Mr Thomas King, the board desires to place on record its keen appreciation of the great services he has rendered to the company. Joining as a boy in 1880 he rapidly advanced and was appointed a director in 1898, managing director in 1917. This period covers many important events in the company's history including the disastrous fire in 1903, additions to the Bedminster works, the building

of Malago and Fishponds factories, and the development and extensions of the company's business in many directions. The company owes a debt of gratitude to Mr King not only for the energy and vision shown in the direction of the business, but for his constant exercise of an influence which is, to a considerable extent, responsible for the happy relations which today exist between all ranks of the company's officers and workers. The board realises with much regret that Mr King's health prevented him continuing his active association with the business he has served so faithfully for nearly fifty years and hopes that he still has many years of happy life before him.

The reference to his influence is echoed in other material, where it is clear that he took a great interest in the welfare of all the Robinson employees, as indeed did my father when he was the director responsible for human resources. TK's influence extended not least to promoting the sports facilities that flourished with the Robinson teams. He gave real moral leadership to the business, introduced pensions for women employees, reduced the hours of work for all, and, together with my grandmother, took a particular interest outside the business in the Adult School Movement. They were strong supporters of Women's Suffrage, and he introduced profit-sharing for all employees, similar to the scheme now operated by the John Lewis Partnership.

This of course became possible because of the success of the business, which started as a paper-merchant specialising in supplying paper and bags to shopkeepers. In those days shopkeepers had reels of paper to wrap the purchases. That moved on to bags, which were handmade. The real breakthrough came with the introduction of bag-making machines, which could work at fantastic speeds to meet the growing demand. I remember, when I joined the company in 1956, seeing two machines in the bag-making factory at Malago, in Bristol, totally committed to producing brown paper bags for Woolworths, millions per order. As retailing changed with the arrival of the supermarkets, so the demand for more sophisticated packaging grew, and Robinsons grew with it into a very big packaging group, with major competitors like Metal Box and Bowater's. One major customer was its Bristol neighbour, W.D. and H.O. Wills, the country's largest cigarette and tobacco company, and Robinson's was particularly involved in the development of cigarette cards, a major feature of early cigarette packaging.

My grandmother was a Walters. Her family had been farming since the early 1800s at Cullompton in Devon, and in the 1850s there were three sons. The eldest inherited the farm, and the second, my great-grandfather, was a carpenter and builder, who moved to Bristol and built some of the fine houses in Clifton. The third had a particularly interesting life. He went into the army and served in both the Crimean War and the Indian Mutiny.

He then returned to England, left the army, and emigrated to Australia, taking his new wife and his horse with him. On arriving in Adelaide, he found his wife a place to stay and then rode out until he found somewhere that looked like Devon. That was Mount Gambier, on the South Australia/Victoria border. He secured some land, and, having collected his wife, proceeded to build a Devon farmhouse. He did it well enough for it now to be listed by Heritage Australia. From this enterprising beginning the Walters family flourished, and when my nephew, Giles Clarke, arranged to visit Mount Gambier to meet some of our relations, 300 people turned up.

Tom King having married Ada Walters, they had one son, my father Jack, although they subsequently adopted the illegitimate daughter of a doctor and a nurse. My grandmother was a strong Methodist, and the baby had been advertised in the Methodist paper. She was my aunt Molly, a very lively and artistic person.

My father gained a scholarship to Clifton College, and he was both a good classical scholar and a keen games player, good enough on the rugger field to play some games subsequently for Rosslyn Park. As well as a good cricketer, he was also a scratch golfer. He left Clifton in April 1918, joined the Army, and was sent to Officer Cadet School in Brighton on 1 May. He cannot have had too many illusions about what might await him in France, as the life expectancy for a young officer in the trenches was said to be ten days, and he had sat in the Clifton College Chapel every Sunday for the last four years, when the Headmaster would read out the names of the Old Boys who had been killed, many of whom had left only the year before and were well known to them all. The Armistice was signed just before he was due to go, but he then caught the Spanish flu. Luckily he survived the epidemic, which in the end killed more people than all those slaughtered in the war.

He left the Army and went to Cambridge, where he gained a double first in classics and English. He used to write poetry and must have been an exceptional scholar as, in 1923, at the age of twenty-four, he was offered the post of Professor of English Literature at Tokyo University. I do not know if he was tempted to take it, but he turned it down, probably because he was an only son of quite elderly parents, and Tokyo in those days was obviously a very long way away. He was very lucky that he did not go. In the 1970s I met a man who had taken up a new position in Tokyo in 1923. He told me how he and his wife had sailed into Yokohama Harbour and were met and taken to their company house. Having barely unpacked, he reported for his first day in his new office in Tokyo, which came to an abrupt halt at 11.30am when the office fell down, and he found himself caught up in the horror of the Tokyo earthquake, which destroyed the whole city. Total chaos ensued, with huge casualties and all normal life destroyed. He set out to get back to Yokohama, to find his wife, but it took him three days through raging fires and total devastation. When he eventually reached his house there was no sign of his wife, and after searching everywhere for her, he finally sought refuge on an American ship in the harbour which took him to the safety of the Philippines. It was weeks before he discovered that his wife had also survived, and had been taken by a Canadian ship to Vancouver.

I subsequently discovered that after my father turned down the offer from Tokyo University, it was taken up in 1924 by the well-known poet Edmund Blunden, which suggests that Tokyo had been remarkably quick in getting back on its feet after the disaster.

Instead of Tokyo, my father went to join E.S. and A. Robinson, and stayed there for the rest of his life, save for serving in the RAF in an administrative role in World War II.

❈ ❈ ❈

I now turn to my mother's family. She was Molly Riches, the daughter of Cecil Riches, a dentist in Cardiff, with a home in Penarth. He was one of seven children of Eliza, Mrs Charles Hurry Riches, a famous figure in Cardiff. Eliza herself had come from a large family. Her father was descended from Fergus I of Scotland, and her mother was a Thomas of Raglan, who claimed descent from Llewellyn, the last native prince of Wales. Whether it was because there were simply too many children for the parents to cope, or for whatever reason, Eliza was subsequently adopted by a Mrs Wyndham Lewis. This lady had started life as a milliner, but had subsequently married a person of considerable wealth, owning substantial property in Wales but also a house at Grosvenor Gate in Park Lane, London. After Mr Wyndham Lewis's death she married Benjamin Disraeli, and later became the Countess of Beaconsfield. The house in London became the scene of much entertaining, and she was an outstanding hostess in top political circles. Eliza grew up in this fascinating environment, and then married Charles Hurry Riches and moved to Cardiff. In later life she used to entertain her friends with stories of the social life of the Disraelis, with such guests as the Duke of Wellington, Sir Robert Peel, the Duchess of Kent (the mother of Queen Victoria), Louis-Napoléon, Marshal Soult, the Shah of Persia, Daniel O'Connell, and many, many more.

My grandmother was the daughter of Canon Bruce, the younger brother of the Marquess of Aberdare, who was descended from King David Bruce, the son of Robert the Bruce. I understand that the Bruce connection with South Wales started when they moved from Scotland at the time that James VI of Scotland became James I of England in 1603. To add to the historical interest, I discovered that her mother, Canon Bruce's second wife, was an Olivier, and a relation of the great actor Laurence Olivier. I wondered how the Oliviers came to be in Wales, but apparently they were originally Huguenots from the Basque Pyrenees near Pau and, to avoid religious persecution, had fled from France, possibly first to Holland and then to England, as in 1688 an Olivier was chaplain to William of Orange.

The Riches family have certainly left their mark in a number of ways, with, more recently, a distinguished general and the captain of Glamorgan County Cricket Club. My favourite is my great-great-uncle, T. Hurry Riches, who was clearly an outstanding engineer and a brilliant teacher. I remember that when I was Secretary of State for Transport I went to make a speech at the Institution of Mechanical Engineers in Great George Street, by Parliament Square. My private secretary noticed the list of previous presidents. She thought that the name Hurry Riches was particularly apt, and was amused to find that he was my great-great-uncle.

I did a bit more research and discovered that at the age of twenty-seven he became the youngest ever superintendent of the Taff Vale Railway. He himself designed the motor trains that were a very important feature of the Taff Vale service. He was frequently consulted on the latest scientific advances, and on one occasion, when interviewed on the future development of British locomotives, he said that electric power would come but that it should be generated by means of the locomotive carrying a steam engine, which would produce enough power to haul the train. Having recently watched the laborious process of erecting overhead electric lines on the Great Western Railway, as these lines move to electric power I find myself wondering whether his idea could have been developed further, and thinking how much time could have been saved.

He held the position of superintendent for nearly forty years, and his fame was such that he became president of the Institution of Mechanical Engineers, in 1907 and again in 1908, having been previously elected as the youngest member of the Council. He was also chairman of the technical education committee of Cardiff Council, and there he gave enormous practical advice to hundreds of students, who subsequently showed their loyalty and respect by keeping him posted about any new development from wherever they were in the world. It was said that he was a student to the last, and that his great hobby was to inspire the young men of the city to seek to succeed in life, and to leave the world better than they found it in whatever spheres they were working. His addresses to the students were regarded as an admirable compendium of instructive facts and sympathetic advice – that sounds a very good combination.

My mother was the third of four sisters. I know little about their early life, except their holidays – because they used to come every year to what was later to become part of my constituency. I found out that they used to travel by steamer from Penarth to Minehead. There they would be met by a horse and cart, on which they loaded their luggage, and they would walk to a cottage they rented in Wootton Courtenay, on the edge of Exmoor. I do recall one story that clearly demonstrated the incredible change in means of transport during the twentieth century. In 1910 my aunt, Bobby, suddenly got appendicitis, and the doctor was needed urgently. The neighbouring farmer quickly saddled up his horse and galloped into Dunster. He woke the doctor, who in turn saddled up his horse and galloped back with him to

Wootton Courtenay, using the means of transport that had been unchanged in country areas for a thousand years. Bobby lived to a good age, and shortly before she died she flew by Concorde to Australia to visit her son and his family, who had emigrated there.

But things changed very rapidly with the onset of World War I, and this was illustrated very clearly by a photograph that I have of my mother dressed in auxiliary uniform, standing by a large army car, when she was the driver of the pilot car on the occasion of the visit by the Prince of Wales, later Edward VIII, to South Wales. The picture came from a Cardiff newspaper in March 1918, when she would have been barely eighteen, and there could not have been many girl drivers at that time. What it also confirmed is that with the huge death toll of men in the war, girls were taking over many of the jobs previously done by men.

❈ ❈ ❈

My father started work with Robinson's in Bristol, but quite soon he was appointed area sales manager for Scotland, based in Glasgow. My father and mother had met before he had gone to Scotland. They married in 1928 and lived in Pollokshields until 1934. They made many good friends and my father certainly made the most of life there, becoming a scratch golfer and playing bridge for Scotland. However, it was the time of the recession nationally, and Glasgow was hit particularly hard. My mother worked as a volunteer in the Gorbals, and she never forgot the impact of the terrible poverty, with forty people sharing one tap in the tenement blocks in that most deprived part of Glasgow, and with the children in rags.

In 1932 my sister, Stella, usually known as Tess, was born and I followed one year later. In 1934 my father returned to Bristol as the director in charge of the colour-printing factory at Bedminster. The family came to live initially at Flax Bourton, just outside Bristol, our home until the war, when my father joined the RAF. In 1940 my mother rented a holiday bungalow at Mortehoe in North Devon, and while we were there the Germans started bombing Bristol. Although our home was a few miles outside the city, a large lighting system was installed on a nearby hill, and was switched on when the German bombers were coming, in the hope of fooling them that this was Bristol and its docks. When the bombing started, my aunt, who was in Bristol, suggested to my mother that we stay in North Devon and keep the bungalow that we had rented for the holiday.

At that time there was a real fear of a German invasion, and a number of schools in Kent and Sussex decided to move to a safer place. The first of these was a girls' school called Bartrum Gables, from Broadstairs in Kent, right on the invasion coast. They found the Watersmeet Hotel in Woolacombe, a large hotel with understandably little business at that time, and moved the whole school there. As luck would have it, it was just down the hill from our bungalow and so Tess joined them. The headmistress said that I could join too, and for one term I was the only boy in this girls' school. It was only one term because almost immediately another school arrived, this one for boys, St Michael's from Uckfield in Sussex, which took over Tawstock Court, near Barnstaple, the substantial home of the Wrey family. My luck was that St Michael's had an outstanding new young Headmaster, Cecil Cook, and was an excellent school. By modern standards it was very small, with only seventy pupils, but that made his impact all the greater. That was borne out for me in a photograph taken forty years later in Northern Ireland with Ian Stewart, the Minister of State, Air Vice-Marshal David Brook, Air Officer Scotland and Northern Ireland, and myself as Secretary of State, all contemporaries from this tiny school.

I was extremely lucky, in this oasis of peace in the North Devon countryside, to have such a good school, and it nearly never happened. With the fear of invasion, arrangements were being made for many children to go to Canada. My mother had in fact arranged for Tess and me to go and we had already acquired lots of warm clothes for the Canadian winter. Three times the sailing was cancelled, and then, fortunately, my mother decided to drop the idea.

At St Michael's I had started to learn Latin and Greek with a delightful elderly master. I found one of his reports on me: 'Considering the amount of time spent (a) chewing his pen, (b) staring out of the window, (c) doing (a) and (b) at the same time, the exam results were surprisingly good!' With that encouraging endorsement I went to Rugby School. An Old Rugbeian friend had recommended to my father that I should go to Sheriff House, which had an outstanding housemaster. Unfortunately, by the time I arrived, he had suddenly died and his replacement, while he had a reputation as a demanding but very effective teacher, was quite unsuited to the wider role of housemaster. However, in my case this was more than compensated by the succession of exceptional teachers that I enjoyed in my various forms. I continued my Latin and Greek with them at Rugby, starting with a delightful man, James Hunt, who later rose to the position of Second Master and combined his classic teaching with producing the school play, in which I briefly appeared as an English soldier in Shaw's *St Joan*.

I moved up a form, where my master was David Ashcroft, who went on to become Headmaster of Cheltenham College; I then joined the lower sixth form, called the Lower Bench, whose master was Michael McCrum. He arrived at Rugby with a first-class degree from Corpus Christi College, Cambridge, a degree course that had been interrupted by a couple of years' service in the Royal Navy. He was an outstanding teacher, as his subsequent career so clearly confirmed. Having married Christine fforde, the Headmaster's daughter, he was invited to return to Corpus Christi as the youngest senior tutor in any college. After eleven years in that role, he became Headmaster of Tonbridge School for a further eight years, and the climax of his career was as Headmaster of Eton for the next ten years, before returning to Corpus as Master. It was an outstanding career, and I was extremely lucky to be taught by him in my last years at Rugby.

I have many humorous memories of Rugby, two in particular. There was a tradition that the Head of House would write brief profiles of the other Sixth Form prefects in the House, and his deputy would write one of him. One year it was memorably said of the current holder, 'He lived in a world of his own, in which he had great influence,' and we have all met others that well fit that description!

Once we had a serious outbreak of athlete's foot in the school, against which the Headmaster launched a major campaign. This couldn't pass unnoticed in the *New Rugbeian*, a literary magazine run by the boys, in a parody of *Jerusalem*:

> *And did those feet in ancient time*
> *Suffer from foot rot worse than ours,*
> *And was that soft and healing balm*

On mantelpieces found in jars?
I will not cease by day or night,
I'll powder yet through cold or heat,
Till we have brought back cleanliness
To Rugby's green and rotting feet.

The particular feature of Rugby was the wide range of activities in which the boys (and in those days it was only boys) could take part. Of course, games were extremely popular, but many other activities flourished as well. One friend of mine from Sheriff went on to teach at Harrow School, and a particular difference that he noticed was that at Harrow then it was only the games players who were respected as the real stars by other boys, whereas at Rugby, if you were a good artist or a musician or had taken the lead in the school play, those achievements were also respected. I plead guilty to the charge that games certainly were my greatest interest, and I was lucky enough to be for two years in the 1st XI for Cricket, in the Rugger XV, and also Captain of Fives, Rugby Fives of course, a game that Rugby had invented. On the rugby field, I had the doubtful privilege in the Schools seven-a-side competition at Rosslyn Park of having to balance one side of the Rugby three-man scrum against the three-stone heavier Ewen Fergusson, a gigantic figure who went on to play for Scotland. We happily met many times again later, in less physically demanding circumstances, in his distinguished career in the Foreign Office, which he ended as an outstanding ambassador in Paris.

My cricket career was commemorated elsewhere in a question in the sports section of the game 'Trivial Pursuits', with the question 'Which Cabinet Minister opened the batting at Lords?' I fear very few would have got that right, unless they happened to know that the high spot of the season for Rugby was their game at Lords against Marlborough, and some smart question-setter had spotted that and linked me to it. A further item appeared in Wisden, the great annual record of all things cricket. As Secretary of State for Northern Ireland, I used to have regular police protection wherever I went. On one occasion in my constituency, in the village of Holford, I was asked to play in a team against the village, which was celebrating its centenary. Unfortunately there was some problem over the umpires, and two of my policemen volunteered to stand in. Wisden discovered this, and reported that it was the first occasion ever in a match where both umpires were armed!

Another enjoyable activity was the Rugby School Jazz Band, founded by a good friend of mine, Tom Lane. An excellent trumpeter, he later went on to start a band, the Red Hot Chillies, which became very popular in the Lincolnshire area where he farmed. He recruited me, with my very limited skills, to pluck the double bass as a noisy member of the rhythm section, and I found my batting gloves the ideal protection for my tender hands. Humphrey Lyttelton was our inspiration, and we made a tremendous noise.

Last of the Rugby memories was the Sheriff House play where I had the role of the bumbling Mayor in Gogol's *The Government Inspector*. Three years later, I found myself playing it again at Cambridge, when Emmanuel College chose it. It would be nice to claim that my reappearance in the part was by overwhelming popular request, but sadly it was pure chance!

As my time at Rugby was drawing to an end, the question of National Service arose, which was then compulsory for men. You were required to serve for eighteen months, and so the plan was that I would sit the scholarship exam for Emmanuel College in October, leave Rugby in December, do my eighteen months' service and go up to Cambridge in October 1953. However, the Korean War and other dramas had put extra pressure on the manning levels in the services, and so National Service was increased to two years. This meant that if I stayed to take the scholarship exam in October and left in December I would lose a year and not go up to Cambridge until 1954. It was then agreed that to avoid this I would leave at the end of the summer term in 1951 without staying to take the exam. I am suitably embarrassed now to say what happened next. As a former Emmanuel undergraduate, my father knew the Master of Emmanuel well, as he had been the senior tutor. My father wrote to the Master and told him that I could not now take the scholarship exam but that he still hoped I could come to Emmanuel. The Master, having heard that I was going to take the exam, and under the serious illusion that I must be a real chip off the undoubtedly impressive scholarship block that was my father, said what a disappointment it must be for me not to be able to sit it, but that I would certainly have a place at Emmanuel after my National Service. I don't think I would ever have got the scholarship, and yet, without any exam or interview, I had a place at Emmanuel.

2 NATIONAL SERVICE, AFRICA, CAMBRIDGE AND FIRST JOB

For my National Service, I had applied to join the Somerset Light Infantry, the local regiment. I therefore started by reporting to the Jellalabad Barracks in Taunton. Our group was quickly transferred to the Light Infantry Training Depot at Bordon in Hampshire. There we spent eight weeks being knocked into shape by some very tough sergeants and corporals, trying their best to make soldiers out of some pretty unlikely material. From there, the depot moved to Strensall in Yorkshire, where I was promoted to a leadership platoon. I went next to Eaton Hall, where all the National Service infantry officers were trained, and four months later, as a second lieutenant in the Somerset Light Infantry, I was ready to join the regiment.

However, there was a problem. At that time the Somersets were in Malaya, on active service against the communist insurgency. They were due back in three months' time, but I would have to do a jungle training course before I could join them. Because this would leave too little time before they returned from Malaya, I was told that I would be attached to another regiment in Germany, to await their arrival there.

While I was digesting this news, a fellow officer cadet, Charles Thatcher, suggested that there was an alternative option, that you could join the King's African Rifles, the colonial regiment whose battalions were based in British colonies in East Africa, with British officers and African troops. His father had been a district commissioner in Nyasaland, so he was keen to return to Africa and encouraged me to go as well. As it happened I had an aunt, my mother's youngest sister, who had gone to Kenya in the 1920s and married a white hunter. The lure of a few safaris and the excitement of Africa had obvious attractions over the reputed boredom of serving in Germany, and I jumped at the idea. As soon as we passed out at Eaton Hall as newly commissioned second lieutenants, it was full speed ahead to get our tropical kit and be ready to sail. And sail it was on His Majesty's Troopship *Empire Ken* for our stately month-long voyage to Mombasa. Gibraltar – Alexandria – Suez Canal – Port Sudan – Aden – Mombasa: one whole month of my year's commission spent sailing.

Once arrived at Mombasa, after a brief but delightful stop at the army Nyali Beach and Transit Camp (now I believe a popular holiday resort) it was off to join my new regiment, the Twenty-Sixth KAR, the Tanganyika battalion based in Dar-es-Salaam. Although Dar was only some 200 miles south of Mombasa there was no road down the coast, and getting there involved a night sleeper train going inland to Arusha, a further train journey to Korogwe, followed by a 200-mile road trip to Morogoro, and then another night sleeper down to Dar.

One advantage of the leisurely troopship journey from England was the chance to work on my Swahili. Although there are many different tribal languages, Swahili, spoken by the coast tribes, was the common language, having been spread through East Africa by the Arab slave traders, and it was used by the KAR. I was very fortunate that on the same troopship and bound for the same battalion was a major, Colin Dees, and his family. Colin had just finished as a company commander at Eaton Hall, having previously served in the KAR, and spoke fluent Swahili. I subsequently became the second lieutenant in the company he commanded, and was enormously grateful to serve under somebody who was an excellent soldier, a fund of knowledge about the KAR, and great fun as well.

The first requirement for a new officer joining the battalion was to test his Swahili. The Colonel's technique could best be described as 'total immersion'. A platoon of askaris, hand-picked for their total ignorance of English, was assembled. I was instructed to take them on a three-day patrol in the bush. Off we set, and amazingly my halting Swahili and some vivid hand signals combined to get us through and almost back safely to base. The only moment I remember when my command failed was on one of the evenings when I had chosen our campsite for the night. I marched confidently into the middle of a suitably large grassed area, followed by my platoon. I stopped in the middle and was just giving the order to pitch the tents when a shout went up from one askari, and the whole platoon turned and ran headlong back to the road. I then heard the shout of '*mwaka*', and realised that I had marched right into a field full of snakes – the askaris had no intention of staying there!

Having survived my initiation without any other untoward events, I settled down into the normal life of a KAR regiment. Because of the climate, we worked from 6am to 2pm and then adjourned to the officers' mess for lunch. One particular regimental tradition was the Wednesday curry lunch, with no less than thirty-five side dishes to accompany it. The Mess President, who had previously served with an Indian regiment, saw it as his personal responsibility to maintain the tradition, and used to spend the whole of his Wednesday morning in the search for all possible ingredients for the dishes from the markets in Dar.

The young officers were all billeted in a building next to the officers' mess, which was overshadowed by a massive mango tree. After the Wednesday feast on a hot afternoon, siesta time was pretty popular, and as we snoozed on our beds, there would suddenly be a thud outside, and to an echoing cry of '*embe*', a rush of naked officers would race out to seize the very juicy fallen mango.

The Ethiopian and Burma campaigns of World War II had shown the quality of the KAR, and the great endurance of the askaris. They were good fighters and excellent peacetime soldiers. One thing they particularly enjoyed was their drill and they took real pride in their appearance on any ceremonial parades. The washing, starching and pressing of their khaki drill, as well as the normal 'bulling' of boots, polishing of badges, *et cetera*, took up a great deal of their off-duty time but was willingly done.

In general, the conduct of regimental work was not dissimilar to that in any British regiment, but one significant difference was the treatment of minor offences. A particular problem was the smoking of *bhang* or hashish, which was strictly forbidden. The penalty for this was six strikes with the *kiboko*, a rhino-hide whip. The particular feature of this punishment was that it administered not in some closed guardroom, but rather in front of the whole battalion on parade. The battalion would march on to the parade ground and form up in a hollow square. The culprit would be marched out to the middle, in his uniform but without his belt, hat, or rifle. The African regimental sergeant major would then ask the Colonel for permission to administer the punishment. He would march to the centre where the intended recipient lay face down on the ground. He would whip him three times from one side, then march smartly round to the other side and repeat the procedure. On completion of the punishment the soldier was handed back his belt, his hat, and his rifle and ordered to fall back into the ranks. The whole battalion marched back to the barracks, with the miscreant back in the body of the regiment, his penalty having been discharged and with no further record against him.

There was another offence that was peculiar to the battalion. It was a fundamental principle throughout the KAR that there should not be too great a concentration of any particular tribe in a section or platoon, but tribes would be mixed. There was one tribe, the Watende, whose particular feature was to distend their earlobes so that they hung down in a loop. On parade they were not allowed to let them hang and they had to be looped over their ears. However, at night, before sleeping, they let them down and if there were two Watende in adjoining beds, a favourite trick of askaris from other tribes was to tie a piece of cotton from the lobe of one askari to the lobe of another and then kick one of them! Very unfriendly and definitely punishable with the *kiboko*.

This leisurely period of colonial soldiering was all too brief. Barely a month after my arrival, the news came from Kenya of the Mau Mau emergency, with an urgent call for reinforcements to support the Kenyan KAR battalions. We were due to take over garrison duties in Mauritius, so it was decided to split the battalion, with two companies going to Kenya and the rest to Mauritius. My company stayed with the battalion, and so after all too brief a stay it was back on another troopship. Any idea of a gentle cruise through the Indian Ocean quickly disappeared as we sailed right through the most terrifying cyclone, which undid us all.

Mauritius itself was a delight, with much of its coastline and beaches quite unspoilt – this was long before the tourist boom that has now enveloped it. Indeed, the very first cross-Pacific air route to Mauritius was opened while we were there, when Air France launched a new service from Sydney to Johannesburg via the Cocos Islands and Mauritius. Part of their advertising of this exciting new route made great play with the fact that the stretch between the Cocos Islands and Mauritius was the longest flight anywhere in the world without sight of land. On the inaugural flight, one woman passenger became so overwrought at this news that the stewards had great difficulty in controlling her, and finally resorted to locking her in the only toilet. This had unfortunate consequences for the rest of the passengers!

The KAR provided the garrison for Mauritius, while the locally recruited Mauritian Guards served in the Canal zone in Egypt. A friend of mine at Eaton Hall, wondering what regiment he should try to join, discovered the existence of the Mauritian Guards and was attracted by the idea that this must be a crack colonial regiment. Just in time he discovered that the largely Creole regiment was hardly a frontline unit, but undertook less glamorous though essential tasks such as road-building, latrine digging and other pioneer tasks in Egypt.

The population of Mauritius was largely Creole, a mixture of the French immigrants who had come to plant sugar during the pre-Napoleonic period, when it was known as the Île de Maurice, and the large number of Indian workers who had been imported to work in the sugar plantations. Successive governors had expressed some concern about the stability of the population and that was the reason for a KAR garrison.

Our duties included ceremonial ones such as the opening of the new session of LegCo, the Parliament, by the Governor. Our company and regimental band provided the guard of honour to greet the Governor's arrival and to salute him on his departure. Our barracks, on a high area of the island, at Vacoas, were pleasantly cool. LegCo was in Port Louis, at sea level, and noticeably warmer. This posed the usual challenges for soldiers standing on parade for a long stretch in the heat, but our askaris coped very well, and the drill was as good as anything at the Trooping the Colour on Horse Guards Parade in London. The particular problem was for officers. For this parade officers carried swords, and when the company was standing at ease, waiting for the Governor to reappear, they rested their swords point down on the road. The trouble was that the tarmac became soft in the heat, so the trick was not to rest your sword on the road but in the welt of your boot. One officer forgot this, and when he stood to attention and raised his sword, a good piece of tarmac came with it. He had to march off with it, unable to shake it off.

We stayed in Mauritius for three months and then swapped with the other two companies that had gone to Kenya, and thus found ourselves on active service against the Mau Mau.

The Mau Mau uprising involved the Kikuyu tribe in particular and was concentrated in the Rift Valley, the Aberdare Mountains and Mount Kenya. Our company was based in Nyeri, at Brigade HQ, and my platoon took over a forward base in the Kikuyu reserve, just behind the forest line of the Aberdares, where many of the Mau Mau – at that time estimated at some 12,000 – were based. Our job was to give support to the local loyal Kikuyu headmen, and to tackle the Mau Mau gangs in the forest. Our base was on one of the spines running down from the Aberdares, with steep river valleys on either side. Our huts were surrounded by a deep, wide trench, at the bottom of which was a mass of sharpened stakes and coils of barbed wire, a most effective obstacle against any night-time intruders. From there we patrolled by day and set ambushes at night in the forest. At that time there was little intelligence on the Mau Mau, whose efforts were concentrated on attacking the farms of European settlers, intimidating their workers, and killing loyal Kikuyu headmen opposed to them. Our presence undoubtedly boosted the morale of loyal Kikuyu, who took part in many of our patrols, and guided us to suitable spots for our night ambushes on the forest paths. Sadly, we were not always able to protect the loyalists. One night we learned too late of an attack on a headman's home. As we rushed to protect him, we saw the flames soaring into the sky and found that he and his family had been burnt to death in their house by a Mau Mau gang, who had also killed those who had tried to escape the burning house.

These were the early and most dangerous days of Operation Jock Scott, the codename for the state of emergency established to confront the Mau Mau threat. As well as the thousands of them in the forests, they also had support lines throughout the Kikuyu Reserve, reaching as far as Nairobi. My own base area included Treetops, the famous tree-house for watching big game. It happened to be the home area of Dedan Kimathi, a particularly violent Mau Mau gang leader who had established his base there. We did have some limited success against smaller gangs, but we did not get close to Kimathi. That took another four years and the creation of pseudo-gangs of converted former Mau Mau, led by that remarkable Kenyan policeman and fluent Kikuyu speaker Ian Henderson GM, to finally capture him.

Two years later Henderson told the full story of this remarkable exploit in *The Hunt for Dedan Kimathi*, which he wrote with Philip Goodhart, the *Daily Telegraph* Africa correspondent at the time. Philip subsequently became an MP and was a very good friend and colleague for many years. Their book brings out vividly the extraordinary feel of the Aberdare Forest, where I had spent so much time in night patrols and ambushes.

Much of our work was physically and mentally pretty demanding, but we did get an occasional break, when we would descend on Nyeri for a few hours' relaxation. I would leave a skeleton guard for our base and then drive to Nyeri in our two three-ton lorries with the remainder of the platoon. In an echo of a Wild West film, we would hitch our waggons to the rail outside the Indian general store of Osman Alu, and I would buy supplies for the next couple of weeks and load them on to the lorries. Meanwhile the askaris had time off for rest and relaxation, with strict orders to be back by 5pm, so that we could return to our base in daylight. Once, come the appointed time, it was clear that we were well short of the full number, and a search party was formed. What was also immediately clear was that the search party, under my command but led by an African sergeant major and two corporals, knew exactly where to go. The red-light district of Nyeri seemed to cover a considerable area of the town. As we moved from hut to hut with our Swahili greeting of *hodi* ('hello') and the response of *karibu* ('welcome'), it was clear that the local ladies had enjoyed exceptional trade with the arrival of my platoon. In hut after hut we extracted askaris until we were at last at full strength, and could return to base fully refreshed in every sense!

After we had been some months on the Aberdares, the activities of another Mau Mau leader, under the intriguing name of General China, were causing some concern. He was operating on the other side of Nyeri in the forests on the slopes of Mount Kenya. My platoon joined the rest of the company when we moved to a farm on the foothills. In contrast to the unimproved nature of the Kikuyu reserve, this farm was a perfect example of how early settlers had transformed the land. In place of scrub and minimal grazing, well fenced and fertile fields sustained good-quality cattle, which they proudly exhibited at the Nairobi agricultural show. Their house was a charming ranch-style single-storey building, looking out over a well-kept lawn and lovely herbaceous borders, as English as could be.

From our base on this farm we became involved in a number of joint operations with other KAR companies. These consisted of major sweeps over very large areas, with a line of stops to catch any escaping terrorists. Over the right terrain these sweeps could be very effective, but in the forests of Mount Kenya and the Aberdares there was one particular problem, namely the abundance of big game. On our silent patrols in the forest, our presence was often betrayed by the shrieks of colonies of Colobus monkeys suddenly jumping from tree to tree high up in the canopy. A sudden disturbance in front could well be a herd of buffalo or waterbuck. While the presence of hitherto undisturbed game indicated that no terrorists were likely to be anywhere close, it obviously in turn betrayed our presence, and coping with this additional problem was a constant challenge. This was particularly difficult for new officers who had had no previous experience of the forest, as a new major, who had just taken over command of our sister company in 26 KAR, soon found out. We were all engaged in a sweep operation on Mount Kenya, and he was leading his group of askaris through the forest. They came to a particularly large mass of thorn-bushes. The askaris showed no great enthusiasm for investigating this large obstacle, so the Major decided to demonstrate the importance of checking everywhere and proceeded to crawl under the thorn branches into the middle of the clump. Unfortunately it was not a terrorist hideout, but the resting place of a rather large rhino. The animal was not at all pleased to be so rudely disturbed, and charged at the unfortunate Major, tossing him with his horn. Although badly injured, he was luckily not killed, almost certainly because the rhino had a broken horn.

Our operations included companies from other KAR battalions. One of these was the company of 5 KAR, a Kenyan battalion. Its company commander had previously served with the KAR in Burma and had developed a particular admiration for the qualities of Somalis as soldiers. He had managed to break the KAR's cardinal rule of mixing the tribes right through a company down to platoons and sections, by creating an overwhelmingly Somali company. This had disastrous consequences in the campaign against the Mau Mau, who were overwhelmingly Kikuyu, a tribe that the Somalis particularly hated. The fact that the majority of Kikuyu were not involved with the Mau Mau terrorists was readily ignored by the Somali askaris, who left a trail of devastation, including rape, behind them. This was very damaging to the KAR's reputation, and led, rightly, to the court martial of the company commander and the disbanding of the company.

After a brief stay at this farm, we moved further up the slopes of Mount Kenya to another farm. Soon after our arrival, my company commander, Colin Dees, developed jaundice and went into hospital, leaving me as acting company commander. The company at that time was on its own in its forest base, the Colonel was with the rest of the battalion in Mauritius, and I answered direct to the Brigadier, who was more than fully occupied with all his many responsibilities. Thus I found myself, aged nineteen, a National Service officer, in command of a company of three Kenyan Regiment sergeants and 120 askaris on active service. I remember, many years later, reading an article by the management guru Peter Drucker, who was asked what in his opinion was the best-run organisation or company. In those days IBM or Unilever or General Motors might have seemed likely choices, but he actually selected the British Indian Civil Service. His particular reason for choosing this was the way in which they gave enormous responsibility to very young people in the challenges they faced in the management of the vast subcontinent. I don't know what Peter Drucker would have made of my position, but it was certainly an extraordinary experience. It was a great responsibility, and I am glad to say that we had no serious disasters in my time, but were able to continue to play our part in protecting the local population, and combating the terrorists in our area.

September finally came, and my two-year service drew to a close. No Troopship *Empire Ken* this time, as air trooping had started, and we flew home, I to return to Jellalabad Barracks in Taunton, transfer to the TA, and go off to Cambridge as a new undergraduate.

One further pleasure of serving in Kenya was the prospect of seeing my aunt, Jane Stanton. I had thought that my service in East Africa would have allowed for one or two relaxed safaris, but the Mau Mau emergency prevented that. I did see my aunt and uncle briefly in Nairobi but I was not able at that time to visit their well-known camp, Bushwhackers, close to the Tsavo National Park. One feature of Bushwhackers was a huge stockade, much used by film-makers who wanted good pictures of charging animals without the risk of dead film crews. The courage of Clark Gable and Ava Gardner in the face of a charging rhino, in the famous 1953 film *Mogambo*, owed everything to the Bushwhackers stockade.

✽ ✽ ✽

After a brief stay at home it was off to Cambridge, to my father's old college, Emmanuel, and back to studies. What was immediately apparent was the difference between the new undergraduates who had come straight from school and those who had spent the last two years on National Service. I had certainly had my share of interest and excitement during my time with the KAR, but it did not compare with other friends whose National Service had found them in Korea. There they had faced a full-scale war, in trenches, dug in at night, facing screaming charges of Chinese soldiers coming at them with fixed bayonets, an experience that not all of them survived. The relief of returning safely home was celebrated vigorously in the pubs of Cambridge, and it was some time before they settled down.

I had decided to continue with classics for my first two years, and I immediately had a problem trying to remember any Latin and Greek. I could conjugate the verbs, but the basic words were wrong, and I realised that I was muddling them up with Swahili words. This suitably confused my erudite supervisor, but fortunately I got back on-stream, and successfully completed Part One after two years. I then switched to one year on Archaeology and Anthropology, where my knowledge of Africa had a real relevance, and it was a most interesting course. I should perhaps confess that the great attraction of Cambridge was all those other activities that I remember best: rugger, hockey, cricket, and even a bit of rowing, including one series of Cambridge bumps in one crew of casual rowers for which I was the heaviest cox. I was also able to recreate my role as the Mayor in Gogol's *Government Inspector* in the Emmanuel College play. Having been quite successful at school in sport, I soon realised how much tougher the competition was at Cambridge. I remember particularly that for cricket, I was offered a Freshman's Trial, the opportunity for new undergraduates to be considered for the Cambridge teams. When my turn came to bat I found I was facing Gamini Goonesena, probably the best spin bowler in the country at that time and already playing first-class cricket for Nottinghamshire, later to become an outstanding Test cricketer. Unsurprisingly against such talented opposition, my Trial innings was extremely short!

One sport that I took up for the first time was skiing. Every December the Oxford and Cambridge ski clubs met in the Alps for an annual race. The first year for me was at Sestriere in Italy, the next year at Zurs in Austria, and finally for the last year back to Sestriere. They were wonderful parties and a great opportunity for me to learn to ski, the start of many happy skiing years. In my third year I reached the dizzy heights of *Times* ski correspondent to report on the races. I had to ring in my report to the paper in London, and they were amused to hear that I was doing it from my bed, as I had broken my leg. I remember that time for another reason. While we were in Sestriere, an Italian crew were filming an episode of Tolstoy's *War and Peace*. This was the retreat of Napoleon's army in the snow from Moscow, as the bedraggled soldiers dragged their guns and other equipment with them, their parts being played by a large number of Italian soldiers. One day a bunch of undergraduates pinched one of the cannons and took it into the Torre hotel where they were staying. The local *carabinieri* spotted this and chased after them. The hotel was a hollow tower, sixteen storeys high, with all the bedrooms facing outwards, and a spiral ramp up the inside. When the *carabinieri* entered the hotel they could see the cannon being carried up the ramp some three floors above and followed it up, knowing that they had now trapped the culprits. They followed them up all sixteen floors, only to discover when they reached the top that the gun had disappeared. They searched all the bedrooms on the way down, but never found it. It subsequently transpired that in one room they were met by a semi-naked student, greatly embarrassed, having been caught in the middle of a private engagement with his girlfriend. The *carabinieri* showed proper understanding of his embarrassment, immediately apologised and withdrew, not realising that the figure hidden under the bed-sheet was actually the cannon!

Cambridge at that time was buzzing with talent – not just sport, but theatre, music and entertainment all flourished. The Cambridge Footlights, a long-established group of outstanding entertainers, included Jonathan Miller and Peter Cook, and I well remember organising the cabaret for the Emmanuel May Ball, with Jonathan Miller and Rory McEwen, a wonderful young folk and blues singer who soon made his name on television.

At the end of our second year four of us who had all served in the KAR decided to drive out to Kenya, take jobs for a couple of months to pay for our journey, and be back in time for the start of the next year in October. We managed to get hold of an old Ford army staff car, which had big bulbous tyres and was very suitable for desert crossing. However, we then received the unfortunate news that, during high summer in July, the Sahara was closed and we would have to go round by the coast. That made it a rather longer journey, but there was no alternative, and off we set. Our passage through France and Spain was blissfully uneventful, and the ferry from Gibraltar to Tangier landed us safely in Africa. We drove to Agadir on the coast, and found a coastal freighter to take us as deck cargo to Dakar in Senegal, bypassing the Sahara. From there we drove inland via Bamako in Mali, Ouagadougou in Upper Volta, Niamey in Niger, and on to Kano in Nigeria. What with having to take the long way round, plus a couple of breakdowns, we had lost a lot of time, so we hastened south through Nigeria via Kaduna and Enugu, where we turned left for the Cameroons. When we got to Ikom, close to the border, our next stop was to be Mamfe in the British Cameroons, from where we would climb some 100 miles to the hill-station of Bamenda. We had planned to spend the night in Ikom, but we were warned that the road from Mamfe to Bamenda was very narrow and one way only, up on Mondays, Wednesdays and Fridays, down on Tuesdays, Thursdays and Saturdays. I don't remember what happened on Sundays, except possibly to hope and pray! Unless we got to Mamfe the next morning, we would lose a whole day waiting for the next 'up' day. We therefore decided to drive through the night on what turned out to be the worst road we had been on. We were well into our journey when we became completely bogged down in deep ruts. We had with us a couple of large steel perforated planks (of a kind that were used by the RAF for temporary landing strips), which could get wheels out of these sorts of ruts. We needed to see how far down the car was stuck, but it was pitch dark and by then none of our torches worked. The only light we had was a small oil lamp, which we lit, and I went round the back of the car to check the situation. We had not realised that the petrol tank had got damaged and had leaked petrol. Suddenly the flame from the lamp ignited the petrol, which had run right under the car. We tried to put it out and rescue what we could of our baggage, but then the fire took hold and our car was destroyed.

By now we were exhausted and no doubt in a state of shock, so we simply lay down with a tarpaulin and fell fast asleep. The next thing I remember was a lot of chattering voices, with a group of African workers looking down at us and wondering what on earth had happened. They had had to get off their bus, as the remains of our car were completely blocking the narrow road, and having established that we were not corpses, they lent a hand to heave it off the track.

I don't remember how we somehow made it to Mamfe, but there we were very fortunate to find an excellent British colonial officer who helped us decide what to do next. Only two of us still had our passports, while the other two had to return to Lagos to get new ones. Having passports meant that two of us could still try to reach Nairobi and this, we thought, could be done by hitchhiking most of the way. We first had to go down to Douala and fly to Bangui, on a branch of the Congo river, the frontier of what was then the Belgian Congo. We spent one night in a guest-house and next morning hitched a lift across the river in a dug-out canoe.

We had been told there would be delivery lorries bringing supplies for stores in the north of the Congo. On the western side of the countries the lorries came up from Brazzaville, on the eastern side from what was then Stanleyville, now Kisangani. This proved exactly right, as the lorries moved from town to town, usually 100 miles or so apart, and were normally very willing to help an unusual cargo of two British students. The only real problem was that when we got to the last town serviced from Brazzaville, we found that there was simply no real traffic between it and the furthest town serviced from Stanleyville, 150 miles away. It took us three days sitting by the roadside before we found a lorry going to this next town. It wasn't an all-day vigil, as they left only in the morning, to reach the next town before dark, and there was virtually nothing in between. Our luck on this occasion was that there was a Belgian Mission handy, which kindly gave us shelter for those nights.

Once we were on the Stanleyville line, things moved quite swiftly and we rapidly went on from there to Uganda, reaching Kampala where we thankfully took the train and reached Nairobi just in time, after a very brief pause, to catch a plane and return to Cambridge for our final year!

At the end of that final year, I drove with three other friends through

Yugoslavia, and on our journey we stopped in a small town called Postonya, famous for the amazing caves that were a great tourist attraction. After we had visited them we spent a little time in the town and were just walking down the road when suddenly a whole lot of police appeared, everybody was pushed to the side, and the road was cleared. We stood there wondering what was happening, when a great convoy of cars came through. There were a lot of escort cars and then in the middle of the convoy we saw the reason for all the activity. In that car were not only President Tito but also Prime Minister Nehru and President Nasser. It was July 1956, two months before President Nasser seized the Suez Canal, and what we were witnessing without realising it was the start of the Non-Aligned movement. Whether or not President Nasser told Tito and Nehru of his plans, I don't think that either of them would have wanted to discourage him!

That was the end of Cambridge and my travels, and I started with E.S. and A. Robinson, where both my grandfather and my father had worked. It was one of the largest printing and packaging groups in the country, with a number of factories in Bristol as well as London and Scotland, and overseas as well. I was first posted to the carton factory in Fishponds in Bristol, initially for a spell of familiarisation with the various processes of carton-making and then in the sales office. Quite early on I was sent to Malmö in Sweden to negotiate a licence for a packaging system that a small Swedish company had developed. The system was called Expresso, designed for powder-proof cartons, and the company was Akerlund & Rausing. Expresso had limited success, but was subsequently eclipsed by their other invention, the Tetra Pak, and later the Tetra Brik, both of which have become huge successes and have made the Rausing family extremely rich.

After this brief introduction to the world of carton-making and selling, I was posted to a small subsidiary in London, the Shirley and Warbey Box Company, as a sales representative. It had a few large customers such as Polyfilla, but specialised in high-quality work for the cosmetic industry in Bond Street. It was a most enjoyable time to be in London, where many of my friends, from both Rugby and Cambridge, were working as well.

The enjoyment was nearly short-lived. Shirley's was based at Colliers Wood, not far from Croydon. During my time in Bristol I had started learning to fly. I had not yet gone solo when I moved to London, so I decided to carry on with flying lessons at Croydon Airport. When the time came to go solo, my instructor said, 'When you are coming in to land, if you get it wrong and cut the throttle back too soon, simply open it right up again, do another circuit, and then come in to land again.' That was indeed what happened: I did cut the throttle too soon and to avoid crashing I opened it fully again. Instead of a steady, smooth ascent from the runway, the sudden thrust on the propeller caused the plane to bank sharply to the right. I was then heading at right angles to the runway. I did manage to level it up, but I succeeded in flying very low straight over a bowling green. When I managed to get on the proper circuit and land the plane, successfully this time, I found that the bowling club had been sending furious complaints about my activities, and rightly so!

I had started my flying lessons at Lulsgate, an old airfield that is now Bristol Airport. One of the other sales representatives at Shirley's was a former Battle of Britain pilot. For a break from the battle, he was sent down to Weston-super-Mare, where new pilots were being trained. Because of the large number of them, Lulsgate was used as an additional landing ground. One day he flew up with a pupil to practise 'circuits and bumps', as they are called. As they were circling, he noticed a large plane on the ground close by the hut where the Home Guard was based to guard the airfield. As he got closer, he realised that it was a large German bomber, and that the crew were standing on the ground, being held by the Home Guard and his trusty rifle.

What had actually happened made a remarkable story. The German plane had apparently been bombing Liverpool docks, but had been chased away by fighters far out over the Irish Sea. They escaped and set off to return to their base in occupied France. Their fuel was getting low, and so their captain decided that as soon as they got over the Channel, they would land on the first airfield they could find. They did indeed do so, but unfortunately for them, they had got the wrong channel – the Bristol Channel. Not realising this, and being thoroughly relieved to be on land again after such a long flight, they had jumped off the plane, only to find themselves facing the rifle of the Home Guard.

The outcome subsequently proved to be hugely important, because the crew, in their relief and thinking they were safe, had left the plane without making any effort to destroy the vital codebooks and equipment that the Luftwaffe had to guide their planes. Getting hold of all this vital information was a huge bonus for the RAF and a crucial turning point in the defeat of the Luftwaffe.

3 SCOTLAND, MARRIAGE AND START OF POLITICAL LIFE

In January 1959, a group of us went skiing in Kitzbühel. I was a day late in joining the others and finally arrived on a starlit night in the crisp snow on a midnight train from Munich. As the train rolled silently into the station, the peace was broken by an extremely noisy welcome from the rest of the group, who had decided, after what had clearly been a very jolly evening, to come down to the station and welcome me to the mountains. We went back to the *pension* where we were staying and somebody decided to wake up the one girl who had sensibly preferred her warm bed to a cold wait at the station. That was the first time I met Jane. A year later we were married, and sixty years later we are still going strong, even if our skiing is a bit rusty now.

When we returned to London, I kept up my pursuit of Jane. However, six months later, after an excellent experience with Shirley and Warbey learning more about packaging and sales, I was appointed by Robinson's as area sales manager for Scotland and Ireland, based in Glasgow. I arrived there on a miserable wet Sunday evening, with the old trams clanking over the cobbled roads, and the contrast could not have been greater from the Swinging London that I had just left. At first I booked into a small hotel while I embarked on my new responsibilities. The very first week, however, I had a great stroke of luck. A couple I had known in London, who had moved to work in Glasgow, invited me for a drink to meet some of their friends. One of them was Nigel Buchanan, whom I had last seen as a fellow member of the Lower Bench at Rugby School, and who was working as a lawyer in Glasgow. He told me that there was a spare bed in the flat, full of 'boys', where he was living. The flat turned out to be in an unlikely part of Glasgow, 245 St George's Road, up a stone staircase above Bell's Bar, a typical old Glasgow bar with sawdust on the floor and no women admitted. There was a flat either side at the top of the staircase, in which an interesting group of young bachelors were learning their trades. Lawyers, distillers, shipping, journalism, were all represented, and it became a focal point for a few girls as well as a social centre in Glasgow.

Employees of Dewar's White Label and Gloag's Famous Grouse whiskies, Stewart and Lloyd's, and a future editor of *The Times* made a very good bunch in these two flats and for me it was an excellent return to Glasgow, the city of my birth. Then it was down to work in charge of six sales representatives with the wide spread of customers for Robinson's packaging range. Macdonald's was our largest customer, with their Penguin, YoYo and Bandit range of biscuits. McVitie's and Macfarlane Lang, also biscuits, J. & P. Coats, the largest cotton firm, detonator boxes for ICI Nobel division, Macfisheries in Peterhead, can labels for Baxter's of Fochabers for their wonderful range of soups, printed plastic bags for all the fine knitwear companies in the Border towns, were among many more. My territory covered Ireland as well, and many years later I was amused to renew my acquaintance with the Ormeau Bakery in Belfast. Visiting these companies with my various representatives was an amazing accelerated course in learning about industry, and was hugely valuable for my future life. I learnt about so many different products with national appeal and real, long-lasting success. I remember being taught one important lesson about the need for a long life for new product, told me by a good friend, Tommy Niven, the buying director of Macdonald's. It seemed that Rowntree's, the leading confectionery company, was in the 1930s having a difficult time, with their range of chocolates and other confectionery looking a bit tired. Tommy told me that because of the considerable capital cost in setting up new production lines, it was essential that any new product must have the prospect of at least twenty years of good sales life ahead of it. Apparently they appointed a new marketing director who came up with four quite original new lines. Not only did he achieve the twenty-year mark for all of them, but they are still going strong, sixty years later. When I tell people this story, I challenge them to guess which they are, and few get them all. The answer is Polo Mints, Aero chocolate, Smarties and KitKat – all quite different, and all huge winners.

As a new manager, I had a lot to learn, and quickly. Our biggest customer in the Borders was Lyle and Scott, for whom we produced millions of printed polythene bags. I was interested to know how this well-known knitwear firm could require so many, until I learnt that they had a most profitable sideline making Y-front pants! Another interesting customer was an Aberdeen fish merchant, Byron S. Bellamy, who had latched on to the potential export market for frozen fish. I was amused to see our cartons, printed in Italian for frozen North Sea calamari, and to think of the British visitor relaxing in a restaurant by the sea in Portofino, under the illusion that his calamari were fresh out of the Mediterranean, when they were actually not quite so fresh and from Aberdeen!

I learned another lesson that I got to know all too well later on in Northern Ireland, when one of our sales representatives asked to see me. He wanted to warn me that we were starting to do business with a company that we should not touch. I knew that in his spare time he was a scout for the Rangers football club, and I realised that the company he was talking about was owned by a Catholic family, unacceptable to somebody steeped in the Protestant/Catholic antagonism of the Rangers/Celtic tradition. That was the only time I saw the depth of hostility between the two traditions while I was working in Glasgow, but I later saw the great support that Ian Paisley and the Free Presbyterian Church had in parts of Scotland.

But amid all the interesting experiences of my new job, there was still one piece of unfinished business. I went back to London to ask Jane if she would marry me. Most happily, she said yes, and on 20 January 1960 at St Margaret's, Westminster, we were married. It was interesting that the ceremony was at St Margaret's, the parish church of Parliament, and it might be thought that it was some early sign of my interest in Westminster. In fact, it had nothing to do with me, and was chosen because Jane's parents had been married there, apparently because my mother-in-law was American and there is an American connection with the church. We got married late in the afternoon, went on to the evening reception and flew to Munich the next day to catch the train to Kitzbühel, where we had met and skied the year before. After a skiing honeymoon, we returned via Paris and on to our new home in Scotland. A friend had told us that there was a house to rent just outside Glasgow, in Stirlingshire. This was the dower house for Duntreath Castle, the home of the Edmonstone family, and we lived there for the next two years. Suddenly being transported from London to

Glasgow and Stirlingshire was a very tough call for Jane, but she coped wonderfully well, and we made a number of good friends.

This was the start of our sixty years together, but it was nearly cut very short. When we first met in London, a group of us used to go and waterski in the evenings on a lake in Berkshire. In Scotland, our house was very close to Loch Lomond, so we managed to get a small cabin cruiser, inevitably named *Kingship*, with a powerful outboard motor, and skied on the loch. For holiday breaks, we used to tow it up to Crinan and cruise around such wonderful places as Mull, Lochaline and Loch Etive.

One Sunday two friends, Nigel Buchanan and Sandy Stewart, were giving a picnic lunch for a large group of friends at Sandy's home at Ardvorlich on Loch Earn. They asked us to bring up our boat so that people could waterski after lunch. After a jolly busking and singing picnic, I launched the boat, but said that, for the engine to be able to pull the skier, I could only take a couple of people with me in the boat. Somebody then said, 'Before we start skiing, why don't we all have a quick trip and get some fresh air?' That seemed a good idea, and all sixteen of us piled on, with a few sitting on the roof. That was my great mistake. When we motored out from the shelter of the trees at the edge of the loch, there was a good wind blowing, which caught us as we tried to turn. With the people on the roof, what had always seemed a very stable boat was not stable at all, and slowly, slowly, we rolled over, finishing upside down. It was only May, there was still snow on Ben Vorlich, and the water was very cold. Suddenly we had a serious crisis: Jane was seven months pregnant, and while we were all hanging on to the boat, it seemed to be very slowly sinking. We knew there was a waterski school three miles up the loch at the Lochearnhead Hotel, and Raymond Johnstone volunteered to swim ashore and send an SOS to them for help. It turned out that he had been a champion swimmer at school, which was just as well. He said afterwards that, with the very cold water and weighed down with his clothes, he only just made it. The rest of us stayed with the boat, singing to keep our spirits up (over lunch we had been singing one very appropriate song, 'Michael, row the boat ashore', and we sang even more vigorously now as we tried to ease the upturned boat towards the shore, without much success). Just as things were starting to look really worrying, a rowing boat suddenly appeared with two men in it. We managed to get

Jane into it, as the most urgent case, and I and some others swam in beside it. As the boat was going back for the rest of the group, there was a sudden roar of engines as two Albatross speedboats arrived from the ski school, and the rescue was complete.

We subsequently found out that the two men who were our first saviours were off-duty policemen, one of whom was convalescing from an illness, and were out with their wives, driving along the side of the loch, when they suddenly saw our misfortune. Being policemen, they used their initiative to try to help. They broke into the boathouse at Ardvorlich, found a rowing boat and started rowing. They then discovered that the boat was starting to leak, so one of them stopped rowing and began bailing, while the other kept rowing, and undoubtedly saved us. When we got ashore, Jane was rushed away by two kind ladies to their nearby house where they stripped her, stood her in front of a warm fire and rubbed her down to thaw her out. I stayed to see the last of the party ashore and to recover the boat. When finally everything was done, we didn't feel up to driving home to Blanefield, so we stayed the night in the Lochearnhead Hotel. I always remember how, despite a load of blankets and the electric fire on all the time, we lay and shivered the whole night, a sign of the hypothermia resulting from our immersion in the loch.

As the area manager for Scotland and Ireland I was involved in a great deal of travel. Our most northerly customer was in Dingwall, the well-respected Rowat's Tea, our most southerly in Cork. Getting around Scotland in particular in the winter had its challenges. On one occasion I had left home very early to drive to Aberdeen. Not far from home, I hit some black ice, and the car went straight into a tree. I don't remember how I got to the hospital in Killearn, but I do remember lying on a trolley in a corridor just beside a telephone on the wall, so I was able to call Jane. At least I could tell her I was not at death's door, which was more reassuring than if somebody else had reported me being taken to hospital. I had actually bashed one knee quite badly. They bandaged me up and sent me home, where I went to bed. I rang my office to tell them, and to apologise to Aberdeen for my non-arrival.

The next thing was that I got a call from the sales director in Bristol, who wanted to know what on earth I was doing still in bed at 10am. He had rung the office, had simply been told that I was in bed, and jumped to the wrong conclusion. He did apologise, and I chided him, as a good friend, that, so far from criticising me, he should appreciate that before he himself had even got out of bed that morning, I had practically laid down my life for the company!

✷ ✷ ✷

I could not have managed the extraordinary twists and turns of my eventful life without the unstinting help and support of my wife Jane. I pay proper tribute to her later in this book (page 197) – suffice it to say here that she coped marvellously with a host of things, including the security challenges of being married to a Secretary of State for Northern Ireland and then Defence, while caring for our family and looking after our farm.

While I was working in Scotland, I had rather lost touch with a small old wine business in Bristol that my brother-in-law, Charles Clarke, had bought with his cousin, John Robinson, which I had joined as a sleeping partner. Howell's had started in 1785 in the house of John Foster, the Mayor of Bristol in 1481, a merchant trading in salt and wine. He had built it with three levels of cellars, with a small shop at street level, and it was the oldest building in Bristol still used by merchants. Bristol at that time had two nationally known wine merchants, Harvey's and Avery's, and Howell's was tiny in comparison. Nonetheless, it had a small band of loyal customers, not least among the lawyers and stockbrokers whose offices were nearby. We found, as well, that it had clearly been very convenient for the sailing ships, being very close to what is now the Centre, but used to be the old Bristol port. In the lowest cellar there were still iron rings in the floor where the slaves from Africa were held awaiting transhipment to the West Indies – Bristol had played a major role in that notorious traffic.

It was in 1961 when I was in Scotland that Charles rang me and said that they were thinking of diversifying into catering as well, using the cellars as private dining rooms, and he asked my views. I thought it sounded a good idea, as our wine trade was never going very far, but I said I would like to take a second opinion. As it happened, my office in Glasgow was on the third floor of a big building in Hope Street, the ground floor of which was a well-known restaurant called The 101. Part of my responsibility involved entertaining our major customers, and I had formed a great respect for the manager of The 101, Peter Healey. I asked him for his views on such a venture. He was very enthusiastic, so I asked him if he would be interested in leading it. He said he could be, so we flew him down to Bristol, for a very successful interview with Charles, and for sixty years since, under the name of that ancient Mayor, Foster's has flourished.

At the beginning of 1962 I returned to Bristol to a new position as sales manager for the colour-printing division and soon after that became general manager of the division. My responsibilities now included the Bedminster factory, an old multi-storey building, with a very substantial range of printing and finishing machines, employing 700 people. We had a comprehensive range of capabilities: litho, letterpress and gravure printing; metallising plant; bookbinding; engraving; artists' design studios; and a reputation for high quality. There were many skilled craftsmen in the design, reproduction, print, paper-finishing and engineering areas, with strict demarcation of their territories. Union problems were never easy and many hours were spent in meetings with the Fathers of the Chapels, as the union representatives were known in the printing industry, a title carrying with it an element of moral superiority. There were nine different unions, the Society of Lithographic Artists and Designers (SLADE), the Typographical Association (TA) of Letterpress and Gravure Printers, Amalgamated Society of Lithographic Printers (ASLP), NATSOPA, SOGAT, the AEU, TGWU, ASTMS, and EEPTU, each jealously protecting their position. In general the meetings were reasonably constructive, but in other parts of the industry, particularly Fleet Street, they were notoriously bad. We had only one direct link to Fleet Street practices, which was the Ink Room, controlled by NATSOPA members, where the wage levels and restrictive practices were a direct feed from London. Otherwise, I had only one chapel that could be difficult, until I discovered that the Father was extremely deaf, had no hearing aid, and in reporting back to his chapel, delivered his own version of what he thought I might have said!

While I tried to get around the factory often and see as many people as I could, I was keen that everybody knew something about how we were getting on: what new business was being won, what new investments and new equipment, but with such a large plant, and working double shift in parts of it, it was a challenge. What I decided to do, once a month, was to use the factory's Tannoy loudspeakers, and to stop all the machinery during the fifteen-minute hand-over period between the two shifts, when everybody was there. While some did listen – I wasn't sure how many – I had one lucky break, which was certainly not in any management instruction book. It happened that I had been talking the day before to Nick Robinson, a colleague in Robinson's and the grandson of the then President of E.S. and A. Robinson, a keen racehorse owner. Nick told me his grandfather had a horse running in the Oaks the next day, called Homeward Bound. At the end of my Tannoy broadcast, I thought it might interest people to know that the President of the company had a horse in that great classic race, being run that afternoon. It actually won the race, at 14–1, and I discovered that a few of the people in the factory had slipped round to the local betting shop and done very nicely! After that, people certainly listened to my broadcasts!

I remember being told of one gem that illustrated the power of the unions in Fleet Street. That power came, of course, because it was always more sensible for the management to make some small concession to the unions than to run the risk that the next day's paper would be lost, and that day's income never recovered. These concessions had steadily accumulated to make Fleet Street notorious for overmanning and poor productivity.

This particular prize involved the bundling and tying up of newspapers off the printing machine for the Sunday edition of the *News of the World*. This once involved a number of men working long hours through to Saturday evening, for which they were paid, I believe, quadruple time for weekend work. Subsequently this operation had been automated, making the men redundant from this rewarding work. This had not been accepted by the NATSOPA union, and so it was agreed that the men should still report for work, to stand and watch the machines doing their job while continuing to receive their handsome pay. Other union chapels learnt about this attractive 'money for nothing' scenario, and so a system had grown up for different Saturdays to be balloted around the country and some of the Bedminster chapel were lucky enough to win the prize on occasions.

Many years later, as Secretary of State for Employment, I was given a vivid reminder of that union power in Fleet Street. I had been invited by the managing director of the *Daily Mirror* to have dinner with his fellow directors and to see the paper being 'put to bed', and the next day's edition being printed. In the middle of an interesting dinner and discussion, somebody came into the room and handed a note to the managing director. He looked rather embarrassed: it turned out that the unions had discovered that I was in the building, and that they would stop the printing of the next day's paper unless they had the opportunity to speak to me as well. I was quite happy to meet them. The meeting was possibly more friendly than it might have been for a Conservative minister when they discovered that I had been in the printing industry for twelve years before going into Parliament, and was very familiar with the unions to which they belonged. The meeting over, and having shown their power, they returned happily to work, and the printing of the next day's paper went ahead.

In taking over the Bedminster factory I inherited a very high standard in all our products. Our range of customers – Cadbury's, Rowntree's, Kellogg's, Max Factor, the Mars subsidiary Petfoods Ltd with their range of Kit-e-Kat and Lassie labels, and many other household names – confirmed our standing in the printing and packaging world. We produced can and jar labels, cigarette coupons, show cards, other point-of-sale advertising, calendars and diaries, and an envelope division that made all the seed packets for the main producers like Sutton's. It was a formidable range of a consistently high quality. My responsibility for the divisions of Colour Printing, Calendars and Envelopes was a real challenge, and my message to everybody was that, as we did not have the comfort of the patented systems and proprietary products of some of our other factories, we had to live by quality and service, and speed in developing new ideas. I was very proud of what we achieved, and the good humour and spirit of everybody working there. However, there was no denying the age of the factory. It was older than my grandfather, who had made some additions to an already existing building. There was space in other much newer Robinson factories in Bristol, and it was decided to move the three divisions into them, although inevitably splitting them up. This effectively, after seven years, finished that job for me, and I was offered the job of running a new company, Wye Plastics, in Hereford, which Robinson's had just acquired. I had no desire to move, and I had anyway realised that I was ready for a fresh challenge, so

I decided to leave Robinson's. I set myself up as an independent consultant, while having a closer involvement in Howell's and Foster's, the wine and catering businesses. I had recently also gone on the board of Sale Tilney. My father-in-law, Robert Tilney, had created this group of companies, but just as it was being floated on the Stock Exchange, he had a serious hunting accident, and could no longer continue in the business. Frances Tilney, my mother-in-law, asked me to go on the board as a non-executive director and family member.

Our MP at our home in Wiltshire was Daniel Awdry, representing Chippenham. I had known Dan for a few years and we had played some cricket together, and in the 1966 election he had asked me to be the warm-up speaker at some of his meetings. He knew of my involvement in industry and particularly of my experience in handling trade union questions, which were becoming a major issue nationally. During the campaign he used to have two or three meetings a night in the villages and small towns that made up the Chippenham constituency, with an opening speaker holding the fort until Dan arrived from his previous meeting. The first one I did for him was in Luckington village hall, chaired by Major General Menzies, the chairman of the Luckington branch of the Chippenham Conservative Association. It started with General Menzies setting out all the arrangements for the election, who then introduced me as the opening speaker. Dan had told me that it would be ten to fifteen minutes before he could get there, and I had prepared accordingly. I started by saying how pleased I was to support Dan, and that there were three particular points that I wanted to make. At that moment the door opened and Dan Awdry came in. Everybody applauded, I sat down, and that was the end of my contribution to the meeting.

A week later Dan asked if I would be the support speaker at his meeting in a secondary school in Wootton Bassett. He had apologised for arriving as early as he did at Luckington, but thought the timing at Wootton Bassett would be closer to his original prediction. The meeting opened in the same way, with the chairman explaining the arrangements for polling day and introducing me. I started to speak and duly completed my ten minutes as I awaited Dan's arrival. No sign of that, so on I went, another ten, and then another, and still no sign of Dan. In the end, I spoke for forty minutes until Dan finally arrived and I could at last sit down. The chairman then introduced Dan, saying that he would first address the meeting, and then be pleased to answer any questions, at which somebody in the audience, suitably provoked by something I had said, jumped up and said, 'Would Mr King answer some questions as well?'

This pattern of village and town meetings was exactly what I did when I was later the candidate in Bridgwater, with three, and sometimes four, meetings a night. I remembered once meeting Lord Mancroft, a well-known and entertaining speaker, and a good friend of my predecessor as Bridgwater MP, Sir Gerald Wills. He had come to speak in support of Gerald in Dunster and then in Minehead. When Gerald had arrived at Dunster, Lord Mancroft had left him there and gone on to open the meeting in Minehead. He did his fifteen minutes, and then another ten, when a note was passed to the chairman, who slipped it to him: it said, 'Gerald's in the ditch – keep it up.' In the end he did forty-five minutes before Gerald arrived. At the end of the meeting, as he was walking out, he happened to hear a good yeoman Somerset farmer in front of him say to his friend, ''E was very interestin', His Lordship, but 'ow 'e do chat!'

In the various meetings where I helped Dan we had a range of different chairmen, but the most intriguing was Major General Menzies. After the meeting, he had kindly asked Jane and me back to his house, Luckington Grange, for a drink. We noticed on a piano in his drawing room a great range of signed photographs of very well-known faces: 'Many thanks for all you did' signed 'Ike', from General (later President) Eisenhower, a similar message from Winston Churchill, and many others. We wondered how he came to have such a collection of tributes, but the next Sunday we got the answer. On the front cover of the *Sunday Times* colour supplement was a picture of General Menzies, with the caption 'The Man Who Was M', and the article revealed that in the last war he had been the head of the Secret Intelligence Service, MI6. The head of SIS is traditionally known as 'C' after the first holder of the office, Admiral Cummings, but Ian Fleming had served in SIS himself, and in his James Bond books he had changed 'C' to 'M' in memory of his old boss.

It subsequently emerged that Luckington had featured in one event involving MI6 and the German Secret Service, the *Abwehr*. Before World War II, there was considerable concern among senior German generals about Hitler, and the risk of war with Britain. Admiral Canaris, the head of the *Abwehr*, was anxious to establish a secret back channel to MI6 to avoid misunderstandings that could provoke war. To establish this channel, and knowing that General Menzies was a keen horseman and hunted with the Beaufort Hunt, he sent a young German cavalry officer to rent a house close to Menzies in Luckington, and to join the Hunt. By all accounts, the Beaufort Hunt, and particularly the ladies, thought the dashing young officer was very good news, but the village did not, as they thought he was a German spy, which, of course, he was!

One night in 1968 Dan and his wife Liz came to dinner, and during it he suddenly turned to me and told me that David Webster, the MP for Weston-super-Mare, had had a skiing accident, and sadly had subsequently died. This would now involve an early by-election for one of the safest Conservative seats in the country, for which they would quickly have to choose a candidate. Dan, having seen me campaigning with him and knowing that this was my old home patch, as my parents lived at Langford in the Weston constituency, urged me to put my name forward. I asked him what the procedure would be, and he gave me what turned out to be a very accurate synopsis: for such a safe seat, with a majority of more than 20,000, as many as 300 people would apply. Of these, 250 would be weeded out straight away on a paper check as unsuitable. The remaining fifty applications would be scrutinised more closely and reduced to a final twenty. These would be invited for interview by a selection committee, who would produce a final three or four to be put before a meeting of the members of the Weston Conservative Association. He added that Ted Heath, then Leader of the Opposition, wanted the earliest possible date for the by-election, to get another vote on his side in Parliament, so things were likely to move pretty fast.

I decided to put my name forward to see how I would get on, and acquire some useful experience for the future. I might try to become an MP, but without thinking for a moment that I could win this time. I learnt that Sir Wilfred Anson, an old friend of my parents and the deputy chairman of Imperial Tobacco, a major company based in Bristol, was, I believe, President of the Weston Association. He discovered that I was going to put my name in, and apparently told Mr Smith Cox, the chairman, that he thought I was worth seeing. So that got me from the original 300 into the last twenty! I took a call from the agent: Mr Smith Cox, who had significant business interests, was a very busy man, and had decided that they would do all twenty interviews in one day, starting at 10am on the following Tuesday, at half-hour intervals. He asked when I could get there, and I suggested 12 noon, when the committee would have had a chance to settle down and before fatigue really set in. As it was, I was only partly right, because when I got there at noon, one lady, well over eighty, had clearly long gone past the point at which she could take much interest, and I fear the later interviewees had an even bigger problem.

Having not done anything like this before, and as a beginner not expecting any immediate success, I was, I suppose, rather more relaxed than some of the other people being interviewed, a number of whom had done it before in trying for many other constituencies. I quite enjoyed it and at the end I thanked everybody for their courtesy and for the interest they had taken in interviewing me. The next day, to my surprise, I got a call from the agent with the result of the interviews. He told me that their plan had been to ask the top three under their marking system to come on Saturday, when the final selection would be made. The candidate chosen would then immediately be fighting the by-election. Because it was such a solid Conservative seat, that person would be virtually certain to become the new Member of Parliament for Weston-super-Mare. He then told me that under the marking system, where they had originally decided to choose the top three candidates, two were much further ahead of the others and, therefore, they had decided to have only two candidates, of which I was one, and would I come back to Weston on Saturday for the final round. This came as a considerable shock, as I had not, even at that stage, decided whether I really wished to do it. I had seen the selection procedure much more as a valuable experience if I decided subsequently to pursue such a career.

Anyhow, Saturday it had to be, and we duly arrived at the Grand Hotel, where some 300 members of the Weston-super-Mare Conservative Association were ready to make the final selection. The other candidate was Jerry Wiggin, who was much more experienced than I was, having already fought two previous parliamentary elections in Montgomeryshire. We both did our stuff, accompanied by our wives, with ten-minute speeches and then questions from the audience. We adjourned to a waiting room while the Association voted. The chairman came in and said, 'Thank you very much for your contributions. It was a close result but the decision is for Mr Wiggin.' I have to say that his announcement did come as something of a relief, when things had been moving so fast: from being an interesting first experience of the selection process to possibly being suddenly elected as an MP. Jerry and Rosemary Wiggin went into the meeting to loud cheers and congratulations, with pledges of support for the coming by-election. We had been left outside, presumably out of sympathy at what must be our enormous disappointment, but I saw no reason to stay out and said I would like to go in and support him. I wished him the best of luck, and said that if I could help him at all in the by-election I would be very happy to do so. The meeting finished and a crowd of people descended together on the small car park, which was jammed. It was some time before we could get out, and as we were manoeuvring the car, a couple rushed up to say they were very disappointed I had not been successful. They added, did I know that Sir Gerald Wills, the MP for the neighbouring constituency of Bridgwater, had just announced that, because of ill-health, he would not be standing again, and Bridgwater would be seeking a new candidate. They had many friends in that constituency and they hoped very much that I would put my name forward. I had not in fact heard the news about Bridgwater, but it was of course a further seat in Somerset, my home patch, in whose regiment, the Somerset Light Infantry, I had served in the TA as well. It took some little time to decide whether I would go forward, but in the end I did and put my name in for the Bridgwater constituency.

4 EARLY CAREER AS AN MP

Once I had taken the step of putting my name forward for Bridgwater, I discovered that even more people had applied for this constituency than for Weston. 360 names were whittled down on paper to sixty-three. I don't know how many were interviewed, but I ended up in the last three and had to come back for a full meeting of the whole Bridgwater Conservative Association. It was a very big constituency and some of the members had to come from miles away on Exmoor. As it happened, Jane had a cousin who was married to a doctor in Porlock. The cousin got into conversation with a keen hunting farmer from Exmoor, who said that he was going to the final selection meeting but didn't know anything about the three candidates and wondered whether they were sound on hunting. The cousin told him that Jane's father had been the Master of the Quorn Hunt, and got the prompt reply 'That settles it then', as it was clearly the most important issue, as far as he was concerned!

The final selection took place in the upstairs ballroom of the Royal Clarence Hotel, in front of a very full house. The bit I remember best was when Jane and I walked out of the room, having done our piece as the second of the three contenders, and two elderly ladies walked out with us. They said some very nice things about my contribution and hoped I would be successful. I said, 'You are going to stay and vote?' to which I got the splendid reply, 'Oh no, it's the last bus to Nether Stowey, but we did enjoy it!' Fortunately, even without their votes, we were successful and I became the Conservative candidate for the Bridgwater constituency, which was the start of a very happy relationship for the next thirty-two years.

I was warned that I could be up against a Liberal candidate, Donald Crowhurst, a Bridgwater councillor, who was taking part in a famous single-handed round-the-world yacht race, and looked likely to win. However, very sadly, realising that his boat was unseaworthy, it turned out that he had decided to stop and to radio back a series of fraudulent locations, and when he probably realised he would not get away with it, he committed suicide.

Our first task was to get to know as much as we could of this vast constituency, more than fifty miles long and with good Conservative branches not just in the towns but in many of the villages as well. We were warmly welcomed, as for some time Sir Gerald Wills had not been well and was unable to visit them, and there was an understandable curiosity to see who would succeed him. The constituency was an area of fascinating contrasts. Politically, you had the staunch Labour town of Bridgwater, with its massive British Cellophane factory, and other major companies; large areas of Somerset farming; the tourist and retirement areas of Burnham-on-Sea and Minehead; and, to cap it all, a nuclear power station at Hinkley Point.

The countryside was fascinating as well. The low-lying Somerset Levels with their elaborate system of drainage ditches, the hills of the Quantocks, the Poldens and the Brendons, Exmoor, the shore of the Bristol Channel, the River Parrett, the Bridgwater docks, the harbours of Watchet and Minehead, made an extraordinary amalgam of contrasts. Nowhere else would you find in the same area the wild herds of deer on Exmoor and the Quantocks; the annual phenomenon of the elver harvest, when millions of these baby eels swim across the Atlantic from their breeding grounds in the Sargasso Sea to funnel up the Bristol Channel into the River Parrett, and thence up the ditches of the Levels; the withy beds for the willow basket industry; the conger eel 'gladding' (hunting) with dogs at low tide at Watchet; and the bittern booming away.

There was plenty of history, too. It was behind the natural defences of the Somerset Levels that King Alfred was able to evade the Viking invaders and burn his cakes, 'as the tide came in faster than a horse could gallop'. And 800 years later came the last battle on English soil, when the Duke of Monmouth was defeated at the Battle of Sedgemoor, and Judge Jeffreys held his Bloody Assizes. This marked the end of the Monmouth Rebellion, but the story is that Bridgwater was labelled ever after in royal circles as the rebel town. When, 200 years later, Queen Victoria was travelling through Somerset on the train and asked what town they were passing, she was told it was Bridgwater, and promptly ordered the blinds to be drawn! I am glad to say that the present Queen had no such reaction when she made a very happy visit to Bridgwater a few years ago.

The town's most famous MP was Robert Blake, a staunch supporter of Oliver Cromwell in the Civil War. He became Cromwell's General-at-Sea, and was considered, next to Nelson, the greatest of the English admirals and the Father of the Royal Navy. He was buried in Westminster Abbey, but I learned only recently that Charles II was determined to expunge from the record any Parliamentarians, and Blake's body was exhumed from a place of honour in the Abbey and buried next door in St Margaret's Church.

The town clearly recovered quickly from the damage done in the Monmouth rebellion, as shortly thereafter a significant number of fine Georgian houses were built, which suggests that the docks were prospering. When the film of *Tom Jones* was made and the director needed a London Georgian street scene, it was Castle Street, Bridgwater, that was used.

The constituency had its literary connections as well. The village of Oare is well known to readers of *Lorna Doone*. William and Dorothy Wordsworth and Samuel Taylor Coleridge lived not far apart on the edge of the Quantocks. Coleridge wrote *The Rime of the Ancient Mariner* there, and also the first verses of *Kubla Khan*, until he was interrupted by a 'person from Porlock'.

It could have been very hard work, but the wonderful welcome we had from the Conservative branches and the other groups in the constituency made it very manageable, and an excellent preparation for the task ahead. Gerald Wills had announced that he would not be standing again at the next general election, whenever it came, and I thought I would have at least a year before that happened. However, in October 1969 he died, and suddenly we faced the prospect of the by-election, which was fixed for 12 March. The Conservative party organisation swung into action, with the regional agent in charge, calling in eight other agents from other West Country constituencies to help. With members of the Bridgwater Association they drew up a detailed plan for the day tours and the evening meetings. Exactly as I had seen in Chippenham, the schedule normally included three meetings a night, as I was driven from village to village, town to town, to cover the huge spread of the constituency. To support me I had the pick of the Conservative team in Parliament: Tony Barber, Keith Joseph, Michael Heseltine, Chris Chataway, and Edward Du Cann from Taunton. For the climax of the eve-of-poll meetings in Highbridge, and then the Town Hall in Bridgwater, I had the star attraction of Iain Macleod, an outstanding speaker, and he didn't let me down. None in that packed audience would have guessed that he would be dead in three months, and that the new Conservative government, in which he had just become Chancellor of the Exchequer, had lost a vital member.

I was very fortunate to have such a good organisation behind me, and we managed to avoid any major disasters. At an evening meeting at Wheddon Cross, a village high up on Exmoor, Jane had been sitting with me at the top table with the chairman. As we walked out, I heard someone say, 'It's nice he's brought his daughter with him.' I used to tell that story at every meeting while introducing Jane, and say that while it could be a justifiable tribute to her, it could have been a reflection of how old I looked!

Another feature of the by-election was that, following a recent change in the law, eighteen-year-olds could vote for the first time. I think it was the *Western Daily Press* that discovered a girl whose eighteenth birthday would be on polling day, and so she would be the youngest person ever to vote in a Parliamentary election. Her name was Trudy Sellick, and as she had told them that she was voting for me, they asked me to have my photograph taken with her outside the polling station just after she had voted, at the very start of the day. Thus I found myself in the North Newton schoolyard at 7am together with a gaggle of TV crews, including some from Sweden and Japan who were intent on capturing the moment of the youngest voter ever in a British election. It would not have been a problem, but it had been a very cold night and then it had rained. The schoolyard had become a splendid ice rink, and TV crews and their equipment were crashing down all around. Fortunately I managed to avoid any serious injury, which would have brought my campaign to a sudden halt.

Otherwise polling day proceeded without disaster and at the count I had a majority of over 10,000. This result was particularly welcomed by the team of Conservative agents who had worked so hard in the campaign. They had found that the local bookmaker, Dave Pipe, thought we would win, but had set up a table of different odds for a range of possible majorities. In 1966, Gerald Wills had had a majority of 3,000, at a time when his illness handicapped his campaigning, in an election which was much more difficult for the Conservatives. I discovered only afterwards that the delight of the agents at the result was not least because they thought the campaign was going well, and when they found Dave Pipe offering odds of 25–1 against a 10,000 majority, they had all jumped in!

This Bridgwater result was later to have a national significance. A week later there was a by-election in South Ayrshire, won by the Labour Party. Labour were in government and had been having a very difficult time, with a substantial swing against them. They had lost a by-election in Swindon with a swing against them of more than 20%, but there had been another by-election three months before Bridgwater, with a swing of only 9%. The swing in Bridgwater against them was also 9%, but in South Ayrshire it was only 2%. It was known that Harold Wilson, the Labour Prime Minister, was looking to have a general election as soon as it was safe to do so. There had been some recovery in the Labour prospects, and the question was how far it had gone. Having two by-elections so close together with such different results convinced Wilson that one must be a phoney and the other a genuine guide to the political situation. He decided that there must have been some freak element in the Bridgwater result, and that South Ayrshire was the correct guide to follow. Assuming that the Labour recovery was continuing, after a further three months he called a general election, when there was still a full year left in that parliament. He lost and Ted Heath became Prime Minister.

The *Economist* magazine set out to discover why Wilson called the election when he didn't need to, only to lose it. They identified that the Bridgwater result was entirely in line with the accepted polling position of Labour at that time, and that the freak result was in fact South Ayrshire. They established that the Conservative candidate in South Ayrshire was a Roman Catholic, and that the age-old Protestant/Catholic hostility in Scotland had been the crucial factor in producing such an unforeseen result.

The tradition in Bridgwater was for the result to be announced first in the hall and then upstairs from the town hall balcony to the crowd in the street outside. Next it was downstairs for the traditional chairing, in which the winner was proudly carried down the street by four stout men to the Royal Clarence Hotel for a lively celebration. The chairing of the Member used to be widely practised throughout the country, but it has largely lapsed except in Bridgwater and a very few other constituencies. There is a famous picture by Hogarth of the chairing, with an extremely fat MP, in a huge armchair, throwing out handfuls of coins to his voters, but the Bridgwater chair was very simple, and did not include any cash provision!

Then it was off to Westminster, where, flanked by my two sponsors, Willie Whitelaw and my old friend Daniel Awdry, I took my seat in Parliament. The first weeks were extremely hectic, with a lot to learn about parliamentary business, and a huge number of people to thank for all their help in the campaign. I immediately started a regular programme of 'surgeries' in ten different locations right across the constituency, as I had promised.

These first months were very exciting and demanding of my time, but everything suddenly came to a grinding halt when Harold Wilson decided to call the general election, and so off we went again, having already done it so very recently. At one of my first meetings, without the cast of stars that had accompanied me in the by-election, I said that I did not want to hold the record of the shortest serving MP. I was quickly advised that there was no prospect of my achieving that record, as it emerged that there had been a by-election many years ago in Cardiff, and while the victorious candidate was being congratulated, his agent whispered in his ear that the Prime Minister had just called a general election. The sad end for him was that in the ensuing election he lost the seat, leaving him with the doubtful privilege of holding the record for the shortest ever serving MP, which was never going to be broken.

The result this time was a slightly reduced majority of 8,000, but I went back to Westminster with the Conservative government. Chris Chataway became Minister of Posts and Telecommunications and asked me if I would be his Parliamentary Private Secretary, to which I happily agreed. At that time the ministry covered the Post Office, which in those days included telecommunications, as well as the BBC and ITV. One of the first pieces of legislation he introduced was for the establishment of commercial radio, for which we were fiercely attacked by the Labour Party during the bill's progress through Parliament, but which they were more than happy to appear on thereafter.

One of the most lively moments during that time concerned the Post Office and its chairman, Lord Hall. He had been appointed by the previous Labour government and there were substantial criticisms of his performance, which finally led to his sacking by Chris. There was a huge row in the Commons, as he was a Labour peer and it was seen as a politically motivated sacking. It was on a Thursday, and Labour immediately moved a motion of censure against Chris, to be debated on Monday. However, the weekend press carried rather more detail of Lord Hall's background, which took the sting out of Monday's debate, and Chris won the day. It emerged that Lord Hall had said he was a company doctor, and had told the Labour Government whips that he was available for public service. They were looking for a new chairman for the Post Office, and 'company doctor' was the phrase used to describe some clever businessman who would sort out a company when it was in trouble. On that basis he was thought very suitable for the Post Office, only for it to be revealed that he was in fact a genuine medical doctor, working for the company Powell Duffryn.

When I made my maiden speech, the next speaker was James Dickens, a well-known Labour MP. He had had the courtesy to do a little research before making the friendly, welcoming remarks traditional from those speaking immediately after a maiden speaker. He said he was pleased to welcome the new member for Bridgwater, a seat that had been almost continuously represented in the House. I don't think anybody else picked up the point, but he had spotted that a hundred years before, in 1870, Bridgwater was convicted of bribery in an election, and the seat was abolished. There had been complaints of bribery, and a parliamentary commission came to investigate. They found that in the election the Liberals had given £5 to anybody who promised to vote for them. In those days there was a very limited electorate, and the votes were published. The Liberals had been confident that they would win, but to their horror they lost, and a number of those who had promised their votes were recorded as voting Conservative. They discovered that the Conservatives had promised £10 to people who could show they had voted for them. The burghers of Bridgwater happily took their £15 and two Conservatives were elected! I am sorry to say that the commission also looked at earlier elections as far back as they could, to 1832, and were satisfied that there was substantial bribery in all of them. My own suspicion is that Bridgwater would not have been at all alone in these practices.

In 1972 Chris Chataway became Minister of Industry, and I moved with him. That Christmas I had a real surprise when my sister Tess told me that she had been invited to be a governor of the BBC. I was both surprised and a little embarrassed, as Chris had previously had the responsibility for appointing governors to the BBC and it might appear that I had arranged it for my sister. After Christmas, when Parliament reassembled, I happened to bump into John Eden, who had taken over from Chris and now had responsibility for the appointments, and I asked him if he realised he had appointed my sister. It was clearly news to him and I am sure that if the connection had been known she would not have been asked. I found out later how it had happened. The Ministry wanted more diversity among the governors and were looking for a woman, politically independent and from one of the regions. One of the people they enlisted in their search was the Vice Chancellor of Bristol University. Tess had been active for some time on the University Council, was a district councillor, elected as an independent, and therefore met all the criteria and was appointed, without my having any idea that it was happening. By all accounts, she did very well, including taking an interest in parts of the BBC that other governors had not paid much attention to, such as local radio and the engineering side, as well as the more glamorous and newsworthy areas of the main stars and programmes.

Once I was elected, it became urgent to find somewhere to stay in London, and we found a tiny flat in Palmer Street, right beside the back entrance to St James's Park tube station. It was a small modern building with one other flat on the floor above, and it was only a few years later that we found that a couple quietly living there were Marcia Williams, later Lady Falkender, Prime Minister Harold Wilson's political secretary and close confidante, and Walter Terry, the political editor of the *Daily Mail*.

Later on we moved to a larger flat in Westminster Gardens, which we discovered had been owned earlier by Denis and Margaret Thatcher. It was on the same landing as one owned by Airey and Diana Neave, and it was in the car park of the flats that the bomb was put in Airey's car by INLA Irish terrorists. It must have had a tilt switch, as it did not explode until he was driving up the ramp out of the House of Commons car park where he was killed.

This happened at the start of the general election in 1979 that led to the Conservative victory and to Margaret Thatcher, of whom Airey had been such a key supporter, becoming Prime Minister. Shortly thereafter there was a big memorial service for Airey, and Diana organised a lunch for some special visitors, for which we lent our flat. Airey had been a prisoner of war and was one of the very few who escaped from Colditz Castle. When he got back to England, he helped set up the escape organisation that assisted many other allied prisoners to pass safely through France and Spain home to England. The elderly French ladies sitting demurely on our sofa had been a key part of Airey's team, and had survived the toughest Gestapo interrogation and torture to protect the escaping prisoners.

During the by-election there were rumours that the Labour government were going to stop funding the railway branch-line from Taunton to Minehead, a vital link for West Somerset to the main line. When they were challenged on this during the campaign, they strongly denied it and said it was a disgraceful Conservative story. When I arrived at the Commons and had taken the oath, I was walking through the Members' Lobby past the letter-boards, which have a slot for every MP, and which light up if a letter is there. I was very excited to see my light was lit, but not when I opened the letter. It was from Fred Mulley, the Labour Minister of Transport, to tell me that the Taunton–Minehead line would be closed. That became my first challenge, and Edward Du Cann, the Taunton MP, and I fought hard to save it. In the end we failed, but a wonderful body of volunteers took it over and created a very popular heritage railway.

One feature of the by-election was a very good poster campaign throughout the constituency, which was vital for me as a new candidate so as to get my name recognised. One morning canvassing, I thought I would do a little market research of my own, and I went into a greengrocer in Highbridge that actually happened to have a TOM KING poster right outside. I asked him what the name 'Tom King' meant to him, and after a pause got the telling reply, 'I'm not sure – is it a new kind of potato?'

Shortly after I became an MP, I was approached by someone who said that they were about to publish the autobiography of one of my predecessors, Vernon Bartlett. I was fascinated to hear this as he had rather disappeared, and since his successor, Gerald Wills, had died after twenty years as MP, I think most people thought that he must have died as well. He had a very interesting history, having been an active journalist in the 1930s, ending up as the foreign editor of the *News Chronicle* in 1938. In that capacity he was a strong opponent of the Munich agreement between Chamberlain and Hitler. In that same year, the Member of Parliament for Bridgwater had been made a judge and there was a by-election. It was a safe Conservative seat and a Heathcoat Amory, of a well-known West Country family, had been chosen as their candidate. However, a vicar from Porlock, similarly opposed to Munich, approached Bartlett and said that, if he would stand as an independent candidate, he was authorised to say that both the Labour and the Liberal parties would support him. He agreed to stand and won the by-election, going on to win it again in 1945. He then stood down and returned to journalism with the *Straits Times* in Singapore. After that he had retired to Lucca in Tuscany, to make wine and to write books, including his autobiography. The publisher told me that Bartlett was coming over from Italy for the launch, and I said I would love to meet him. I invited him to have lunch at the Commons, and asked whether there were any old colleagues he would like me to invite as well. The result was that I hosted a fascinating occasion with Vernon Bartlett, the left-wing Labour MP Tom Driberg, and the Conservative MP Angus Maude. They had all been journalists together in the 1930s, on the *Daily Express*, the *Daily Mail* and *The Times*, and Maude had also had a spell overseas editing the *Sydney Morning Herald*.

I remember particularly that when Bartlett responded, accepting my invitation, he added a footnote, 'I hope you are enjoying being MP for Bridgwater, I didn't!' From a discussion with him later, it was clear that it was a lonely position to be in – an Independent surrounded by the organised groups of Conservative, Labour and Liberal MPs – and he was happy to return to journalism.

While Vernon Bartlett didn't enjoy being MP for Bridgwater, this is perhaps the moment to record that I certainly did, and I have always been grateful to all our many friends whose support and encouragement over so many years made possible not only thirty years as the MP, but also the wider role that I have been lucky enough to play.

❋ ❋ ❋

During the 1960s there was growing concern over the impact of militant trade unionism and the damage it was doing to British industry. This was recognised by the Labour government and in 1969 Barbara Castle, with the support of Harold Wilson, published proposals in a paper, *In Place of Strife*, for proper ballots before strikes, to replace the notorious 'car park' meetings, where militant shop stewards intimidated their members into supporting strike action. When she put her proposals to the Labour Cabinet, Jim Callaghan strongly opposed them, and they were withdrawn. When we came into government the next year, Robert Carr, supported by Geoffrey Howe as solicitor general, introduced the Industrial Relations Bill, which focused particularly on the abuses of the closed shop. This met strong opposition from the unions and the TUC ordered them not to comply. Because of my previous practical experience of the challenges for management, working in the printing industry – one of the most unionised – I became quite involved in the different stages of the bill, and it was an excellent and early opportunity in my parliamentary career to learn a lot about Parliament. I realised that, on our benches, there were a number of company directors but very few with factory management experience, and on the Labour side plenty of trade unionists but with virtually no management background. The bill was very hard-fought, and to defeat filibustering, a timetable motion was imposed. However, the motion had one serious flaw, in that while there could be no debate after 10pm, there could still be votes on any outstanding amendments. The Labour opposition seized on this by tabling a vast number of amendments and then insisting on voting on them all. What happened, which I believe was quite unprecedented and has never happened since, was that we proceeded to vote throughout the night. A vote takes about fifteen minutes and requires every MP to walk through the voting lobby, so every quarter of an hour it was on our feet and then back to whatever refuge one could find to rest. It was an appalling experience, and certainly the complete opposite of the current practice of 'family-friendly hours'.

It illustrated the serious breakdown in relations within Parliament over the union challenges. Two years later we had the miners' strikes and the three-day week, the disastrous election under the slogan 'Who governs Britain', and the election of a Labour government that immediately repealed our Industrial Relations Act. Meanwhile the crippling damage to British industry, particularly the car industry, continued. Michael Edwardes, who took charge of British Leyland in 1977, made two comments to me that explained it all too well. He said that a German manager would be spending 5% of his time on industrial relations matters, whereas a British manager was spending 60%, and that there wasn't a single day in his first year in charge of that enormous car company when there wasn't at least one of their factories on strike. At the end of the 1960s Britain produced more cars than Japan. Thereafter it was downhill all the way until at last under Margaret Thatcher we got going again.

One of the most pleasant discoveries on becoming an MP was to realise that it wasn't all work – there were occasional opportunities for sport as well. Tennis, golf, cricket and skiing all featured at one time or another. One tennis match I took part in was in Deauville against the French Parliament, where the French team was led by a very charming *député*, Bernard Destremau, who had actually been a semi-finalist at Wimbledon. He played a singles match against our best player, John Hannam, the MP for Exeter, who had himself played in the junior Wimbledon championships. It was a very informal occasion, and one of our team was umpiring. I was playing on the next-door court and, wondering how the big match was going, was encouraged to hear Bernard complaining that the umpire was not scoring in French!

In golf, Willie Whitelaw, a fine golfer, set up an excellent week in the summer recess, playing against three English and three Scottish clubs, one of each a year on a three-year cycle. His criterion was that it should be not only a very good course, but a good club as well. His choice of Lytham St Anne's, Hoylake and Ganton, and Prestwick, Muirfield and St Andrews, could not have been better, and I was very lucky to take part.

On the cricket field, the Lords and Commons have maintained an excellent fixture list for a team that is a healthy mixture of Lords, MPs and parliamentary staff, including one or two very helpful policemen, and an occasional ringer. For many years I had the privilege of running the match at Highclere, which, in addition to being the location of the fictional Downton Abbey, has an excellent cricket ground and team. On one occasion an MP, Graham Allen, brought his friend Phil Edmonds, the Test player, to sharpen up our bowling. He certainly did very well, but we paid the price for it the following year when the Highclere team was reinforced from the Hampshire

County squad; Phil Edmonds had to cry off, and we were soundly thrashed! One particularly enjoyable game was when we commemorated the publication of a book marking the history of Lords and Commons cricket from 1850 to 1988. I had the honour of captaining the Lords and Commons team, a wonderful medley of Lords, MPs, a Cabinet Secretary, eldest sons and two policemen, against a splendid team of Lords Taverners, which included the Test cricketers Colin Cowdrey, Derek Underwood and John Snow, mingled with the world of entertainment, represented by Tim Rice, David Frost and Willie Rushton.

The other great sport was skiing. Originated by Ernest Marples in Davos in 1956, the Anglo-Swiss Ski Week is still going strong. Over the years some 200 parliamentarians from each country have skied together, and great friendships have formed. The week culminates in the giant slalom race, which in the earliest years the British used to win. At that time the Swiss team was rather older, but then it was noticed that there was an increasing number of younger, more athletic Swiss MPs appearing, and we learnt that this was because women had now been given the vote, which previously had not happened in many parts of Switzerland. As the younger MPs appeared, Switzerland quickly asserted its superiority as an Alpine nation and the lowland Brits were soundly defeated. A handicap system was then introduced to keep the spirit of competition alive, which it certainly is. I had the honour for a few years to be captain of the team, due purely to seniority and not skiing ability! One year I realised that while we were in Davos, down the valley in the neighbouring village of Klosters Prince Charles was on holiday with Princes William and Harry. As Prince of Wales he was totally eligible to ski in the Lords and Commons team, and I was delighted when he immediately accepted my invitation to race. He did extremely well, and did it again the next year, too.

❋ ❋ ❋

During my later years at Robinson's and my first years in Parliament I had also taken on an additional responsibility on the board of Sale Tilney. This was a small group of companies created by Jane's father, Robert Tilney, of which he was chairman. He had started it in the 1930s, had it managed by others while he was away in the 1939–1945 war, and had built it up successfully to the stage where it was floated on the Stock Exchange in 1965. This involved a public advertisement offering shares in the company under his signature as chairman. At the very moment when these advertisements appeared in the principal newspapers he was actually lying unconscious in Nottingham Hospital, having had a serious fall out hunting with the Quorn, of which he was Joint Master. He was unconscious for many weeks: he did in fact survive till 1981, but he was never able to contribute again to the running of the group that he had done so much to create.

He was succeeded as chairman by his good friend David, Viscount Hampden, but Frances Tilney, his wife, was concerned that there should be some representation on the board to reflect the substantial Tilney family financial interests, and asked me to be a director. I was at that time a full-time employee of Robinson's, but I talked to John Robinson, the chairman, and he helpfully agreed to my doing this. I served as a non-executive director for the next six years, which involved travelling to London once a month for a board meeting, and a certain amount of midnight oil for board papers.

In 1971 the chairman retired because of ill-health, and I was invited to succeed him. By that time I was an MP and spending most of every week in London, and when we subsequently decided to move the head office from near the Tower of London to Queen Anne's Gate, just by Parliament Square, it made life a lot easier. In those days there were no offices for back-bench MPs, so it was a great luxury to have an office close by, and to fit in my work at Sale Tilney with my far greater commitment as an MP, and later on the front bench.

Robert Tilney had created the group from two main elements. The first was a very old British trading company based in Japan. Its origins went right back to the 1860s when foreign companies were first allowed into Japan, and its original address was No. 5 Yokohama, which indicated that it had the fifth warehouse to be built on the quayside in Yokohama. It suffered a major setback in 1923 with the Tokyo earthquake, which did such enormous damage to the city and all the businesses there. The company must have been quite successful, as they had seventeen Rolls Royces in stock, which were all destroyed – and they discovered that their insurance did not cover earthquakes! They subsequently developed a substantial trade in salmon, and Robert Tilney went to the Russian peninsula of Kamchatka as a young man to help establish a canning factory for the salmon caught by the Japanese fishing fleet. I subsequently met his companion on this lonely mission, a gentleman called Haratsika, known as the Father of Japanese Fishing. Mitsubishi became the exclusive selling agents for the canned salmon; Sale Tilney became the agents for half the exports to the UK, and John West for the other half.

The second element of Sale Tilney was Henry W. Peabody and Co. of London. They were a leading firm of brokers, specialising in dried fruits and canned goods, who took on the sale of the salmon. This became the most important business for Sale Tilney, until the next disaster struck: when World War II broke out, the business with Japan disappeared overnight, and the British staff in Japan were interned for the duration. Thirty years later I met the man who had been the head of Sale Tilney in Japan. Now retired and living in Kent, he told me how punishing it had been. While the Japanese staff from the company tried to help him, there was very little they could do, and it was starvation rations all the time. The one relief they had was when they were ordered to work picking the mandarin harvest. He said that for the first five minutes they were allowed to eat mandarins, and so desperate was he for any nourishment that in those few minutes he used to eat nearly a hundred!

Later on, of course, the Japanese themselves suffered greatly. We had an excellent Japanese non-executive director that I used to meet on my visits to Japan, who before the war had been general manager of the Bank of Tokyo in London, but who, by the end of the war, had been reduced to scavenging through the dustbins for any scrap he could find.

When peace came it was some years before trading could be resumed with Japan, but in October 1949 Chris Lepper, who had already experienced the earthquake and then the war in his service with Sale Tilney, was appointed as the representative in Japan, where he continued until his retirement in 1963. Before the war, there had been some kudos in Tokyo in working for a British company, but after the war, as Japanese companies rapidly grew in strength, that kudos faded. I found on my annual visits, however, a real measure of goodwill towards Sale Tilney for the support they had given their old trading partners like Mitsubishi and Marubeni as they strove to

My mother, *née* Molly Riches, driving the pilot car for the Prince of Wales's tour of South Wales in 1918.

My father (seated, centre) as President of the Literary Society at Emmanuel College, Cambridge, 1922.

© *Stearn & Sons, 72 Bridge St, Cambridge*

Thirty-three years later, in 1955, I, as Chair of the XII Club, was photographed in the identical spot!

© *Stearn & Sons, 72 Bridge St, Cambridge*

In the Rugby School 1st XI (standing, centre), 1951.

Aged nineteen, in the King's African Rifles in Kenya during the Mau Mau campaign.

Jane Tilney and I are married on
20 January 1960 at St Margaret's,
Westminster.

An Eve of Poll meeting for the Bridgwater
by-election, March 1970. Jane and I with
Iain Macleod, who became Chancellor
of the Exchequer three months later; a
month after that, he died suddenly.

© *Evening Post, Bristol*

As Shadow Energy Secretary, visiting Hinkley Point in 1978 with Conservative MPs and (far left) the excellent Research Department Energy specialist, a young Michael Portillo.

Meeting a suitably armed Saddam Hussein, Baghdad, 1982, with the city's Lord Mayor and an interpreter.

Helping the international swimming star
Sharron Davies to open the giant flume
at Butlin's, Minehead, Somerset, 1980s.

Remembering my earlier days in the
jazz band at a constituency party in
the 1990s.

Meeting Her Majesty The Queen on her
visit to Bridgwater in 1986.

Saving the West Somerset Railway: Sir William McAlpine
(foot on step), a well-known steam railway enthusiast, with
Robert Adley MP (left), David Nicholson MP and me, 1989.

The Staffordshire figurine, one of several presented to me over the years, of the highwayman Tom King, friend of Dick Turpin.

The apple press given to me in 1995, which makes wonderful apple juice and not yet wonderful cider!

Jane and I with our son Rupert and daughter Elisa, 1979.

As Minister for Merseyside, on the site of the Liverpool Garden Festival, 1983. © *Liverpool Daily Post*

With James Sherwood, Chairman of Orient Express and Sea Containers Ltd, a major figure in the transport world, 1983.

With Bob Reid, Chairman of British Rail, when I was Secretary of State for Transport, 1983.

The signing of the Anglo-Irish Agreement at Hillsborough, November 1985: Margaret Thatcher and Garret Fitzgerald, with Dick Spring (left), deputy Prime Minister of Ireland, Geoffrey Howe, UK Foreign Secretary (right), and me.
© *Associated Press*

With Lord Hailsham (left) at the funeral of Lord and Lady Gibson in Belfast, following their murder by the IRA, July 1987. Also shown is Northern Ireland's Lord Chief Justice, Lord Lowry (right).
© *Pacemaker Press Intl.*

Prime Minister Margaret Thatcher receives the wreath from me at the memorial service held at the Cenotaph in Enniskillen on 22 November 1987, for those killed in the bombing atrocity there on Remembrance Day.
© *Pacemaker Press Intl.*

Being winched down on to a Royal Navy minesweeper in Carlingford Loch in 1988, when the IRA inaccurately claimed to have machine-gunned me.

© *Naval Intelligence Section, c/o Senior Naval Officer Northern Ireland*

Presenting the Speaker of the US House of Representatives, James Wright, with the book of his family history, tracing their origins in County Tyrone. London, 4 July 1988.

Ed Koch, Mayor of New York, finding
out for himself the true story of
Northern Ireland.

© *Century Newspapers Ltd*

Launching a keep-fit campaign in Northern Ireland on
the steps of Stormont, 1989, with Richard Needham,
one of my ministers, and plenty of help!

© *Pacemaker Press Intl.*

Addressing the workforce of Shorts, Belfast, in 1989,
after signing the take-over agreement with Bombardier,
and introducing Laurent Baudouin, their new boss.

Meeting Chairman Kim of Daewoo in Seoul,
Korea, in 1989, before he opened a video-
recorder factory in Antrim, creating 500 jobs.

With Brian Lenihan, the Tánaiste or deputy
Prime Minister of Ireland, my co-chair of the
British/Irish Intergovernmental Council, at the
England v. Ireland rugby match in Dublin, 1989.

With Peter Brooke at Harland and
Wolff, 1989, as he succeeded me as
Secretary of State for Northern Ireland.

With the Earl of Home, a keen cricketer in his time, a
great Foreign Secretary and then, as Sir Alec Douglas-
Home, Prime Minister.

The Lord's Taverners v. the Lords and Commons match: the latter side included
Tim Rice (front, second left), Colin Cowdray (second right), David Frost (second
row, right), Derek Underwood (back row, right) and Willie Rushton (back row, left).

The Ski Race against the Swiss Parliament:
with HRH The Prince of Wales and
Winston Churchill (at left).

About to take my introductory
flight on a Tornado.

rebuild their previous powerful positions. By the time I was visiting Japan in the 1970s they were once more established as massive corporations, vastly bigger than Sale Tilney, but still very friendly.

I did wonder if that early support had been rather too generous, as I discovered that Sale Tilney had sold some land to Mitsubishi in Marunouchi, the commercial heart of Tokyo, where land had subsequently become extremely valuable.

One of the agencies that Sale Tilney held in Japan was for Morris Mini Minors, and I remember the clever TV commercial that sought to show how much room there was in this apparently small car, as it drove up and four massive sumo wrestlers got out!

In addition to its continuing trading business, Sale Tilney had a factory making adhesives under licence from Evode. I discovered that the origin of this came from the hunting field in Leicestershire. As Master of the Quorn, Robert Tilney knew Geoffrey Bostock, who hunted regularly with the Quorn and whose family owned Evode, the leading British adhesives manufacturer. A chance conversation led to Sale Tilney making Evode adhesives in Japan.

In the UK the company had acquired some very interesting engineering businesses. First it was to become the licensee for an American company, Ransburg of Indianapolis. They had originally been manufacturers of saucepans, but in the process had invented an electrostatic spray-painting process whereby the paint particles were charged with a high voltage and attracted on to the object being painted. This achieved a very even coating and a saving of up to 70% of paint. Whatever cost benefit it achieved for saucepans, the motor industry immediately seized on it, and this became a very profitable licence, with all the major car companies as customers. It would have generated even greater profits had there not been extensive pirating of the Ransburg patents, and a long series of infringement suits by Ransburg to protect its position.

The second engineering business was Badalex, which produced machines for the high-speed production of light-bulbs, fluorescent tubes and vacuum flasks. During my time it was a successful business built on the high quality of their equipment. It would have done even better if we could have developed the Chinese market. We had got our first order from the major Chinese light-bulb company, and knowing the size of the market in China, and hearing very good reports of the performance of our equipment, we knew that this would be the start of substantial further orders. When our sales director visited the company to discuss this, he was waiting to see the purchasing director when he felt the call of nature. The receptionist kindly indicated that there was a toilet just inside the factory on the production floor. As he went in the first thing he saw was our machine, not operating but stripped down, with every piece of it carefully labelled. We never got another order, and I suspect we were not the only foreign company to receive this treatment in China at that time.

In addition to trading in a wide variety of foods from all over the world, we also had one manufacturing company, Newtime Foods, which specialised in producing a whole range of jams under their own labels for the major supermarket chains. I remember they said they were also going to produce mincemeat. When I visited the factory I noticed they had acquired two new large cement mixers, and I assumed these must be for some construction for enlarging the factory. I discovered that they were in fact for mixing the mincemeat, and very successfully they did it.

I stayed as chairman until 1979 when, following the Conservative victory in the election, I joined the government, and therefore had to relinquish my outside activities. I shall always be grateful for my time with Sale Tilney because, while I was actively involved in Parliament and on our front bench in opposition, dealing first with Industry and then Energy, I was able to keep in touch with the outside world, and the practical problems that British companies were facing.

5 TRADE AND INDUSTRY, ENERGY AND ENVIRONMENT

During the Industrial Relations Bill in 1971, the business motion had prevented any debate after 10pm, but allowed outstanding amendments to be voted, which led to the all-night sittings that I have described. For the European Communities Bill there was no such prohibition, and we debated and voted through the night on a number of occasions. On one day, or rather night, we voted at midnight, at 2.30am and at 3.30am, and did much the same on the following night. With so much time being spent on the European bill, there were great problems with fitting in other important legislation. I remember one night we had finished voting on the European bill at 10.45pm, and we then started on another bill. We had votes on this at 3.10am and 5.30am, when we moved on to the adjournment debate, in which my neighbour, Edward Du Cann, raised the issue of the state of West Country roads. I wanted to support him and at 6.12am I rose to speak. Later that afternoon we returned to the European Communities Bill, and when I rose to speak on one of the amendments, I thought the time on the clock looked familiar, 6.12, exactly twelve hours later!

During my first years in Parliament I solidly backed the Conservative party and government and voted steadily in its support. That was until a bill was introduced to reorganise local government which included among other changes the creation of a new county of Avon. This was centred on Bristol but it included slicing off a substantial piece of north Somerset. The Somerset County Council and all Somerset MPs were strongly opposed to this, and launched a vigorous campaign, culminating in a crucial vote in Parliament, in which we, all Conservative MPs, voted against our government and persuaded a number of our colleagues to support us as well. It was a knife-edge result, 175 to 172, but sadly we were three votes short of victory.

Every week I used to write a column for the *Bridgwater Mercury* and for the *West Somerset Free Press*, the two weekly newspapers in the constituency. I am writing this in the midst of the Brexit controversy, and came across the report that I wrote in 1972 when we were debating the European Communities Bill, for our entry into Europe. In that particular week the key item was the final vote on a clause which set out how we were going to incorporate all the European regulations into our domestic legislation. The similarities with the events on the Brexit Bill are all too clear in my report:

> There was considerable interest in the result as it was known that the majority would be close, and in fact my own forecast of eight turned out to be correct. However, I think this close result may have misled many people into thinking that the government might have been defeated, but the situation is rather more complicated than that. What is happening in the European Communities Bill is that there are a large number of Labour members who believe very firmly that we should join Europe, but at the same time are under great pressure from their party to oppose the Bill. Likewise, there are a number of Conservatives who are opposed to our entry but are under equal pressure to support the government. The result of this is that at each of these critical votes, the two groups are watching each other very closely: the Labour members to ensure that there are sufficient abstentions on their side to prevent the bill being defeated and the Conservative opponents of entry being influenced by their actions as to whether they abstain or vote against the government. It is certainly a most complex situation and one which makes the whips' lives very difficult.

Forty-seven years later in the European Withdrawal Bill we saw it all again!

❋ ❋ ❋

In 1972 Chris Chataway had moved to a new position of Minister for Industrial Development in the new Department of Trade and Industry, with Peter Walker as Secretary of State. In 1973 we had joined the European Community and Peter had just returned from a visit to Canada, where a worried British High Commissioner complained of the feeling there that, in joining up with Europe, we were turning our backs on the Commonwealth.

He said the only time they ever saw British MPs were occasions when some of the more elderly of them might visit for some largely social junket, but that nobody had come to talk about UK/Canada relations in the future. Peter had just become Secretary of State of this new large department, with four Ministers of State, each with an MP as their Parliamentary Private Secretary. He decided that the PPSs, all young, newish MPs on the bottom rung of the ministerial ladder, would be the ideal team to go and carry a warmer message of our abiding interest in the Commonwealth at this critical time of our new relationship with Europe. The PPSs were Cecil Parkinson, Richard Luce, John Hannam and me. The proposal was that if we gave up some of our holiday, a two-week visit to Canada would be arranged for us to speak at different gatherings across the whole country, to see something of it, and to take our wives as well. Without being absolutely clear exactly what we were letting ourselves in for, we agreed to do it and I think that overall it was a great success. Certainly we had a very warm welcome. We started with a joint meeting in Toronto, went on to Ottawa, and split up to cover all the provinces, ending together in Vancouver. Hard work, and never done before, but a classic illustration of Peter's creative mind. I myself took on the French-speaking part of Canada, and in Quebec City I was the guest of honour at the annual dinner of the Chambre de Commerce de Québec. After a little practice with our excellent Consul General beforehand, I spoke at this huge gathering in French, and I can still remember the response of my host: '*Nous voulons remercier Monsieur King pour son allocution très intéressante, et parce qu'il a parlé en français*', at which the hammering on the table showed all too clearly the strength of feeling on that issue. Whether what I said was interesting or not to a large part of the audience was clearly of secondary importance compared to the language in which it was delivered. It was six years earlier that General de Gaulle, the President of France, had caused a major diplomatic incident during a visit to Quebec, when his speech included the cry '*Vive Québec Libre!*' By speaking in French, I was certainly not supporting the campaign for Quebec's independence from Canada, but simply did it as a courtesy to my hosts.

The start of my front-bench experience was as Shadow Minister of State for Trade and Industry in 1975, working with Michael Heseltine as Shadow Secretary of State. This became a very high-profile activity because the Labour government had just introduced the controversial nationalisation bill for aircraft and shipbuilding companies. Michael had the advantage of having been Minister of Aviation in the DTI in the previous Heath government and, as gamekeeper turned poacher, was able to organise a very effective plan of opposition to fight this damaging bill. Part of the plan was, while avoiding a guillotine motion, to prolong the committee stage until it ran out of time. In those days guillotine motions were used only sparingly and so the plan we worked to was to organise the committee stage so that we appeared to be making good progress in the initial stages but that when we got to clause 43, some two thirds of the way through the bill, we put the brakes on. Eric Varley and Gerald Kaufman were the front-bench team on the Labour side. They went to their business managers to try to obtain a guillotine motion to get the bill through, but were refused on the grounds that the bill was well on the way to completing its committee stage and they should just get on with it. Our other line of opposition was to claim that the bill was a hybrid one. This means that not everybody covered by provisions in the bill was being treated equally. When that was the case, such a bill had to go through a completely separate procedure, with it first being considered by a Hybrid Bill committee, who would hear representations from individuals who felt themselves unfairly treated in comparison to others affected by the bill. This procedure had to be completed before it could come forward for the normal bill procedure of the second reading and the other stages. This additional requirement meant that a lot more time was needed and the bill would have run out of time in the parliamentary session.

Our claim that this bill was hybrid was because we had discovered that the list of shipbuilding companies and ship repairers to be nationalised did not include one or two makers of mobile floating oil-drilling platforms, which were classed as ships and should have been included. We made our submission to George Thomas, the Speaker, and he agreed that it was hybrid and so declared it. When the Speaker made his announcement in the House, Michael Foot, the Labour Leader of the House, immediately announced that there would be a special day's debate to pass a motion that for this bill the standing order for hybrid bills should be set aside. When the debate occurred, it ended with two votes. The first was on our amendment saying that the hybrid rule should apply, and that was tied. Under the conventions of the House, because the vote had not been carried, the Speaker duly gave his casting vote to the government. The excitement mounted, because we knew that when we tied again on the government motion, the Speaker would have to give his casting vote to us and the government would be defeated. However, when the result of the vote was announced the government had won by one vote, and we quickly discovered that it had won only by cheating and breaking a pair. That led to riotous scenes in the Chamber, with individual members coming to blows, a group of Labour MPs singing *The Red Flag*, and Michael Heseltine lifting up the Mace and offering it to the Labour Party, as the respected symbol of parliamentary democracy that they had abused.

It was a very busy period in Parliament, with far too many late nights. One night when we were still voting at 3am, Michael came up to me in the voting lobby and said he had a problem over a speaking engagement the following night. At that time he was attracting attention as a star speaker, and was receiving a whole raft of invitations. He was still also much involved in the Haymarket Press, his very successful publishing business, for which he had to go urgently to South Africa. The engagement was a dinner in connection with the timber industry, and his secretary would send me the papers the following morning. The next day, after the all too short night's sleep, it turned out that the dinner was for the Timber Trade Federation Panel Products Division, which sounded fairly modest, until I looked further at his original invitation, which said, 'Dear Mr Heseltine, we are delighted that you are able to come to our annual dinner. We sit down 750 strong in the Hilton Hotel. Previous speakers have included Harold Wilson and the Archbishop of Canterbury.' I had never spoken at such a large dinner before, but I followed the old rule that in the end there is no great difference between a large audience and a smaller one in holding their interest and attention. It was helpful that that year's President of the Panel Products Division spent some time discussing the changes of their Articles of Association. Most of the audience were customers of the members of the Panel Products Division, and after some refreshment were not very interested in the changes to the Articles. They were more than ready for a little light relief, and with the generosity shown to understudies, I survived.

Among those at the top table was the Czech ambassador, who approached me afterwards and invited me to lunch at his residence. I accepted and was curious to see who the other guests might be. However, it turned out to be rather different from what I expected. When I arrived in Kensington Palace Gardens, the outer gate was firmly locked. I had to announce my name over an internal telephone and walk across an open forecourt before arriving at the front door. This was noiselessly opened, with the ambassador ready to greet me. It was apparent that I was the only guest, and after a brief moment in a small, intimate room with old Czech furniture, we went into a large, gaunt, square room with a small table in the middle. There were two chairs, and a ceiling light shone straight down on to the table. There was no sign of any service until a figure suddenly appeared behind me, a look-alike for Rosa Klebb, James Bond's sinister adversary in *From Russia with Love*, who proceeded silently to serve our lunch. It was clear from the position of the table and the lighting that I was being carefully recorded, and being checked out as a possible contact for future use.

When we came into government two years later, the new ministerial team at the Department of the Environment were being briefed by the Security Service on the threats we might face of subversion by foreign powers. We were told that the people particularly active in this field and in some ways proxy for much Soviet activity were the members of the Czech embassy, and we were advised that their preferred instruments of subversion were substantial money or sex. Until that moment the new ministers, having got over the first excitement of their appointments, were looking suitably depressed at the scale of some of the responsibilities they had taken on, but they did seem to cheer up considerably at this helpful piece of information!

I worked for two years with Michael on Trade and Industry and then Margaret asked me to join the shadow cabinet as shadow Secretary of State for Energy. Tony Benn was my opposite number and I had a number of amicable meetings with him, because he was looking for my support for legislation to reorganise the Electricity Council and the Central Electricity Generating Board, in which he was battling against what he called 'The Gang of Four', Frank Tombs (Electricity Council), Glyn England (CEGB), Frank Chapple (the electricians' union) and John Lyons (the electricity managers' union). He needed my aid because the Labour government at that time had no real majority and their business managers would not allow any new legislation unless the Minister concerned could guarantee that it had cross-party support. In the end, nothing came of it, but we had some good mugs of tea and friendly chats, as he had been a Bristol MP for nearly thirty years, so we had a lot of memories in common.

It was a busy time for me, getting to know a whole new range of activities, much helped by a bright young member of the Conservative Research Department, who covered energy, called Michael Portillo. The successful development of the oilfields in the North Sea was still relatively new, and I had a most interesting helicopter ride to one of the BP platforms in the Forties field. BP were keen to show me more of their activities, and arranged a visit to their remarkable project at Prudhoe Bay in Alaska. This became possible because I was returning from a visit to Sale Tilney in Tokyo, and in those days to fly from Tokyo to London you flew to Anchorage in Alaska and then on to London, so I was able to change there and join a flight making the ninety-minute trip north to the BP operation.

The basis of our energy policy was described as Co Co Nuke, standing for Coal, Conservation, and Nuclear. On the nuclear side, I took our conservative energy team down to see Hinkley Point B Station in the constituency. We also went to see the Fast Breeder Reactor, located at Dounreay in the extreme north of Caithness, apparently for safety reasons, in case there was an explosion, which I learnt only after our visit! In respect of coal, we took a much more active interest than previous Conservative teams, visiting a number of deep mines as well as open-cast mines, and clocking up a useful mileage on the moving belts that carried the coal back from the coal face, the return loop taking the miners often long distances along the mine shafts out to the coal-face, sometimes right under the sea. We also held a very successful Conservative Coal Conference at Nottingham University. In addition to talking to the National Coal Board management we met the union leaders, and I had an interesting meeting with Arthur Scargill, the President of the Yorkshire branch of the National Union of Mineworkers. He was keen to show me the impressive system he had for pursuing claims for compensation for any injury or sickness that his members incurred in the mines, and this was clearly one reason he enjoyed such loyalty from them.

After two years the election came, and Margaret Thatcher became Prime Minister. Her first task was to appoint her cabinet, and she decided to make Michael Heseltine Secretary of State for Energy. Although he had been Shadow Environment Secretary, she had remembered how he had complained about being moved from Trade and Industry to Environment when we were in opposition, and thought that he would prefer to take on Energy. Michael, however, made clear that he did not want to go to Energy and would rather continue with Environment. She agreed to that. Michael asked if he could have me as his No.2 in Environment, and that was the start of nearly four years of close partnership.

One of the characteristics of the British political scene is that, depending which party has been in government for a while, the chances are that the bulk of local government will be in the hands of the other party. This was demonstrated when we came into government in 1979. Labour had been in power for the previous five years and so increasingly major councils were now in Conservative hands. We had a number of very good Conservative councillors leading major authorities and Margaret chose one particularly good leader from Leeds City Council, Irwin Bellow, to be a minister with me in the Department of the Environment, where his great experience of local government was a real asset. To do this he had to be made a lord, and while this procedure can normally take a little time, it was obviously important for him to be able to start his work, both in the department and in the Lords, straight away. He therefore had an immediate meeting with the distinguished figure of Garter King of Arms to make the necessary arrangements, only to find that there was apparently a difficulty over what his title would be. There was already a Lord Bellew, and indeed a previous Garter was a Bellew as well, and Bellow was thought to be too similar a name to be permitted. He was under great pressure to start his work in the Lords, and was told that to keep to the timing of his introduction into the Upper House he had twenty-four hours to decide what his name was to be. He had urgent discussions with his wife, who, in all the excitement of his new appointment and promotion to the Lords, now faced the unpleasant and unexpected consequence that they would have to change their name. In the end he had to compromise, and Irwin Bellow duly became Lord Bellwin at the start of an excellent period of office.

The strength of Michael's position was that not only had he been a minister in the department during the Heath government but he had been shadowing it from opposition in the previous three years and thus was very well prepared for his new responsibilities. That sort of continuity and preparation very rarely happens in government. All too often people are moved after very brief periods in one office or another and as a result are ever more dependent on their officials to guide them in their work. Very often the same officials have had all too short a time in their positions, and that is a recipe for bad government.

I have a couple of particular memories of occasions when lack of continuity and experience was very evident. One goes right back to when I was the PPS to Christopher Chataway, who was Minister for Industrial Development. The Triumph motorcycle company had just gone bust and I remember one official saying that while these new Japanese competitors, with strange names like Suzuki and Kawasaki, might be able to compete with Triumph for the smaller 250cc bikes, they would never be able to challenge the Triumph on the big powerful 750cc bike: a classic illustration of an official who had just been moved from some quite different area of responsibility and who had no real understanding or background in the new area.

A second occasion was when I had been in post in the Environment Department for some four months and I asked for a meeting to discuss the vexed issue of local government finance. This was a very critical issue and I discovered that the meeting had attracted an exceptional number of attendees, I think about twenty, including the permanent secretary and his deputy, who decided to attend as well. In my naivety, I assumed that this would mean that we had brought together the largest possible gathering of knowledge on this vital subject, and I was looking forward to learning a lot from it. Early on in the meeting I raised a query on some particular point of information that I was anxious to know, and asked the permanent secretary. He turned to his deputy who turned to the under-secretary, who turned to the assistant secretary, who turned to a principal, who turned to the most junior official, who was actually able to answer the question. I realised that because of my particular interest in this subject after four months I was already further into it than almost all the people at the meeting. Their knowledge and experience were certainly much wider but not with the depth on that subject that I needed.

Michael Heseltine and I worked well as a team, partly, I think, because we both had a business background before we came into Parliament, Michael with the very successful creation of the Haymarket group, and I with twelve years in the printing industry and then being chairman of Sale Tilney for eight years before becoming a minister. When I first came into Parliament, most people had had some outside experience before becoming an MP, but increasingly I worry that more and more have had no outside experience and their whole previous activity has simply been in politics as a researcher or special adviser to an MP or a minister. There is no special training or qualification to become an MP or a minister. The only criterion for a minister that seems to count is whether the person is 'politically sound' in the view of the Prime Minister, and far less consideration is given to whether they would be any good as a minister.

Michael was a junior minister in the Department of the Environment during the Heath government. This gave him a priceless advantage: when he reappeared in 1979 as Secretary of State, he had had the chance to reflect on the lessons previously learned. He was committed to maximum delegation to his ministers, and wanted no frontline responsibilities for the department's many and varied activities. This gave him the time and opportunity to keep progress under review and to examine more critically the activities and functions of the department. This meant, for instance, that he played no part in the committee stages of bills. John Stanley took on the vitally important legislation for council tenants' right to buy. I had four bills, the massive Local Government Planning and Land Bill, Wildlife and Countryside, Local Government Finance, and a Water Bill, all of which took a good part of my time.

By all accounts, there could not have been a bigger contrast than between Michael and his predecessor, the Labour Secretary of State, Peter Shore. Michael, in his memoir, referred to Peter as a 'don manqué'. Apparently he used to take home with him in the evening as many as five full red boxes to study late into the night, giving rise to a series of questions to officials, stimulating yet more papers to be read. So far from five large red boxes, Michael had an especially small one made, which effectively limited its load!

One of the consequences of the semi-paralysis that the Labour government suffered in those years, aggravated by their lack of an effective majority in the Commons, was that we inherited a huge backlog of measures that the department was anxious to legislate. This became apparent in the Local Government Planning and Land Bill, which appeared with a monster 550 clauses and assorted schedules. At the start of a new session of Parliament the majority of bills are scheduled to start in the Commons but a few, normally less controversial, start in the Lords. It was true that significant parts of the local government bill were uncontroversial, and it was therefore proposed to start it in the Lords. This required the agreement of the opposition and Labour immediately indicated that it was quite unacceptable to start such a substantial bill in the Lords. The problem then was that the government business managers, appalled at the size of this monster and the time that it might take up, insisted that a substantial reduction was made to it. We had no choice but to agree and so 150 clauses were removed. On that basis the bill started in the Commons, and I was in charge for the committee stage. The original bill in full size had already been published before it was withdrawn and the 150 clauses removed. The first thing that happened when we started in committee was that Peter Shore, leading for the Labour opposition, immediately tabled as amendments the 150 missing clauses, which we could hardly vote down, as they were our own, and so the Bill returned to its original size!

Meanwhile Michael was able to look at the wider issues in the department and to give personal leadership where needed. We found that there was an urgent need for savings in public expenditure and Michael introduced a completely original approach for a secretary of state. Previously the concept was that ministers do policy, and officials execute and administer. Michael initiated a programme called MINIS, which stood for Management Information System for Ministers. This involved each part of the department reporting on what people were doing and what the cost was. Undoubtedly in many parts of the department, as widely throughout government, there was a far greater focus on policy and administration, and far less on organisation and expense. This was certainly proved by Michael with the Minis exercise, which reported directly to him, and which resulted over some three years in the reduction of numbers in the department from 52,000 to 39,000, without any evidence of real damage to its performance.

Margaret Thatcher was so impressed by his work that she asked him to make a presentation to the whole Cabinet. He did not have great success with his audience, many of whom clearly regarded it as not their job at all, encouraged, I suspect, by their own officials, who had no desire to see their Secretary of State interfering in this way.

In those days, Environment was a massive department. John Stanley was responsible for the critical areas of Housing and New Towns, and I covered virtually all the rest. The most important of these was Local Government, its structure and finance, but I also had the water authorities, nuclear waste, ancient monuments, Royal Parks, nature conservation, the urban programme, and more. One of our most successful initiatives, following a conference that I chaired at Sunningdale Civil Service College, was Business in the Community, led initially, and most successfully, by Sir Alistair Pilkington and Sir David Sieff. Within two years they had established enterprise agencies in every town with a population of 200,000 or more. This partnership of local government and local businesses has now spread much more widely, under the active patronage of the Prince of Wales.

In a successful Urban Programme we gave extra financial help for worthwhile projects that were above the level that local councils could manage. One was the Nottingham ice rink, which was rapidly crumbling away but which had been the starting point for Torvill and Dean, the wonderful stars of British skating, and we helped to ensure its survival. Another came up in an interview on the *Today* programme with the famous presenter Jim Naughtie. I was boasting of the success of our urban programme in rescuing important old buildings when he said, 'The next thing you're going to tell me is that you're doing something about Manchester Central station.' He was referring to a famous, long derelict railway station in the middle of the city. Luckily I was able to tell him that we had just decided to do precisely that! I had been shown the pictures of the station with its wonderful vaulted roof but with its steel bases all rusting away. Unless urgent and quite expensive action was taken, it was about to be condemned and then demolished. I believed it was too good a structure to lose, and we put up the funds to repair the bases, without, I must admit, being sure what future it might have. I'm delighted to say that it lives on now as the Manchester Central Exhibition and Conference Centre and is a valuable asset for the city and the region.

Another responsibility was for nuclear waste, and we did have on one occasion a serious spillage from a tank containing high-level radioactive waste. This was at Sellafield, where the spent fuel from the nuclear power stations was being processed. What was particularly disturbing was that the leak came from a tank whose dial indicated that it was only a quarter full. In fact, it was one and a quarter times full – the needle had gone round once already – and the tank was consequently overflowing. Understandably, this led to a major review of procedures at the plant after this extremely serious event.

We brought in measures to stimulate efficiency in local government. One was a requirement to maintain a register of derelict land, to encourage the development of brownfield sites, particularly those in public ownership. Another was the establishment of the Audit Commission with the responsibility of auditing local authorities, to obtain a sharper awareness of cost-effectiveness and value for money. This had a particularly significant effect in exposing the inefficiencies of the direct labour organisations, the in-house contractors that most councils had, which were notoriously uncompetitive, and which then largely disappeared.

The most significant change in the structure of local government concerned the Greater London Council and the Metropolitan County councils. It became increasingly clear that this additional level of local government was unnecessary, and made for a source of great friction with their lower-level councils. We decided to disband them and Margaret Thatcher announced this in our manifesto launch for the 1983 election campaign.

One story illustrates the extraordinary range of responsibilities that the department covered at that time. Before the water industry was privatised, there was a National Water Council, which kept a large cabin cruiser on the Regent's Park Canal, used for entertaining official guests. I had been invited to join the Council for lunch as we travelled along the canal. My timetable was too tight to complete the journey and it was arranged that I would disembark at the Regent's Park Zoo stop. I was surprised to find a welcoming party of zoo officials, and I then remembered extensive correspondence in the department about which minister would be responsible for zoos. As we got off the boat, I asked my private secretary if it had yet been decided and received the prompt reply, 'You are, Minister.'

One important item in the Local Government Planning and Land Act was the establishment of Urban Development Corporations, of which the first was the London Docklands Development Corporation. Michael had first identified the 5,000 acres of derelict former docklands, close to some of the most expensive real estate in the world in the City of London, in 1973 when he was Minister of Aerospace. He was in a small plane on his way to look at the possible site on the Foulness mudflats for a third London airport, and passed over this huge derelict area. He had already investigated the concept of a UDC for the south bank in London but unfortunately the election intervened and so the idea had to lie dormant until we came back into government. Michael had a real fight on his hands to introduce it. Geoffrey Howe and the Treasury were opposed to opening the doors to too much expenditure; Keith Joseph opposed it as too interventionist, and argued to let the market take its course. They put forward their arguments at a special meeting with Margaret, and, faced with two of the most senior ministers, Michael had a real challenge. However, he had the brilliant idea of consulting Reg Prentice, who had been the Labour MP for East Ham, but was now a Conservative MP and a minister of state. Reg Prentice's advice, having been MP for part of the area, was to tell Margaret, 'They're all communists down there!' So Michael said, when his turn came, that if nothing was done, nothing would happen, it was publicly owned land, polluted, and under the control of extreme left-wing councils, and that Reg Prentice had told him it was almost certainly controlled by the communists. Margaret had a great respect for his knowledge of the area, and that and the spectre of communists swung the day for her. Michael won!

Five London boroughs each had a piece of these empty areas. As some were run by militant Labour councillors, no government had previously been willing to entrust them with the very substantial sums of public money that were required for their redevelopment. Having created the LDDC, we gave it planning powers over that derelict dockland area, and substantial funds to tackle the large areas of contaminated land and to make them fit for development. To lead the new Corporation we chose as chairman Nigel Broakes, a very successful property developer in the private sector, and to give him good local support we chose as deputy chairman Bob Mellish, the former Labour chief whip and MP for Bermondsey. They had never met and I shall always remember the meeting in Michael's office, with Nigel already there, when Bob Mellish walked in. Michael introduced them and the first thing that Bob noticed as Nigel stood up was the smart-looking buckle on his belt. Bob looked at it and, knowing Nigel was a pretty rich man, said, 'I bet that's bloody gold!' Nigel was not the least abashed, and immediately replied, 'Yes, it is, and I made it myself!' I then remembered that he was a goldsmith. Bob enjoyed Nigel's smart reply, and that was the start of an excellent partnership, the fruits of which can be seen in Canary Wharf, and the wider Docklands area.

Little did I know that I myself, a couple of years after I had left the government, would become involved again in Docklands in the project to build a new exhibition centre for London in the Royal Victoria Dock. It happened that Andrew Mackay, who had been my PPS, thought, after my close involvement all those years before in the rebirth of the derelict docklands, that becoming their non-executive chairman could well make an interesting challenge for me. It did indeed, and for the next fourteen years I served as chairman of Excel London, and still continue as a director, as its Exhibition Centre and International Convention Centre bring ever-increasing and exciting life to the old Royal Victoria Dock (see Chapter 10).

One particular feature of the Docklands transformation that is often overlooked against the huge commercial developments that have sprung up is the great increase in housing. When we started the redevelopment, virtually all the people living there were council tenants. When we started talking about land being made available for private housing development, the local councillors told us that nobody in Docklands wanted to buy their own homes and they all preferred to be council tenants. That of course gave councillors considerable power, and some of the councils were virtually one-party states. We were determined to see that, in the new Docklands, there would be a choice of different types of housing, and we allocated an initial amount of land for 2,000 homes to buy. Five major housebuilders each undertook to build their share of the 2,000, and when their show homes were first open for inspection, with priority given to those already living in the area, the queue down the road stretched as far as the eye could see. So much for people not wanting to buy!

One new feature that Peter Walker introduced, that Michael Heseltine carried on and that I also operated in the departments when I was Secretary of State, was what we called 'morning prayers'. There was nothing religious about it, but simply a couple of times a week all the ministers in the department and PPSs got together, without any officials, to have a political review of whatever was happening. It was a very good idea as it was important for people to know what others were doing in other areas of the department, and to get across the right messages to the rest of the party in Parliament. It helped to avoid misunderstanding, and to keep a better relationship throughout the team. It is obviously important that you work as a team. I was very intrigued to hear one story from a former private secretary during the previous Labour government who had by our time moved on to a more senior position in the department. He told me that he was amazed how well we all as ministers seemed to get on. I replied that surely that was pretty essential and was it not always the case? He told me that in the previous administration when Peter Shore was Secretary of State, part of this person's duties as private secretary was to keep one Minister of State out of Shore's office, as he was apparently continually trying to get in. Why, I have no idea.

I cannot claim that the matters discussed at these 'prayers' were always simply departmental business or politics, and often interesting gossip crept in. I remember the start of one prayer meeting was somewhat delayed at Employment when Peter Morrison, the Minister of State, recounted the successful sale of a family picture at a Christie's auction the previous evening for a rather substantial sum of money, only to be outdone by Alan Clark. Alan had himself recently sold a Turner, I think of Folkestone, which his distinguished father, Lord Clark of the TV series *Civilisation*, had had hanging over the fireplace at Saltwood Castle, but which Alan had sold for an even more substantial sum.

One feature of Michael Heseltine's approach to his work was that he was never frightened to use the prestige and position of Secretary of State to enlist outside help to tackle some of our challenges. One illustration of this approach concerned a serious problem with the water authorities. When we came into government inflation was running at a ruinous 15% and it was vital to get it down. I received a report from the section in the department responsible for water authorities to say that they had been checking on the likely scale of increases in water rates for the coming year and that the figure was an average of 21%. That was clearly unacceptable if we were to have a real impact on getting inflation down. I discussed the problem with Michael and he suggested getting an outside scrutiny of their proposed charges. We contacted Ian Hay Davison of the accounting firm Arthur Andersen and asked for his help. Ian in turn approached the other major firms of accountants and asked them each to provide two of their brightest young accountants to help on this short-term assignment. We told the chairman of each of the water authorities that we would appreciate their cooperation in enabling these special teams of accountants to do their work. The chairmen were charming people but not all of them had much financial background. However, they made clear that they had personally challenged their finance directors on this important matter, and that there was simply no way in which they could avoid proposing the sort of increases of which we had been warned. They welcomed in our special teams, confident that they would be proved right. What the teams found, as they anticipated, were the extra safety margins of contingencies piled on contingencies, the well-known precautions that experienced finance directors are so skilful at making. Eliminating those reduced that year's increase from a disastrous 21% right down to 13% and initiated a downward path thereafter to more acceptable levels. Michael's initiative was in no ministerial handbook or departmental guide, but drew on his own previous commercial background and enterprise.

I don't think that had ever been done before, and Michael did it again when he took over responsibility for the government response to the Liverpool riots. Having seen the damage to the commercial infrastructure of Liverpool and the risk that it could happen elsewhere, he invited the chairmen of some of the best companies in the country to come with him on a bus tour round the city to see it themselves. It was clear that they had never received a request like this before and were initially pretty hesitant, but in the event the bus was full. I think they all expected that Michael was going to ask them for money, but instead he asked each of them to second one of their brightest young executives to the department to help see what could be done to restore the confidence of the city. Once again this was an original idea, using the authority of a Secretary of State for a most worthwhile objective.

One of the legacies that we inherited on coming into power in 1979 was the vexed issue of domestic rates. The 1974 Conservative manifesto had contained a commitment for the abolition of these, before any work had been done on how that might be achieved. We went into the 1979 election with the more cautious position that 'cutting income tax must take priority for the time being over the abolition of the domestic rating system'. Once in government we proceeded to consider the possibilities for the abolition of domestic rates. There were three effective options: local income tax, a local sales tax, and a poll tax. Michael Heseltine and I separately conducted a series of meetings with virtually all Conservative backbench MPs. We found that, while there was support for each of the options, there was also, unhelpfully, a blocking minority for each of them. Each group made clear that, whatever happened, one of the possibilities would be totally unacceptable and they would be strongly opposed to it. They divided more or less equally between the three options, although the poll tax was certainly the least popular, and it showed all too clearly how difficult the abolition of domestic rates would be. We therefore went into the 1983 election having failed to get agreement on an alternative to the rate and published a White Paper after the election stating that 'rates should remain for the foreseeable future the main source of local revenue for local government'.

After this election I had moved on to be Secretary of State for Transport and was therefore no longer involved, but I did hope that this policy, the legacy of all the exhaustive discussions we had had, was how the matter would be laid to rest. Sadly, this did not happen, and the community charge or poll tax emerged. The decisions to introduce the community charge were the product of an exhaustive number of meetings of E Committee, the ministerial economic committee chaired by Margaret Thatcher. By that time I was Secretary of State for Northern Ireland, and as the matter did not involve the Province I was not involved in the committee. I remember being outside the Cabinet Room and taking the opportunity to tell Nicholas Ridley, who was then responsible for Environment, of my worries about the proposal. He sought to reassure me that it would be all right because the amount per head would be only £150. In the event, after strong pressure from the Treasury, it ended up as more than double that, and was directly responsible for the sad consequences, not least to Margaret Thatcher.

✷ ✷ ✷

The House of Commons now rises each day much earlier than was the case during most of my time there, when we regularly sat till 10pm and often later. One consequence of this was that we used to eat together in the members' dining room, sitting wherever there was a spare seat. This had the good effect of regular contact between ministers and backbenchers, in a far friendlier atmosphere. One evening in 1982 I happened to be sitting next to Cecil Parkinson, an old Emmanuel College friend, who was then a very energetic Minister of Trade. He seemed to be permanently travelling overseas in his efforts to support our companies that were fighting for orders at a critical time for the economy. I asked him whether there were missions that other ministers could take on to support companies in the different areas for which we had responsibility. As my remit covered the water industry, which had a very high reputation worldwide, I offered to lead a mission if he would identify for me the countries that might have the best potential for further British exports. He welcomed the suggestion and I got a message shortly thereafter that the Department of Trade and Industry were very keen for me to lead a mission to three countries in the Middle East: the UAE, Jordan and Iraq. A mission was organised with representatives from eight different companies and water authorities covering every aspect of the provision and treatment of safe water.

We flew to Abu Dhabi and, after a briefing from our ambassador, attended our first meeting with the Lord Mayor. We were greeted by rather worried looks on the faces of the Mayor's staff and an even more worried look on the face of our ambassador, who had organised the meeting. We were immediately offered the usual Arab cups of coffee while the Mayor's staff huddled together trying to decide what to do. It turned out that he had just been given a new hawk; he had been extremely keen to try it out hunting in the desert, and had taken the day off! This was not a good start, but I understood subsequently that the embarrassment of the Mayor over the mix-up did lead to some excellent commercial opportunities in Abu Dhabi.

From there we went to Amman in Jordan and then, late at night because of the threat from Iranian fighters, we took off with no lights and blinds drawn, bound for Baghdad, which was the prime purpose of our mission.

Iraq had been identified as the number one priority opportunity for exports for the UK water industry. At that time Saddam Hussein had embarked on a disastrous war with Iran. He had attempted to take advantage of what he thought was a moment of Iranian weakness under the new rule of the Ayatollah, and to seize back disputed lands in the south of the country. In the process he had committed Iraq to an extremely costly war, in which both sides suffered enormous numbers of casualties. However, Iraq at that time was extremely wealthy as considerable funds had been accumulated by the previous government from its oil riches, and Saddam Hussein had embarked on a major programme of civic works to enhance Baghdad. As you flew into Baghdad you could see the dust cloud from forty miles away from all the construction work taking place. I had the opportunity before my visit to meet the Lord Mayor of Baghdad and the Iraqi Minister of Trade, who had come on an earlier mission to the UK. The Lord Mayor was my host for this return mission. The programme for the refurbishment of the city included the restoration of the historic part, new housing projects, motorway flyovers and a new metro system, but, most importantly for us, new sewage works and opportunities to enhance the clean water supply for the whole of Baghdad. The potential was indeed huge and it was an extremely successful visit. However, one was immediately aware that this was not like other countries. I had an immediate illustration of that from the secret police who escorted our ambassador's car after he had met me at the airport. The way they drove anybody else off the road who didn't immediately get out of our way showed a much more aggressive policing style and revealed just how ordinary citizens were treated in Iraq.

An even clearer mark of a rather different country was the news from the ambassador that, since my earlier meeting in London, there had been something of a Cabinet reshuffle, and it was alleged that some minister, a close supporter of Saddam, had himself shot three other members of the Cabinet. It was well known that Saddam had no compunction about executing people himself, including those of his own Cabinet, but this seemed to involve a new level of delegation on his part!

The various meetings of my team with different officials progressed in a perfectly normal way, with encouraging signs of future business. There was one useful gap in the timetable which I was able to spend talking to Stephen

Egerton, our ambassador, about the Iran/Iraq situation. As we were talking, we suddenly got a message that Saddam Hussein would like to meet me. The problem was that our secret police escort, who knew from our programme that we were not going out that afternoon, had disappeared. However, the summons had come and so we got into the ambassadorial Rolls, and in solitary splendour drove down to Saddam's palace. We were greeted and marched through a long, ornate audience chamber lined on both sides with those small gilt chairs that I think came from Asprey's in London. They had apparently been ordered by King Faisal before his assassination, and now rather incongruously lined both sides of this great audience hall. At the end of the hall in a room to the left was a small sitting room and there was Saddam Hussein, my host the Lord Mayor, and an interpreter. The reason Saddam wanted to see me was to ask me to convey a message of thanks to Margaret Thatcher for the support we had given to Iraq in arranging the refurbishment of some of their tanks in the Iran/Iraq war. The Iraqi army had British Centurion tanks, which had been acquired during King Faisal's reign, when relations between the UK and Iraq had been very good. They needed urgent maintenance and repair, and we had arranged to ship them to Jordan for the work to be done. This was, of course, at a time when the greater worry for the UK was the growing threat of Ayatollah Khomeini after the expulsion of the Shah of Iran, and the great danger it was posing for all our Arab friends in the Gulf region. Saddam had provided the vital defence against invasion from Iran.

The one moment I do remember from the meeting was when Saddam Hussein was sitting there in his habitual battledress uniform with a belt and holster. At one point he slapped the pistol in its holster, accompanying it with the words, 'I have the greatest respect for Mrs Thatcher.' The gesture and remark combined were clearly a sign of respect for another strong leader, even if Margaret Thatcher did not actually resort to firearms in pursuit of her objectives!

At the end of this interesting meeting and the conclusion of a very successful visit we flew back to Amman. Once again the flight was at night. What I do remember was how full the aircraft was of Iraqis in obviously poor health, who I learnt were on their way to hospital in London. This was at a time when there had been a close relationship between Iraq and the UK, and for those Iraqis who needed treatment, and could afford to travel, it was to the UK that they would come.

After I had spent a couple of years as Minister of State in the Department of the Environment, Margaret Thatcher intimated that I would be the next to be appointed when the next opportunity arose. When Peter Carrington resigned as Foreign Secretary over the Falklands, Ian Gow, Margaret's Parliamentary Private Secretary, came to see me with a personal message from her saying that she had hoped to appoint me next to the Cabinet. However, she had had a serious complaint from the Lords that where they had had three members in the Cabinet, with Peter's resignation they now had only two, and they said the next appointment must be from the Lords. She had therefore decided to appoint Lord Cockfield. I had no reason to challenge this, and accepted what Ian said. I happened to mention this very recently to Michael Jopling, the Chief Whip at the time, and he gave me a quite different story, to the effect that Margaret had been having real problems in Cabinet between the 'wets' and the 'dries'; she needed Arthur Cockfield as a confirmed 'dry' to strengthen her position, and it was nothing to do with the number of Lords in the Cabinet. Whichever was correct, the story given to me was much easier to deliver than the alternative one.

One of our responsibilities at Environment was looking after the Royal Parks in London, and we were approached by the committee that had raised money to put up a statue to Lord Louis Mountbatten, Earl Mountbatten, the Supreme Commander in South East Asia in World War II and subsequently the last Viceroy of India. His statue now stands close to Horse Guards Parade, just behind 10 Downing Street, on a well-mown lawn. The many visitors admiring it now may not know about the problem that had to be addressed before it could be set up there. When the committee applied to erect it, some alert person in the Treasury raised the question of the higher cost of cutting the grass. The mower, instead of being able to run up and down an uncluttered lawn, would now have to cope with the statue and its large plinth right in the middle, and there would be a lot of extra work clipping round it. The committee were told that they would need to cover the cost, in perpetuity, of the extra work. I believe the public appeal had raised some £70,000 to pay for the statue, but the committee were advised that the calculation of the extra cost of mowing, in perpetuity, was a further

£250,000! While there may have been some logic in charging something for the extra costs, the figure was so large that it only caused great hilarity. There was no way it could be paid, and very quickly it was agreed that the nation would nobly undertake, in recognition of Earl Mountbatten's great service, to carry the cost, for ever, of the extra mowing!

During our time at the Department of the Environment it was decided to open the former Cabinet War Rooms as a tourist attraction. These rooms, in the basement of the old Treasury building, were first used by Churchill in the bombing blitz on London, but had remained unused ever since. It was clear that people had just walked out of them one day and never come back, as soon as it was again safe to work in their offices above ground. You could also see what a rush it must have been to set them up in the first place. A wall in one office was covered with a giant map of the whole of Europe, created by tearing pages out of a large atlas and sticking them on the wall. There were separate rooms in the basement and very tight security, with separate entrances. People working in the various rooms had no contact with each other, as I learnt from somebody who had worked there. It was his responsibility to make regular reports to another official who he thought was many miles away in a different building, but he subsequently discovered that the person he was talking to had been on the other side of a very solid wall in the same basement.

Churchill had his own bedroom, and a small room beside it which looked like his lavatory because the door bore a Vacant/Engaged sign. It was actually a soundproof room with secure telephones, including one with a direct line to the White House in Washington. When the first person from our team went down into the War Rooms to see what needed to be done to open them to the general public, he picked up that telephone and a voice immediately said, 'White House here'. It must have been a real shock for the telephone operator in the White House when a light came on his switchboard that had not lit up for nearly forty years!

It was a good decision to open these historic Rooms, and they have now become a major tourist attraction.

My responsibilities as Minister for Local Government and Environment included the water authorities, the precursors of the present water companies. As a consequence I received the unusual invitation to be the guest of honour at a party in a sewage works. The Thames Water Authority had just completed extensions to the enormous Longreach sewage treatment works in Dartford, and had decided to host a lunch party for 300 people in a marquee at the works to commemorate this achievement. It was indeed a significant milestone. Previously a twenty-five-mile stretch of the River Thames through London was heavily polluted, practically devoid of oxygen and unable to support any fish, except, it seemed, a few extremely robust eels, and most of that pollution was coming from sewage works. The site itself had previously served 60,000 people but there were now 800,000 people in its catchment area and clearly substantial improvements had been needed.

It was certainly a bizarre location for a lunch with all the elements of a garden party, and it reached its climax with an incident involving the attractive Lady Mayoress of Dartford. I had admired the charming straw hat she was wearing. After lunch we embarked on a tour of the site, when she suddenly came rushing up to me and said, 'Minister – Minister, something terrible has happened', and I noticed that she was hatless. The truth dawned that, in her enthusiasm to examine more closely an enormous sewage digester tank with its massive sweeping arm agitating the sewage, her hat had unfortunately blown off and was now being rapidly digested as well!

One feature of our time in government was how often reshuffles of ministers became a muddle. Douglas Hurd used to say that it was because these were party political moves, and therefore officials were not involved and able to help control them. Douglas, having been political secretary to Ted Heath, the Prime Minister, before becoming an MP and subsequently a minister, had been able to see it from both sides. They are certainly complicated events because the resignation or dismissal of just one Cabinet minister can have the knock-on effect of five or six further necessary changes down the line. These new appointments have to get to know their new responsibilities, in many cases subjects of which they have no previous knowledge, and in those early days there are high risks of banana skins. All of this is a powerful argument for a good measure of continuity in government, and recent experiences of continual changes have not been happy. Margaret Thatcher recognised this when she promoted Michael Heseltine from Environment Secretary to Defence Secretary, and then made me, Michael's No.2, Environment Secretary in his place. Normally for my first job in the Cabinet I would not have been given this major department but since I clearly knew it extremely well after three and a half years, she wanted maximum continuity in the months ahead before her planned election. She made clear at the time that after the election she would want me to stay in the Cabinet but in another post.

Government reshuffles are always newsworthy, when gossip and rumour abound. Governments like to avoid this and maintain the picture of calm and efficient administration. This nearly came unstuck over Michael's and my appointments. As I understand it, Margaret and Willie Whitelaw met in Number 10 at the end of the Christmas holiday following John Nott's resignation as Defence Secretary. They agreed the various appointments and broke for a friendly lunch, before Margaret was to telephone Michael and then me to advise us of our new appointments. The calls were put in to us both, with confidence in the legendary efficiency of the Number 10 operators always to find their man or woman. This time they really met their match. Michael was a keen birdwatcher, and was on holiday in Tobago; I was in Davos at the Anglo-Swiss Parliamentary Ski Week. I don't know how long they took to reach Michael, but in my case it was not till the late afternoon after a suitably exhausting day's skiing that I came back to our hotel. I was met by a thoroughly excited concierge, who had been bombarded all afternoon by calls from Number 10. When I called them, I thought the operator was going to pass out with the relief of finding me and putting me straight through to a highly impatient Prime Minister! When I then had to return quickly to London, and somebody asked who the new Secretary of State was, he got the smart reply, 'He's the one with snow on his boots!'

Michael Heseltine inherited from Peter Walker two particular attributes. They were both hands-on ministers and very good delegators. Moreover, they were not frightened to use the prestige and position of a Secretary of State to get people to work for them on good ideas of their own.

My own career is a classic illustration of the long and the short in the appointments that I held. Having started in May 1979 as Minister of State in the Department of the Environment, and because of Michael's very sensible policy of maximum delegation, I found myself responsible for some two thirds of the department's activities, and continued in that office for some three and three-quarter years. When in January 1983 Michael became Secretary of State for Defence, it did make sense for Margaret to decide that, instead of bringing in somebody more senior to take over the major Environment department, she would ask me to take it on just until the election that she was planning to hold in June. After the successful election she then asked me to take over Transport and to reorganise that department by bringing in aviation as well, which had not previously been covered by it but had been under Trade and Industry. When I moved to Transport, I discovered that there had been fourteen ministers of transport in as many years. In my speeches as the new Secretary of State, I drew attention to this, emphasising the need for much greater continuity, which I was determined to provide. Four months later, following the resignation of Cecil Parkinson, another reshuffle became necessary and I became Secretary of State for Employment, in the process becoming the shortest-serving Transport Secretary of all. Then after an eventful two years including the miners' strike, and the successful passing of the Trade Union Reform Act, Margaret asked me to take over in Northern Ireland. Four years there, and of necessity working closely with the security services and the army, were an ideal preparation for becoming Secretary of State for Defence.

6 TRANSPORT AND EMPLOYMENT

After the election in June 1983, when I became Secretary of State for Transport, my department's new additional responsibility for aviation was immediately highlighted by a bizarre incident right at the beginning of the new administration. There had been a federal grand jury investigation in the United States into alleged price-fixing and collusion between Laker Airways and other airlines, including British Airways, in connection with an agreement called Bermuda Two. British Airways was at that time state-owned and it had been summoned to give evidence to the federal grand jury. This was regarded as an unacceptable intrusion into legitimate British interests and Cecil Parkinson, as Secretary of State for Trade and Industry, issued an order under the Protection of British Interests Act ordering British Airways not to give evidence to the federal grand jury.

Shortly afterwards, the then US Vice President, George H.W. Bush, visited the UK in connection with US proposals for the stationing of cruise missiles in Europe, wishing to seek the agreement of the other NATO countries. His first call was on Geoffrey Howe, newly installed as Foreign Secretary. After the meeting George Bush and his team walked across with Geoffrey to Number 10 for a meeting with Margaret Thatcher. Geoffrey's private secretary rang ahead to say that it had been a very good meeting and that no difficulties had arisen. Margaret duly welcomed George Bush, but was then extremely surprised to receive a stern statement from him, saying that he was instructed to complain in the strongest possible terms about the interference by the British government in the proper process of justice in the United States. This caused great consternation. It was apparent that in the short distance between the back entrance to the Foreign Office and the door of Number 10, an urgent messenger had arrived from the US embassy with a request from Washington that the Vice President should deliver this complaint. The US ambassador was badly caught out, as neither he nor indeed the other members of the party knew anything about the matter and were left with no alternative but to deliver it as requested. Understandably the team at Number 10, equally in the dark, were not amused by this bizarre development at the start of what was intended to be an entirely friendly call.

One of my first tasks at Transport was to appoint a new chairman for British Rail. There had been a lengthy consideration of the alternative candidates before the decision was taken to offer the post to Bob Reid. Because of the delay I needed to establish as quickly as possible whether he would be willing to take it on. It turned out that he was a keen climber and was away on holiday, somewhere in the Dolomites in Italy. Some smart detective work established that he would be available later on in the evening, and he had to take my call in an extremely noisy *albergo* bar. Fortunately he heard enough of my offer to be able to accept it, and he became a very well-respected chairman of British Rail.

One of my last visits as Secretary of State was to go with him to the British Rail research laboratory in Derby. I suddenly realised that our train was going straight through Sutton Bonnington, Jane's old home. I remembered that the railway line ran right beside the garden of the house, and there was an old private platform. I had been told that the family used to be able to get the train to stop specially for them. I mentioned this to Bob Reid and he kindly sent me later the details of the involvement of the Pagets, one of whom was Jane's grandmother. Between 1843 and 1919 three Pagets had been chairmen of the railway, initially called Midlands County Railway, and then Midland Railway, which became later the much better-known LMS, and they had indeed had the power to stop a train, either to go to London or to travel north.

What turned out to be my last speech as Secretary of State for Transport was made to the Conservative party conference in Blackpool. Transport had been given the final slot of the day and the remaining audience, suitably exhausted, were listening with modest interest to my speech, in which I described the various strands of our transport policy and its relationship to the economic and social life of the country. The audience were sitting quietly until I added one last item which had just crossed my desk. It related to the unacceptable disregard of parking regulations in London by various foreign embassies, who made use of their diplomatic immunity and CD plates to escape prosecution. One could sense a quickening of interest in the hall. My statement that this flagrant disregard of parking regulations could not be tolerated, and that I was determined to take action on it, immediately provoked a thunderous round of applause, whereas my much more significant comments on general transport policy had passed without a murmur!

My brief time at Transport coincided with Greece's tenure of the Presidency of the EU. A meeting of EU transport ministers was hosted by the Greek government in Athens, and included in the programme was a fascinating visit to the newly discovered tomb of Philip of Macedon, father of Alexander the Great, at Vergina. I was particularly pleased to see that one distinguished English professor who was closely involved at Vergina was Frank Stubbings, who had been my classics tutor at Emmanuel College.

When we came into government in 1979, the memory was all too fresh of the disaster of the previous miners' strikes in 1972 and 1974, with the three-day week and the failed election under the banner of 'Who governs Britain'. The coal industry was still making great losses and it was clear that some pit closures were unavoidable. This came to a head in February 1981. Faced with an imminent strike by the National Union of Mineworkers and knowing that the government was not ready to deal with one, Margaret Thatcher dropped the proposed programme of pit closures. It was clear that action was essential to put the coal industry on a sound footing, but it was equally clear that, as this would involve closing a number of pits, there would inevitably be the threat of strike action once again. This was made all the more likely by the election of Arthur Scargill as the new President of the NUM, somebody well to the left of his predecessor, Joe Gormley. This time it was essential that the government and the country were organised to face the situation, and so plans were made to ensure that a strike would not shut the country down again. This involved the build-up of substantial coal stocks at the power stations and at the pitheads, and the need to ensure that the law properly distinguished between lawful and illegal picketing, so that the transporting of stocks was not impeded. Critically also, as it proved, the police had to be given the authority and resources to enforce the law.

Just as I became Secretary of State for Employment after the reshuffle in October 1983, the first signs of trouble emerged with rumours of the pit closure plans by the Chairman of the National Coal Board, Ian MacGregor, which led to an overtime ban by the NUM. On 6 March 1984, MacGregor announced that 20,000 jobs would go that year, and on the 8th the NUM declared official strikes in Yorkshire and Scotland, significantly without a ballot. On the same day a special committee, MISC 101, was set up, which effectively resembled a war cabinet, with the Prime Minister; Nigel Lawson, ex-Energy and now Chancellor; Peter Walker, the new Energy Secretary; Leon Brittan, the Home Secretary; Norman Tebbit, Trade and Industry; and me. It continued to operate until the following March, when the NUM voted to return to work. Under the Prime Minister's leadership, the key roles fell to Peter Walker dealing directly with the National Coal Board and Leon Brittan with the police.

There was no question about the gravity of the situation that we faced, with the real risk, if we had failed, that the government could have collapsed and Margaret Thatcher would certainly have been destroyed. Part of my concern was to try and ensure that no other unions joined in a wider battle, and apart from the brief period of a dock strike that was achieved. We were right to be worried, since early on Scargill stated that the downfall of the government was a specific objective of the strike. He immediately embarked on mass picketing and aggressive intimidation of the Nottinghamshire miners, who did not support the strike. Picketing reached its peak at the Battle of Orgreave, where 5,000 police found themselves facing the mass picket there, possibly as many as 10,000. This was a coking plant, producing vital material for the steel industry, for which reliable, regular deliveries were essential, and fortunately the substantial police numbers were able to keep the plant working, and the necessary deliveries made.

This robust action against illegal picketing, the determination of many miners to keep working, and the high level of coal stocks at the power stations avoiding any risk of power cuts, all contributed to the eventual collapse of the strike. What also caused it to fail was the lack of any great political or public support, noticeably from Neil Kinnock, the Leader of the Opposition, who was particularly critical of Scargill's failure to put it to the vote of the whole NUM before calling the strike.

It was certainly very tough in the early months of the strike, but we had no choice other than to resist it, or it would have been an open invitation to other more left-wing union leaders to join in the attack on the government, and do huge damage to the economy. In the end it lasted a year, and Margaret Thatcher rightly got full credit for her resolute leadership at this critical time.

In between the more serious events of my time at Employment, I remember well two entertaining incidents. The first was when I attended an Anglo-French conference held at the Palais des Papes in Avignon. This was an interesting gathering that included politicians and figures from the media, education and industry, and climaxed with a dinner attended by Margaret Thatcher and the French Prime Minister. We split into a number of different groups to discuss a range of topics. I attended one on employment and next door there was another group talking about cultural exchanges. I remember this well, as in our group the French minister opened the discussion and the first contribution from the British side would come from David Lea, then the deputy general secretary of the TUC. The French minister spoke for some ten minutes, but I could see that David was getting increasingly agitated by his remarks. He began his reply with a strong complaint that the Frenchman's contribution had been quite irrelevant and that visits of ballet companies or orchestras between our countries had nothing to do with solving the serious problems of unemployment. It transpired that in listening to the interpreter he had unfortunately been switched to the wrong channel and had heard a speech from the room next door about cultural exchanges! Not the best of starts, but normal service was quickly resumed.

The second incident was a bizarre event when President Mitterrand of France came on a state visit in 1984. It started in the normal way with a state banquet at Buckingham Palace. The next day he went to Dartmouth to commemorate his sailing from there to join the French Resistance in the Second World War. While he was on his way, the lead story on the BBC News was the shock discovery of Semtex explosive in the garden of the French embassy, with more of the explosive found in a bedroom at the Grosvenor House Hotel. It turned out that this room had been occupied by a French police inspector, a member of President Mitterrand's escort. It was some time later that I discovered the whole story. The inspector had applied to bring his own dogs for the visit, but, under the quarantine rules, he was refused permission. He was convinced that only his dogs were good enough to find the explosive, and that the British police dogs were not up to the job. He therefore decided to bring some Semtex and plant it in the embassy garden – but he was proved wrong, and the British dogs passed the test! Margaret Thatcher was understandably shocked by the behaviour of this man on the President's team, and President Mitterrand, if clearly embarrassed, was said to have thought that the government should have prevented the BBC from reporting the story. It did indeed lead to a temporary diplomatic frisson, but quickly the antics of this latter-day Inspector Clouseau were not allowed to interfere with the successful achievement of an important state visit.

When I became Secretary of State, I introduced a bill that required trade unions to have a proper set of rules, to be registered, and to require a properly conducted secret ballot to be held before a strike could be called, if they wished to preserve their legal immunity as a trade union. Failure to do so would put union funds at risk. This became the Trade Union Act 1984 and the importance of the secret ballot was to tackle the tyranny of the open-air 'car park' meetings, which had done so much damage, not least to the car industry with its frequent strikes. Barbara Castle had tried something similar in her plan *In Place of Strife*, in 1968, but had been defeated by her Labour Cabinet colleagues. I remember well when I introduced the bill in the House, the impassioned speeches of two new Labour members denouncing this gross interference in the internal affairs of trade unions. They were a Mr Blair and a Mr Brown, and I was interested to see that when they came into government, the right to a secret ballot lived on.

During my time as Secretary of State for Employment a sudden problem arose over union representation at GCHQ. In those days far less was known about GCHQ and the absolutely critical role it plays in our security. Most MPs knew that it was an organisation in Cheltenham, that it was the successor of Bletchley Park – which was so good at breaking German codes in the war. Unfortunately there had been instances of industrial action in 1979 and later which had threatened to interrupt the continuous effective operation of the organisation. What was not known more widely at that time was that it was a vital element in the Five Eyes intelligence network between the United States, Canada, Australia, New Zealand and the UK. It was a global network in which different countries took responsibility for continuous surveillance of different areas of the world, and the United States in particular was concerned about the risk that industrial action could undermine that vital continuity.

It had long been accepted that for both MI5 and MI6 union membership was not appropriate, and successive governments had recognised this, but it had never been applied to the third critical leg of our intelligence and security, GCHQ. Once the government saw the unions calling for industrial action there, the risk of interruption to its operations was clear, not just to ourselves but also to our partners in the Five Eyes alliance. It was therefore decided to put GCHQ on the same basis as the other intelligence agencies and to remove from its staff the right to union membership and to set up instead a staff association. Geoffrey Howe, as Foreign Secretary, had ministerial responsibility for it, and told me that he wished as a courtesy to explain our proposed action to Len Murray, the well-respected General Secretary of the TUC. Because of my responsibility for industrial relations, he asked me to arrange the meeting in my office, to which I could also invite just one senior official from my department. This reflected the enormous secrecy and sensitivity of GCHQ at that time. To be honest, I had very little knowledge then about GCHQ, and it was clear at the meeting that Len Murray didn't either. Geoffrey explained the problem very well, that action was essential for our national security, and Len, as a good patriot, listened politely to all he said, including his final request for confidentiality.

That was indeed the calm before the storm, which came in full force when Geoffrey announced the change in a statement in Parliament. The Labour Opposition reacted with fury to this proposal to remove the right to trade union membership from all those working at GCHQ, and they were joined from our benches by Charles Irving, the MP for Cheltenham. In his criticism he made the point that he was doing it on behalf of the people at GCHQ, all of whom, he stated, were his constituents. This was indeed the impression at that time, but it was quickly found not to be true. That weekend, when some MPs were having their regular surgeries in their constituencies, small groups asked to see them. Correctly observing the Official Secrets Act, they were very discreet about their work but wanted the MP to know of their objection to the proposal. All too quickly the range of GCHQ outstations was suddenly revealed in Yorkshire, Cornwall, Somerset and Staffordshire.

The Labour opposition and the trade unions refused to accept the argument that GCHQ was a special case; they believed that it was just the start of a Conservative government attack on trade unions in general and demanded an urgent debate. This took place the following week, with Geoffrey Howe opening for us; I had the responsibility of doing the wind-up. Facing us were the heavyweight team of Denis Healey opening and John Smith winding up, with a number of interruptions from Jim Callaghan, the former prime minister, who had long-standing union connections. While we held our own in the debate, and the changes from union membership to a staff association were carried through, the Labour Party took on a long-standing commitment to reverse it, which they subsequently did.

✼ ✼ ✼

In my second year as Employment Secretary in 1984, the party conference took place in Brighton, with our headquarters in the Grand Hotel. Whether there was particular intelligence of a possible IRA attack, I don't know; I certainly noticed far tighter security around the hotel. I remember it well, as my driver found he could not reach the hotel since all the roads around were closed, and I had to walk some distance, lugging my suitcase, to get to it. Nobody realised that the bomb was already in place, having been planted some four weeks before. It used to be said in the earlier days of the Troubles that one of the things that made some attacks less effective was the 'Paddy Factor', what the British soldiers saw as the Irish tendency to make mistakes. This was certainly not the case in the Grand Hotel, where not only did they use an extremely efficient timing device, but it was set to go off at the right time. That was in the middle of the night before the Prime Minister's speech to the conference, when she was most likely to be staying in the hotel. What they could not overcome was the very solidity of the Victorian pile that was the Grand Hotel. While, sadly, there were tragic casualties, Margaret Thatcher survived, but it could have been a completely different story if it had happened two years earlier. In 1982 the hotel was being refurbished and we were based in another, much more modern and much flimsier hotel, where I suspect a similar bomb would have caused vastly more damage and loss of life.

7 NORTHERN IRELAND

In September 1985, after I had done two years heading the Department of Employment, Margaret Thatcher asked me to be Secretary of State for Northern Ireland. Two months earlier, Douglas Hurd, then the Secretary of State, had briefed the Cabinet on the secret discussions that had been taking place with the Irish government, and had set out the basic outline of what was to become the Anglo-Irish Agreement. In the September reshuffle, he had become Home Secretary and Margaret asked me to succeed him. The one question I asked her, having so recently heard the outcome of the secret negotiations, was whether she was determined to see it through, and she assured me that she was. She then insisted that I was not to accept her proposal without first consulting Jane, a very good illustration of her constant concern for families.

What Margaret understood well was how significantly our lives would be affected by this new appointment. When I asked Jane, she immediately and very loyally supported my acceptance, but to be honest, neither she nor I really appreciated at that time what a difference it would make to our lives. The immediate introduction of tight security, with close police protection not only at home but wherever we were, and the amount of travel between London, Belfast, the constituency and our home was a major burden. The security arrangements for the Northern Ireland Secretary in those days were of an order entirely different from those for any other Cabinet minister except the Prime Minister. In London it meant leaving our flat and moving into secure accommodation, where we were to stay for the next seven years, covering my time in both Northern Ireland and Defence. At home, the police moved into a small cottage right beside the house and stayed there for the next twenty years. Although we were extremely lucky with the excellent people involved in our protection, it was a major loss of privacy, and particularly tough for Jane to endure.

I accepted it as a major challenge, in which the rewards of success would be worth so much for the whole United Kingdom, suffering, as it had, the long years of the terrorist campaign. If the new initiative could be successfully introduced, it would be a great step forward and its problems well worth tackling.

After speaking to Jane and confirming to Margaret that I was happy to accept, I stayed in Number 10 having a cup of coffee with Willie Whitelaw, to pick his brains as a former N.I. Secretary of State. The fact that I didn't leave Number 10 for some time gave rise to the rumour that it had taken a long time to persuade me to accept, which was not true, but an early example of how easily fake news could be spread, not least in Northern Ireland!

The challenge was clear enough: the many years of communal strife with a continuing terrorist threat, and in 1984 the Brighton bomb, designed to kill the Prime Minister and her Cabinet; 20% unemployment; little inward investment; and the two largest companies, Harland & Wolff and Shorts, widely perceived as the heartland of the Protestant majority's jobs, both facing serious problems. On top of that, the large numbers of unemployed provided a ready recruiting ground for criminal and terrorist groups. Complaints by the minority Catholic community of discrimination against them in employment, and their lack of confidence in the justice system, were regularly advanced by Dublin, and backed by the powerful Irish-American lobby in the United States. This whole depressing picture had existed for far too long, and now this new initiative offered the prospect of real change for the better.

The learning curve for a new Secretary of State was steep enough. I had only ever made a couple of brief visits to Northern Ireland, once for a most enjoyable holiday when our parents took my sister and me to Newcastle in County Down to enjoy a wonderful golf course and to stretch our legs on the Mountains of Mourne, and once in connection with the wedding of an old friend close by that beacon of the weather forecast, Malin Head. The politics of Northern Ireland had been a separate world, with a Governor and its own Prime Minister and Stormont Parliament quite separate from the members of Parliament that it sent to Westminster, and there was a lot to learn. The very first brief I received started with a vocabulary: the important nuances between unionism and loyalism, and nationalism and republicanism. What

I also found was a quite different range of responsibilities from those of a Secretary of State in London. I became in effect both the Governor and Prime Minister of Northern Ireland, well summed up in an *Observer* article describing me as the embattled Viceroy of Ulster.

During the next two months I was busy meeting as wide a range of people as possible from both communities, and the police and the army in their vital role. At the same time the discussions were continuing between London and Dublin on the Agreement, and while unionist suspicions were growing about what might be proposed, it was indeed the lull before the storm.

The background to the Anglo-Irish Agreement was an attempt to resurrect the discussions on how a closer relationship between the Republic of Ireland and the UK could have a major impact on the very unsatisfactory state of continuing terrorism and the feelings of alienation among Catholics in Northern Ireland. These discussions had followed the publication of the report of the New Ireland Forum, which had proposed three options: a united Ireland; a federal Ireland; or joint Anglo-Irish authority. Garret Fitzgerald, the new Fine Gael Prime Minister, had hoped that progress could be made in his talks with Margaret Thatcher, at least in respect of the third option. However, subsequently, each option was summarily dismissed by her in Parliament: 'Out – Out – Out'. In spite of the abruptness of this dismissal, Garret Fitzgerald was determined to try to reach an agreement, because it was clear that terrorism and the gangster-like politics of the IRA and Sinn Féin were a threat not just in Northern Ireland but to the whole of the island of Ireland.

Official discussions continued, led on the British side by the Cabinet Secretary, Robert Armstrong, and on the Irish side by their Cabinet Secretary, Dermot Nally. Margaret Thatcher's key interest in reaching some agreement with the Irish government was to improve security, and the terrorist attack on the Grand Hotel in Brighton made her all the more determined to beat terrorism.

These discussions were conducted in great secrecy and the presentation at Cabinet in July 1985 was the first that other ministers knew about them. I discovered, as soon as I went to Northern Ireland, that the unionist parties had not been consulted for fear that the previous unionist veto would once again be applied. Against that, the unionist confidence in their position was reinforced by the memorably blunt rejection by Margaret Thatcher of the previous Irish proposals, and by the formidable presence of Enoch Powell on their unionist benches in Parliament.

I understood why it was decided to proceed without consulting the unionist majority representatives, but it did inevitably result in a far greater sense of outrage and hostility felt widely across the unionist community, and it made my time that much more difficult in the earliest months. The anger was increased by the discovery that John Hume of the Social Democratic and Labour Party had been kept closely informed of the progress of the Agreement by the Irish government.

When I became Secretary of State the negotiations were in their concluding phase. As I studied the Agreement and the arrangements around it, I insisted that Ken Bloomfield, the head of the Northern Ireland Civil Service, should be included so that I could have the fullest briefing on all the aspects that would be involved in introducing it. With his advice I subsequently pressed for certain late amendments, and my actions have since been misrepresented as trying to derail the Agreement. I was trying in fact to minimise what were clearly going to be serious problems over its introduction. One particular point concerned the location of the permanent secretariat of the intergovernmental ministerial conference. It had been proposed that it should be based at Stormont Castle, the seat of government in Northern Ireland. The thought that senior Irish officials would be based there would have been bound to inflame unionist feelings, and the likely outcome would be major demonstrations disrupting the work at the heart of the Province's government. Fortunately an alternative site at Maryfield was established. When the totally predictable demonstrations and picketing ensued – while it was not a very enjoyable experience for the officials working there – at least it did not disrupt the whole of government.

The warning of the unionist hostility to come occurred on the day before the signing of the Agreement during Prime Minister's Questions in the House of Commons when Enoch Powell, then a unionist MP, got to his feet and said in the iciest of voices: 'Does the Prime Minister understand, and if she does not, she soon will, that the penalty for treachery is to fall into public contempt.' There was a rumble of disapproval from the Conservative benches at his question. The Prime Minister was clearly shaken by this aggressive statement but rose to her feet and replied, 'Does the right honourable gentleman understand that I find his remarks deeply offensive,' and sat down to a roar of approval from the benches behind her.

The final question was where the Agreement should be signed. Security concerns suggested that Aldergrove Airport might be the best location, but it was finally agreed to hold it at Hillsborough Castle, my official residence as Secretary of State. Margaret Thatcher, Geoffrey Howe, the Foreign Secretary, and the Irish delegation of Garret Fitzgerald, Peter Barry and Dick Spring were safely delivered to Hillsborough the next day before the news of the meeting spread more widely in the Province. When Margaret arrived she went immediately upstairs to make a telephone call. I discovered that she was talking to Ian Gow, her former PPS and most loyal supporter, now a minister, who was resigning in protest over the Agreement. She was not able to persuade him to withdraw his resignation, and notwithstanding that unfortunate background the signing ceremony went ahead, against much loud noise from the crowd protesting at the gates, led by Ian Paisley.

The signing took place in front of the television cameras and Margaret Thatcher spoke first. She then invited Garret Fitzgerald to speak, and to my consternation and, I think, hers, he started in Gaelic, so we had no idea what he was actually saying! It was subsequently confirmed that he had said, 'Nationalists can now raise their heads, knowing their position is and is seen to be on an equal footing with that of the members of the unionist community,' which was perfectly acceptable.

It was the first time I met Garret Fitzgerald, for whom I developed real respect and affection. I was always conscious of his particular strength as Taoiseach in understanding the two traditions in Ireland, as his father was a Fine Gael minister in the Republic and his mother a Belfast-born Presbyterian. He recognised the significance of four centuries of Unionism and the Protestant fear of the element of authoritarianism in Catholicism. His great ambition was for peace and stability in Northern Ireland and, with the reconciliation of the two major traditions, to create a new climate of friendship and cooperation between them.

The final shape of the Agreement fell some way short of the separate ambitions of each side. On the British side, a particular prize would have been the amendment to Articles 2 and 3 of the Irish constitution, which described the national territory as the whole of Ireland. This would have answered a long-standing complaint of unionists and would have been very helpful in selling them the benefits of the Agreement. The right to the hot pursuit of terrorists by our security forces for up to ten miles over the border was never achieved, nor were improved arrangements for extradition of 'on the run' terrorists seeking refuge in the Republic. On the Irish side, they sought the introduction of three-judge courts for terrorist offences, with one of the judges an Irish judge, but this was strongly opposed by Lord Hailsham, the Lord Chancellor, and the Lord Chief Justice. The other ambition was to achieve a high measure of joint authority, which we were not able to accept. In its place there was an Anglo-Irish Intergovernmental Council, at which the Irish could put forward proposals on a wide range of issues and in which the British government committed itself to determined efforts to reach agreement where possible. This fell short of joint authority, because the final decisions rested with me as the British Secretary of State.

What was achieved in Article 1 of the Agreement was the principle of consent, the confirmation that Northern Ireland would remain part of the United Kingdom if a majority of people in Northern Ireland so wanted, and it included the important recognition by the Irish government that that was indeed the present situation. In addition it included the recognition by both governments that, were the situation to change, and a majority wished to join the Republic, both governments would respect that democratic wish and facilitate it.

The failure to amend the constitutional Articles 2 and 3 led to an ingenious challenge by two Ulster unionists in the Irish Supreme Court, who claimed that Article 1 of the Agreement contradicted Articles 2 and 3 of the Irish constitution, since it recognised the right of British sovereignty over Northern Ireland subject to the democratic wish of its people. They lost their case but in their judgement the Supreme Court stated that the articles were not just an 'aspiration' but a 'constitutional imperative'. The articles remained unamended until the Irish referendum following the 1998 Belfast Agreement recognised the consent principle.

Notwithstanding all the difficulties that followed, with the hostility of hard-line unionists and the continuing terrorist violence, the key ingredients of the Agreement, with the principle of democratic consent at its heart, have endured and have been the foundation of the peace process that has since ensued.

One noticeable feature of the background to the Agreement was the close interest in it taken by the leading members of Congress who led the Irish-American lobby. The Speaker of the US House of Representatives, Tip O'Neill, was a staunch supporter of Ireland and indeed owned land there, and he and two senators, Teddy Kennedy and Pat Moynihan, were extremely influential in forming Irish-American opinion. They pressed President Reagan to demand changes from the UK and he in turn pressed Margaret Thatcher hard. In February 1985, the Prime Minister had the honour of addressing the Joint Houses of Congress, where she said that she would cooperate with Dublin to reach a political accord, and hope to get continuing US support to find a way forward. That American support and pressure did indeed continue and some years later Margaret said that it was pressure from America that made her sign.

As an aside, I noticed that taking an interest in things Irish had not been a lifelong obsession for President Reagan, as is clear from a quote by Conor O'Clery, the Washington correspondent of the *Irish Times*, who interviewed him in 1979. Reagan said to him, 'Your paper is in Dublin, that's south of the border, right?'

Tackling the very negative Irish-American view of Britain and Northern Ireland was an important responsibility for me, and it was quickly apparent after the signing of the Agreement that the strong support from the leading figures of the Irish-American lobby began to transform the attitude to Britain and against the campaign of terror being waged by what they saw as the Marxist grouping of the IRA and Sinn Féin. This led to better cooperation on intelligence and security issues, and a great reduction in the funds that organisations such as Noraid had been raising on allegedly humanitarian grounds, when in fact we believed that the bulk of the money was going to support the terrorist campaign.

I had had an early experience of that negative view on a visit to New York. Our Consul General gave a dinner for me with a number of significant guests to whom I was able to explain the Agreement. Included among the guests was a very senior executive from IBM, who was initially perfectly courteous; but later in the evening, after some refreshment, he launched a violent diatribe against the whole history of the British in Ireland, all the way from Cromwell to Bloody Sunday! During my visit, as well as meeting politicians it was important to talk to the Catholic Church, and I had valuable meetings with both Cardinal O'Connor in New York and, particularly helpfully, with Cardinal Law in Boston.

In Northern Ireland and in London we had a number of visitors from the United States. One in particular whose visit caused considerable controversy thereafter was the three-times Mayor of New York, Ed Koch, memorably described by the *Daily Telegraph* as 'the fastest lip east of the Pecos river!' He left New York reaffirming his view that the British should be 'ashamed' of their role in the violence in Ulster. He spent six days fact-finding for himself in Dublin and Belfast, and I had a particularly interesting meeting with him at Stormont. It pleased me that on his return to New York he announced, 'I do not believe that the British are occupying forces. My impression is that they are trying to play a constructive role.'

It was a very brave statement to make in the face of a long tradition of anti-British sentiment among New York's Irish population. Only rarely did the British viewpoint get a sympathetic hearing in newspapers and on local television channels, where commentators with Irish surnames and strong views about Ulster abounded. There was a maxim in US politics that no one had ever won an election being pro-British, and the Ancient Order of Hibernians immediately set out to bar Koch from the next St Patrick's Day parade, in which the Mayor of New York traditionally has a central role. It brought home to me very forcibly the recognition that Irish-Americans were considerably 'greener' than the Irish themselves. I remembered an interesting comment to me by Senator Teddy Kennedy that Irish immigrants and their descendants were not so interested in current Irish affairs, but preferred to keep alive the memories of the grievances that caused them or their ancestors originally to leave. It was pointed out to me that whatever picketing or protests I might experience in the United States, I was not alone, as Charles Haughey, the Taoiseach, was facing demonstrations as well.

One particular illustration of American interest in the Anglo-Irish Agreement was the establishment of an International Fund for Ireland. Back in 1977 President Jimmy Carter had expressed his concern about the Irish situation and promised support in cash if agreement could be reached.

President Reagan reaffirmed this and in the Agreement both governments agreed to work together for those parts of Ireland worst affected by the Troubles on both sides of the border, particularly in the areas of high unemployment. The first chairman of the fund, Charles Brett, found it very tough at the start as the unionists hated the Agreement and saw the Fund as blood money to get acceptance of cross-border structures. However, it became truly international, as in addition to the United States, contributions came from the European Union, Canada, Australia and New Zealand. Its aim was the reconciliation of unionists and nationalists in Northern Ireland, including the border counties. Thirty years later more than £700 million had been subscribed and invested in some 6,000 projects, creating more than 55,000 jobs and with 15,000 young people in training. This funding over the years had leveraged additional support to bring the total up to more than £1.5 billion.

The fund continues to encourage economic and social advance by contact and dialogue and to promote reconciliation between unionists and nationalists throughout the island of Ireland. While it has certainly made substantial progress, major challenges still remain, as evidenced by the continuing need for Peace Walls in parts of Belfast to protect vulnerable communities from hostile sectarian neighbours.

I have referred to the two months before the signing of the Agreement as the lull before the storm, and storm it certainly was. The succeeding months were marked by continuing and growing unionist and loyalist hostility. Ministers were boycotted; outside visits were picketed and disrupted, often because details of the visits had been leaked to protesters. I had one early experience of this when I was the guest of Ulster Television at a lunch for the visiting members of the Independent Television Authority. It took place in a large room on the first floor of Belfast City Hall, and it was clear as soon as I arrived that some protesters had managed to get into the room. They were removed, but as the large gathering sat down we became conscious of loud hammering on the doors at the back of the room, with more protesters demanding entrance. It became clear that the lunch could not safely continue while I was there, and my RUC team were keen to get me out before an even bigger mob assembled. As they hustled me out down a back stair to a side door, I noticed on the landing an angry Ian Paisley standing in front of an equally furious bunch of people. We just made it to the car, and after a lively start we got safely away.

I learned afterwards from my RUC team that Paisley had then come down and done a television interview in which he denounced the RUC for betraying Ulster by protecting me. Apparently he then got into his car with his own RUC escort and roared with laughter that it had been the best 'craic' he had had in years. Having heard the interview, his policemen knew that it would inflame the more extreme loyalists, and they were right, as two RUC families were burnt out of their houses that night. The power of his oratory was undoubted, and I remembered it when a year later I suspended the operation of Stormont. Paisley staged a sit-in and the police had to carry him out. As they did he said to them, 'Don't cry to me when your homes are attacked.' He added that Northern Ireland was on the verge of civil war and facing possible hand-to-hand fighting in every street.

I learnt only much more recently of the prayer that he apparently uttered from his pulpit in his Martyrs' Memorial Church in Belfast against Margaret Thatcher: 'We pray this night that thou would deal with the Prime Minister of our country. Oh God, in wrath take vengeance upon this wicked, treacherous and lying woman: take vengeance upon her, oh Lord, and grant that we shall see a demonstration of thy power.'

I never knew what prayers for my divine punishment were being offered at that time, but I was certainly the subject of continuing abuse, nicknamed King Rat, Tom Cat King, and many more! I remember the aggressive poster campaign that sprang up very quickly with the simple slogan 'Ulster Says No', although this was rather undermined by a witty addition by somebody, 'but the man from Del Monte says Yes!' – a well-known advertising slogan.

City Hall was later the location for a massive rally, with anything between 100,000 and 200,000 addressed by Ian Paisley and Jim Molyneaux, well remembered by the oft-repeated clip on news broadcasts of Paisley bellowing 'Never – Never – Never'.

One obvious consequence of the unionist/loyalist hostility to our steadfast support for the Agreement was a marked improvement in nationalist sympathy for the government. The history of Northern Ireland had been the supremacy of the majority, and Workers' Strikes and Days of Action had ensured over the years that their will prevailed. This time it was different, and I was interested when John Hume, the leader of the SDLP, said that I was the first Secretary of State not to accept the Orange card. When, in December, all the unionist MPs resigned as part of their campaign of civil disobedience, it did have some impact in emphasising the total breakdown of relations between government and unionists, but the only net effect was that when they stood again, they lost the seat of Newry and Armagh, and so returned to Parliament with one fewer than when they had left. This gave an early boost to the SDLP, who won the seat, and the reward from nationalist voters to the SDLP for their support for the Anglo-Irish Agreement was that the latter did even better in the general election in 1987, winning four seats, and then in 1992 defeating Gerry Adams, the Sinn Féin leader, in West Belfast. John Hume's involvement in the Agreement gave him added authority in the nationalist community, and he could justly claim that the principle of consent enshrined in Article 1 removed any possible grounds for violence, and that now, to achieve the nationalist ambitions, 'it was for Irishmen to persuade Irishmen'.

By the time I went to Northern Ireland, I had already been Secretary of State in three other departments, and I found that my new post involved a quite exceptional authority and independence. In the period of direct rule the Secretary of State assumed the responsibilities previously held by both the Governor, as the Queen's representative, and the Prime Minister of Northern Ireland, coupled with the responsibility of chairing the Security Policy Meeting, which was attended by the Chief Constable of the RUC, the general commanding the army, and the intelligence services.

In addition to the responsibilities in Northern Ireland I did of course have to report to Parliament and attend Cabinet every week; I tried to ensure that I did not neglect my constituency as well. It did mean a lot of travel, but the excellent support of the RAF and my own security at either end really eliminated the hassle that constant travelling would otherwise have involved. I can hardly believe it now, but I think on one occasion a clash of engagements in Cabinet, an important meeting in Northern Ireland and a statement in Parliament involved me crossing the Irish Sea four times in one day!

What helped a lot, in tackling what at times was a very difficult job, was the high degree of cross-party support in Parliament, plus a great fund of goodwill in the country more generally, stemming from our efforts to defeat terrorism and to improve the lives of everybody in Northern Ireland. That support certainly started at the top. A comment by Margaret Thatcher was reported to me after some bad incident: 'Tom's got a very tough job, and our job is to back him up', and I couldn't have asked for more. The Treasury certainly got the message: while in other departments they were very insistent that money could not be moved from one heading to another, in Northern Ireland I had a single block grant which enabled us to take advantage of an underspend in one area and move it somewhere else where it might be urgently needed.

When I took over I wanted to continue the practice of 'morning prayers' (see page 82), our regular stock-taking meetings, which we had had in Environment. It was important to keep in close touch, because every minister had considerable responsibilities and often very challenging ones. Peter Bottomley, now the Father of the House as the longest-serving MP, had been one of my ministers in Northern Ireland and remembered that, when I gave him full authority for his area of responsibilities, I told him that if he did make a mistake, or some major problem arose, he should not hesitate to talk to me about it. We would sort it out together, and the one thing I did not want was that the first I would know about it would be to read it on the front page of the *Guardian*. I was impressed that twenty years later he still remembered that, which I had quite forgotten.

These meetings became much more difficult in my new post, when ministers might be in either London or Belfast, with our offices in both places. We overcame that eventually by introducing a system called Confravision, with which we could link up a studio in Stormont Castle to one in the Northern Ireland office in Admiralty House in London. It was a pretty crude system, with basically just two television sets side-by-side, but it worked remarkably well. We used to meet first thing in the morning with a cup of coffee and it was so realistic that you almost started passing the sugar to those on the other side of the table. This system proved a huge benefit not just for our prayer meetings, but for a whole range of other meetings between officials from the Northern Ireland office and other Whitehall departments including, particularly, the Treasury. Previously a huge amount of time had been wasted with officials having to fly backwards and forwards, often finding themselves stuck at Heathrow or Aldergrove if there was fog or other disruption. Nowadays it would seem incredibly primitive, but these were the years before any idea of the internet and all the other new systems, and it did the job.

When I became Secretary of State for Northern Ireland in 1985 unemployment was running at over 20%, higher in nationalist areas, and provided a fertile recruiting opportunity for terrorists. I therefore gave top priority both to promoting existing Ulster industry and to bringing in more investment from overseas. Having come to Northern Ireland from two years as Secretary of State for Employment, I found it a familiar task. One of the first who showed solid support was Marks & Spencer's, led by Richard Greenbury, major customers of a number of Northern Ireland textile and clothing companies. Ford, Du Pont and Standard Telephones made valuable investments, and we succeeded in attracting more investment from overseas, which involved a number of interesting journeys for me.

One of the first was to Boeing in Seattle, from whom Shorts had had some valuable orders. On my visit I was accompanied by our consul general from San Francisco. One particular comment by a Boeing director stays in the memory: that Boeing and Shorts had one thing in common, most of their senior management having been with the company for a good number of years, which meant that as new projects came forward, they were dealing with the same people they had worked with before, and not some new figure they had never met. He put this down to the fact that both Seattle and Belfast were somewhat removed from the main centres of their countries, and that people were less likely to move. This emphasis on the value of longer service surprised the consul general, who said that in San Francisco, if someone was in the same job for more than two or three years, people started to wonder about them!

Later on I visited Bombardier in their impressive plant in Montreal to discuss the possibility of their taking over Shorts. This did indeed happen, and I had the pleasure of welcoming Laurent Baudouin, the head of Bombardier, to Belfast. I believed that this was an excellent opportunity for Shorts, as indeed it proved to be, but I also knew there would be great suspicions in the workforce that the government was no longer going to support them. I therefore decided I would give them the news myself, and introduce their new owner. In a vast hangar at Shorts on Queen's Island a platform was erected, Roy McNulty, the head of Shorts, introduced me and I addressed a mass gathering of their workers. I wasn't sure what reception I might get, as Queen's Island was known as a loyalist stronghold and very hostile to the Anglo-Irish Agreement, but their jobs were obviously at stake, and they listened attentively to what I said. I then introduced Laurent Baudouin, who nobly came forward and, in his slightly halting English, told them of his plans for investment in the company. This was well received and the meeting ended successfully. I did think at the time that it was very possible that Laurent Baudouin, as a French Canadian from Montreal, could be a Catholic, and was now taking responsibility for a company in which, in earlier years, it could have been unusual for any Catholic to get a job.

The other major company in Belfast was Harland & Wolff, and both it and Shorts depended heavily on support from the Treasury, as it was vital to maintain the substantial degree of employment that these two companies offered. Just before the deal with Bombardier, Harland's, led by an energetic chief executive, John Parker, was sold to a management buy-out in partnership with the Fred Olsen Line. When I reported in Cabinet on the successful transfer of both companies, which had involved a write-off of government loans of no less than £1.25 billion, Nigel Lawson, the Chancellor of the Exchequer, slipped me a note of thanks across the Cabinet table, which confirmed what a weight had been lifted from the public purse.

Another, rather longer, journey was to Seoul, the South Korean capital, where the hard work of officials had opened up the possibility of a major investment from Daewoo. This company was expanding very fast under the dynamic leadership of the company's chairman, Kim, and it was proposed to build a new factory at Antrim where Daewoo would manufacture video recorders. I met Chairman Kim and he agreed to our proposal; the investment duly went ahead. I had never been to Korea before, but I took the opportunity to see something of the area where some good friends of mine from school had found themselves in the trenches in the Korean War, straight out of school and before going to university, during their National Service.

When I arrived in Seoul, I was shown the headline in the Korean English-language paper announcing my visit, as the Minister from the land of *Danny Boy*. It turned out that that wonderful Irish song was number three in the

Korean schools' book of favourite songs, so I was easily identified! In the evening, at the end of our successful visit, I had a nightcap with my team in the bar of the Seoul Hilton Hotel, and we were entertained to a very special rendering of *Danny Boy* by an impromptu quartet of a Filipino pianist, an Indonesian girl singer, and my two RUC protection officers, singing a song known and loved all round the world.

During the months of boycott and political tension, I was very anxious to meet as wide a range of people as possible from all walks of life and communities, and for that purpose Hillsborough Castle was invaluable. As the old seat of the Marquis of Downshire and then of the Governor, the fine house and gardens were a great attraction, particularly for the garden parties when I welcomed various members of the Royal Family as guests of honour. I also gave a considerable number of dinner parties. The first couple of dinners seemed to drag on far too long, so I devised a scheme with our excellent young butler, David Anderson, to keep things moving. There were usually about thirty guests from a wide range of backgrounds. I would sit in the middle of the long table and at a time after everybody had been served, David would stand opposite. When people had mainly finished, I would give him a nod, and the staff would start clearing away. The few people who had not finished – some, indeed, having been happily chatting away, were barely halfway through – when they heard the sound of plates being removed, either started to gobble up their food or simply stopped. In this way the momentum was kept going and a small minority was not allowed to drag things out too long. This contradicted what I believe is the training in many catering colleges, that you don't take plates away until the last person has finished, a practice that has ruined far too many dinners! By keeping the momentum going we were then able to move back to the drawing room at a reasonable time. One excellent quality of Northern Ireland was that, almost without exception at every dinner, I found one of the guests could play the piano and round it others joined in to sing some of the marvellous Irish songs, possibly *Danny Boy* or Hillsborough's own love song, *In the Gloaming*, subsequently wonderfully recorded by Gloria Hunniford. And so the evenings ended, not too late and achieving just what I wanted in bringing together in a friendly atmosphere many people who might never have met before and who would possibly never otherwise meet.

This has had one unfortunate legacy, as far as Jane is concerned, that I tend to import my 'keep it moving' policy into other people's dinners as well. However, I do claim some royal precedent for my practice, in the delightful and quite informal dinners that Her Majesty gave at Windsor Castle. The pattern for the dinners, for which you stayed the night, was that the guest list was made up of a most interesting cross-section of people. The conversations over dinner were always interesting and as a result people were quite slow in their eating. Her Majesty not being a big eater, the Windsor staff followed their long-standing tradition that soon after she had finished all the plates were removed. This could catch some people out, but they were well cared for, as when they finally retired to their rooms each one had a packet of biscuits to meet their needs!

It was a great pleasure to attend such a dinner with Her Majesty and other members of the Royal Family, and certainly a great advance on earlier royal practices, as I noticed once in a room in Hampton Court Palace. There, it was said, Charles II used to dine, but strictly on his own, and if you were particularly privileged, you could watch him dine!

The launch of the Anglo-Irish Agreement so soon after my installation as Secretary of State meant a very steep learning curve for my new responsibilities, with, I admit, one or two mistakes on the way. However, although it was agonisingly slow, I did feel as we moved through 1986 and into 1987 that things were developing. There were signs of a change of attitude by the unionists from outright opposition, and a sign that Sinn Féin/IRA were changing too, with their recognition that the government was not weakening in its determination to defeat terrorism. We were approaching a general election. I knew that Margaret Thatcher held the view that two years was a reasonable length of time to serve in Northern Ireland, with the extra pressures of travelling and absence from the family, in addition to the obvious pressures of the job itself. I therefore told her that if she would like me to continue, I would be happy to do so and that I believed real progress was now possible. She was glad to agree, and so after the election I continued as Secretary of State. It was interesting that it leaked out somehow that it had been my request to continue, and I was pleased that it received a very favourable response in Northern Ireland, and, I think it fair to say, from both sides of the community.

I would add, as a general point, that ministers change far too often, and that spending longer periods of service in a particular office generally makes for better government. It does take time to take on new responsibilities and too frequent changes are very damaging, as has been all too apparent recently.

The 1987 election was an extremely busy time for me. My continuing responsibilities as Secretary of State for Northern Ireland were coupled with my own campaign in Bridgwater, and I was also supporting other Conservative candidates, including some in Scotland. I remember in particular campaigning for a promising young candidate in the Scottish Borders, Dr Liam Fox, who, while unsuccessful there, was subsequently elected for a neighbouring Somerset constituency. After the final meeting in Galashiels, a car took me to Edinburgh Airport to fly back to Northern Ireland to host the annual garden party at Hillsborough, at which Princess Alexandra was the guest of honour. Because my visit to Scotland was party-political and not government business, my normal arrangements for flying with the RAF were not available, but the Conservative party had hired a small private plane to fly me back to Aldergrove. When we got to the airport there was some confusion as to where the plane was. My police eventually found the pilot, who was certainly rather untidy-looking, wearing a cap with a bit of gold braid on it which looked as though somebody had just stuck it on. He said in a rather charming way, 'I've come to take you away.'

We duly set off, and I discovered afterwards that my Special Branch people had suddenly become very worried as to who the pilot was. They called my office in Northern Ireland and said, 'The Secretary of State has just been taken away on a plane by somebody who we don't think anybody recognises,' and the office, under the impression that it was a different plane, said, 'The Secretary of State knows him very well.' In fact I'd never seen him before in my life. It then did occur to me that this might be the ultimate IRA sting – hijacking the Secretary of State and doing a nice forced landing somewhere in County Monaghan, never to be seen again! Fortunately it wasn't; he flew me very calmly into the setting sun right over the Clyde Valley, out over the Isle of Arran and down into Aldergrove, and all was well.

I am afraid my campaigning in Scotland proved less than successful, as one of the unplanned consequences of the Anglo-Irish Agreement was the loss of Conservative seats in Scotland in the 1987 election. Ian Paisley's visits to Glasgow and the West of Scotland demonstrated very clearly the strength of his support, and his fierce opposition to the Agreement meant the loss of a large amount of support for the Conservative party in that area. I remember one Scottish Conservative MP telling me that he had previously had very good working-class support in his constituency, and understood why after a visit to the house of a chairman of one of his branches, when he noticed a large collection of orange collarettes, the uniform of the Orange Order of staunch unionists in Ulster.

One feature of my security was the advance searches by local police of anywhere that I was due to visit. I never saw these people, but I used to learn afterwards of their activities, and it seemed to add a certain excitement for the organisers of what might have been quite a small event. The searches did occasionally have unexpected consequences. Once when I was opening a Conservative fête in the gardens of a rather handsome property in Devon, it transpired that the police had decided also to search the house. They discovered a rather elderly elephant gun, which had belonged to an earlier generation of the family but unfortunately had never been licensed. The gun was removed by the police, a most unfortunate outcome for the family for their generosity in allowing their home to be used for the fête.

Sometimes we felt there wasn't really the need for such security, but then there would be some unexpected incident which made us very thankful for it. In 1987 early in the morning in the woods overlooking our house the police came upon two people. They started talking to them as though they might be poachers. This clearly relaxed the two, who chatted away, thinking that they could fool these local policemen. It was clear to the police that they were young Irish people, but they simply told them that they would be taken into the local police station on suspicion of poaching. Once there, they were much more intensively cross-examined, culminating in their being advised that they would be arrested under the Prevention of Terrorism Act. From that moment and during the period that they were on remand, they never spoke another word in any interrogation. That was of course precisely the instruction in *An Phoblacht*, the Sinn Féin newspaper, on how to handle interrogation by the police, with the slogan 'Whatever you say, say nothing'.

The IRA had learnt the importance of this the hard way, when in the earlier years of the Troubles the basis of the evidence for their convictions had often come only from what they had said in police interrogations.

It took a long time for their trial to come forward, but some thirteen months later the two, together with a third person who had been arrested in their tent at a campsite near Wells, were tried in Winchester Crown Court and sentenced to twenty-seven years for conspiracy to murder me. Three years later after a successful appeal they were released. The basis of the appeal was that I had improperly influenced the jury by announcements that I made at the very moment when they had retired to consider their verdict.

What had actually happened was that a change in the law was going to be introduced to qualify the absolute right to silence. In general the legal position is that a defendant has the right to remain silent, and the court may not draw any inference from that. The change we were proposing was that in terrorist cases, if there was *prima facie* evidence connecting the defendant with a terrorist crime, and if he or she then insisted on remaining silent, the court could draw an inference from that. It so happened that on the very day that the judge completed his summing up and the jury withdrew to consider their verdict, I made a statement in the House of Commons announcing our proposal, and subsequently did a number of interviews on television and radio about it. In these I drew particular attention to the IRA practice of exploiting to the full their right to silence. The essence of the subsequent appeal was that the members of the jury that evening would have listened to my broadcasts, and knew that the defendants had indeed maintained to the full their right to silence, exactly as I had indicated was the IRA practice. On the basis of my words thus improperly influencing the jury, the appeal succeeded.

It was unfortunate that my statement should have coincided so exactly with the point at which the jury were considering their verdict. The trial was in England, at Winchester, while I and my officials were fully occupied dealing with issues in Northern Ireland. It had been going on for a very long time and I had long ago put it out of my mind.

As it happens, I do not think that the final outcome was unreasonable. I did not believe that these young people were the 'hit squad', but rather the reconnaissance unit for others who might come later, and the fact that they had already served three years seemed to me more appropriate than the twenty-seven years of the original sentence. However, I had no doubt that they were certainly not innocent back-packing tourists. I was confirmed in my view by something that a Catholic priest said to me, when he told me his first inclination was to believe that they were simply three harmless students being picked on by aggressive British police. He had had second thoughts when their tent was found with £5,000 in cash hidden in its lining. As we all know, terrorism needs cash to operate.

That was not the last of my near-encounters with the IRA, as in the mid-1990s, some years after I had stood down from government, I was advised that I remained prominent among potential targets for assassination by Irish Republican terrorists.

❋ ❋ ❋

During my time in Northern Ireland there were a number of particularly distressing terrorist outrages which were damaging to public morale. It was critically important to maintain public confidence that terrorism would be defeated and that there would be a better, safer future for all the people. Over these years, in response to different incidents, we brought in a number of measures to help the security situation. These included tighter border controls, longer prison sentences, improved arrangements for intelligence-sharing between the army and the RUC, the addition of a further army brigade to the two already stationed in the Province, that change in the law to qualify the absolute right to silence that had been so successfully exploited by the IRA, and a broadcasting ban on certain individuals publicly believed to be associated with terrorist groups, as well as the ban on the fertiliser used in bomb-making.

One of the continuing challenges was to prevent the terrorist groups on both the republican and loyalist sides getting access to weapons and explosives. The republicans tried to bring in weapons from the United States, the loyalists from South Africa. In addition, on the republican side the IRA had a supply line from Libya until we managed to intercept the large shipment on the *Eksund* (see below). In Northern Ireland they tried to steal explosives from quarrying companies, but they also learnt how to make very powerful bombs out of stolen agricultural fertilisers. Some excellent scientific work helped ensure that new fertilisers became available in Northern Ireland that could not be used to make bombs, and we introduced a ban on the previous variety.

These different measures and actions were each designed to address a particular problem, and provided positive evidence to the public of government determination to succeed and defeat terrorism. What we did not do, although the idea was raised, was to reintroduce internment without trial, which had been such a breeding ground for terrorists in the past.

One of the essential ingredients for a terrorist campaign is money, and we were constantly looking for ways to block funds going to the IRA. As I said earlier, a lot of their funds had come from the United States, and the Anglo-Irish Agreement was very helpful in changing American opinion and reducing fundraising there. In Northern Ireland itself there were clearly protection rackets in which companies were threatened that their premises would be burnt down unless they paid up – indeed, some were. In addition, the existence of the border between Northern Ireland and the Republic provided considerable opportunities for smuggling. One famous example was a farm owned by a significant figure in the Sinn Féin/IRA world at which the border went clean through his farm, in fact right through one of his barns: animals could go in one door in the Republic and walk out through the other end in Northern Ireland. We did have a particular problem at one time when there was a significant difference in the subsidy available for cattle either side of the border. There were stories of cattle being transported north over the border, qualifying for an extra subsidy of £100 per animal, and then, a little distance further north, the cattle being released and walking their way back to the south, for the merry-go-round to be repeated again.

The most amusing example reported to me was when there was a queue of lorries waiting to cross at the border post, and a very impatient driver stormed in to complain about the delay and demanded to have his papers stamped immediately. The border official took some offence at this aggressive approach and decided to check whether the lorry concerned did indeed contain the number of animals that the driver claimed. He heard considerable noise from the cattle inside, but when the lorry was opened up it was revealed to be quite empty except for a large tape recorder blasting out suitable cow noises!

The difficulty about tackling smuggling and other illegal activity was that many parts of the border area were in a real sense 'bandit country', and it was very difficult for officials to operate without considerable police and army protection. I decided to set up an Anti-Racketeering Unit. I remember one particular foray into, I think, Crossmaglen, one of the most difficult and dangerous border towns. With the protection of a company of soldiers, 100 strong, a very thorough investigation was carried out and uncovered a whole range of illegal activities in the area. One of them involved stealing from pubs in the Republic large numbers of aluminium beer kegs which were then melted down and the aluminium sold to double-glazing window manufacturers. Another involved fraud over commercial fuel. Diesel for private cars was taxed at a much higher rate than diesel for agricultural or commercial use, and to distinguish the two, a red dye was put into the commercial diesel. The unit discovered a fuller's earth filtration plant that filtered out the dye, and thus enabled the low-tax diesel to be passed off as regular diesel and a handsome profit to be made. The other item that the team found was an electricity meter reversing unit. I cannot remember if the evidence was that it resulted in surprisingly low electricity bills in the area, or whether the meter had been used even more aggressively and Northern Ireland Electricity had been sending out a steady stream of credit notes!

In 1986 the IRA introduced a new tactic: to destroy police stations, and to intimidate the workers contracted to repair them. Initially they had some success and, as well as damage to some police stations, there were a number of casualties before security was improved. One technique developed for attacking police stations was the use of mortars. I visited the RUC station at Middletown, which had been attacked. Middletown was right on the border with the Republic and the mortars had been fired from a field on the other side of the river that formed the border. The police told me that the farmer had been making hay in this field and the bales were still lying there. The police had seen a van driving into the field and parking very carefully between two rows of bales. The van's roof was open and mortars were fired from what, it was then clear, had been a position carefully marked with the bales to ensure the right trajectory to hit the police station.

I was later to have my own experience of the ballistic skill of the IRA in the mortar attack on Number 10 Downing Street in 1991. I was then Defence Secretary and was with John Major, the Prime Minister, at a meeting of the War Cabinet in the Cabinet Room at a critical moment in the Gulf War. Unbeknown to us, a van had parked in Horseguards Avenue, close by the Ministry of Defence and opposite the Household Cavalry mounted sentries at the entrance to Horseguards. A large hole had been cut in the van's roof, through which three mortar bombs were fired clean over Whitehall and straight at Number 10. The first fell just outside the high garden wall, which blocked the full force of the blast. Two however fell right in the garden close to the Cabinet Room, but fortunately only the detonators exploded and not the main charges, otherwise the damage to us in the Cabinet Room would have been considerable. It was certainly an impressive piece of aiming, and we were very lucky that there were no casualties.

One interesting legacy of the IRA campaign against those repairing the police stations was a sweater I was given that came, I have to believe, from the Protestant heartland of the Shankill. On the back in large letters was the slogan 'I'M PROUD THAT I HELP BUILD POLICE STATIONS', and on the front the same slogan and a list of no fewer than thirty-five police stations on which extra security work had been done.

During their campaign against police stations, the IRA suffered their greatest loss of life in a single incident when they attacked an unmanned RUC base at Loughgall, Co. Armagh, in May 1987. They filled the front bucket of a tractor with a great load of explosive and aimed it at the police station, but were then ambushed by the SAS and all eight IRA members were killed. I was never entirely clear whether it was a chance ambush, as we were seeking to provide extra protection for border police stations, or whether the army had advance intelligence. I was interested to see a suggestion recently that the source of the intelligence could have been from a senior level within Sinn Féin/IRA, as this Monaghan IRA Active Service Unit may have been undermining the leadership's new approach of moving from violence to a political campaign, with rather less Armalite and more ballot box. I cannot believe that this was the source, but it does illustrate how extensive the world of rumour and counter-rumour was in Northern Ireland, with no shortage of fake news.

It drew attention to how relatively few IRA fatalities there had been during the Troubles, compared with the number suffered by both the RUC and the army, which made the shock for the terrorists all the greater on this occasion. A further setback for them came in October 1987 when the French customs successfully intercepted the *Eksund*, a boat that had come from Libya loaded with what proved to be the largest shipment ever for the IRA: two tons of Semtex, 1,000 AK-47 rifles, 1,000 mortars, and twenty SAM 7s, a lethal threat to the army's helicopters. It turned out that this was in fact the fifth shipment from Libya, but by far the largest, and it was a major blow for the IRA to have this supply line blocked. It is impossible to guess just how many lives were thus saved. It was a great success for British intelligence, well supported by the French authorities' interception. Worse was to follow for the IRA as, following the seizure of the *Eksund*, further intelligence led to a massive Garda/Irish Army search, which found no fewer than five weapon-storage bunkers in the Republic.

Barely a month later there was one of the worst outrages of all the Troubles when the IRA bombed the Remembrance Day parade in Enniskillen, killing twelve people and wounding another sixty-three. Quite apart from the tragedy of so many being killed or seriously wounded, the fact that it occurred without warning at a Remembrance Day parade significantly further weakened support for Sinn Féin, the political wing of the IRA.

I was myself at a Remembrance Day service in my constituency in Bridgwater. When I came out of the church at midday, my police escort told me that my private secretary was trying to contact me. I called him immediately and, with the excellent service of the RAF, I was in the square at Enniskillen that afternoon. It was immediately clear that, in this appalling outrage on the most unsuitable of days, intended to kill members of the security forces, the overwhelming number of casualties were civilians. It was universally condemned north and south of the border. It was also marked by a remarkable BBC interview that attracted massive attention and respect throughout the world. A young nurse, Marie Wilson, was fatally injured in the explosion. In the interview her father, Gordon Wilson, described her last moments in his arms, and most movingly went on to express forgiveness towards his daughter's killers, and to urge loyalists not to seek revenge. I heard it the next morning while having a shower, and the tears welled up as I listened to this wonderful and inspiring interview. Gordon Wilson became a leading peace campaigner and was later, very appropriately, appointed to the Irish Senate, which amply illustrated the huge respect for him throughout the island of Ireland.

The Remembrance Day parade, as always organised by the local branch of the British Legion, was of course totally disrupted. The Legion quickly announced that they would not be defeated by terrorism, and that in two weeks' time they would hold a further parade. Throughout the United Kingdom other British Legion branches pledged their support and announced that they would be sending their standard-bearers to stand shoulder to shoulder with their Enniskillen colleagues. More than 300 standards were due to attend, and I confirmed that I would certainly wish to support it. I thought that it would be excellent if Margaret Thatcher, the Prime Minister, could come as well to underline the total commitment of the government to the people of Northern Ireland in the fight against terrorism. I asked Charles Powell, her private secretary, if she would be able to come that day. He told me that she was committed to a meeting in Paris with President Mitterrand. I asked him what time the meeting was. He replied that it was in the afternoon, and so I asked whether she would be willing to come to Enniskillen in the morning and then fly on direct to Paris. Charles immediately agreed to put this to her, and typically, and to her immense credit, she agreed.

The due day arrived. On that Sunday morning I met her at Aldergrove Airport, and we flew by helicopter to the army base at St Angelo, just by Enniskillen. There she and I were briefed on the proceedings for the parade and our role in it, but unfortunately the official was making rather heavy weather of the briefing, and neither I nor the Prime Minister were entirely clear about it. It was vital that we did understand it completely. There happened to be a plate of McVitie's assorted biscuits on the table, and we quickly established, using the digestive biscuit as the Cenotaph, and the custard cream and the chocolate biscuit as the Prime Minister and me, with other biscuits for the other participants, a much better picture of where we were to stand and when!

We drove to the square in Enniskillen, where the whole parade was drawn up with an enormous array of Legion standards from all over the United Kingdom, and with the atmosphere reinforced by the knowledge that both the BBC and ITV had cleared their programmes to cover this most moving occasion. I shall always remember the gasp of astonishment from the whole crowd when we got out of the car, when they realised that I was not on my own, but that Margaret Thatcher had come personally to show her support to the Legion, to the people of Enniskillen, and to Northern Ireland.

It was estimated that some 7,000 people attended this second Remembrance Day, and the gasp of surprise confirmed how successful the security had been, without any leak of the Prime Minister's visit. There had been questions at the lobby briefing in Number 10 earlier in the week as to whether she would be going, to which the simple reply was that she had a meeting with President Mitterrand in Paris that day, a correct and truthful answer, providing a perfect cover story for her visit to Enniskillen.

We walked to our places facing the Cenotaph, next to the new Lord Lieutenant of Fermanagh, the Earl of Erne. He was so recently appointed that his first engagement as Lord Lieutenant had been the very parade when the bomb had exploded, and instead of a calm opening ceremony for his first official duty he had spent the day visiting all the injured in hospital. The service proceeded, notwithstanding a particularly nasty dose of Fermanagh weather with bouts of bitterly cold rain lashing us. Then came the wreath-laying, with the first one to be laid by the Lord Lieutenant as the Queen's representative and the second by Margaret Thatcher, supported by me. He duly marched forward, laid the wreath and marched back to our line, halted and did an about-turn. He was smartly turned out in his brand-new Lord Lieutenant's uniform, complete with a large sword hanging loosely at his side. As he did the about-turn, the sword came swinging wildly round to smash into the Prime Minister's legs. In the split second when I realised the danger, I was too late to intervene – there was a loud bang but Margaret remained upright, and I realised that we had been saved by her famous handbag, which took the full force of the blow!

At the end of the parade in the square, while everybody else was moving into the cathedral for the remainder of the service, the principal guests waited in the reception room of the manse, the Bishop's house. It had been bitterly cold outside, and in this room, with its single-bar electric fire, it didn't seem much warmer. Margaret had arrived wearing smart black court shoes, ready for her meeting with Mitterand, and it was clear that she was extremely cold and her feet were frozen. I had no desire for her to arrive in Paris as a hospital case so I told her to take her shoes off immediately, which she readily did, and we warmed them up. That done, it was into the cathedral for the rest of the service, back into the cars, and then the helicopter to Aldergrove, from where her plane took her on to Paris.

It was a tough morning for her, made even tougher by the rough weather, but it was very important for her to do, and it was enormously appreciated by people in Northern Ireland at a sad and worrying time.

I tried to visit our security forces frequently, both to keep up to date on the challenges they were facing and to show my appreciation of the vital work that they were doing. I remember one particular visit to see the Royal Marines who were patrolling Carlingford Lough, on the border with the Republic. I took off by helicopter from Belfast and flew down to the lough, where we found a small minesweeper mothership awaiting us. I was winched down on to the deck, and after meeting the Royal Navy commander and his crew I transferred to one of the rigid raiders, the small assault craft that the Marines used to patrol the lough. They loved to demonstrate the speed and agility of these boats and I had a pretty exciting and suitably terrifying ride up and down the long border lough. The visit was otherwise uneventful, and I was winched back into the helicopter and returned to Belfast. I was amused to learn when I got back that the IRA had contacted Downtown Radio in Belfast and informed them that they had got word of my visit and had machine-gunned me as I was being winched down into the ship. They must have spotted me leaving Belfast, but in their enthusiasm to convey their message their reported firing at me was a quarter of an hour before I ever got there – long live fake news!

During all my time in Parliament and in government, for obvious security reasons I had never published my home address in any reference books, and this clearly became even more important when I became Secretary of State for Northern Ireland. It worked well until there was a bizarre event at my home. For our protection at that time we had made available a small cottage just beside the house for a police post, with two policemen there at all times, and two others on a roving patrol. One evening, the two in the cottage were discussing the firearms tests that they were shortly due to take. One apparently said to the other, 'I always find the correct unloading very confusing with these new pistols.' His colleague said, 'It's not difficult if you stick to this simple, clear procedure.' He then went on to show it to him, with the final movement of raising the pistol in the air and pulling the trigger, thus demonstrating that the chamber was clear. Unfortunately it wasn't, and he put a bullet clean through the ceiling. This became the subject of a detailed police practice, in which the incident had to be reported as an accidental discharge with one round now not accounted for. They were suspended from duty, and their uniforms removed from their homes, until the matter was further investigated.

It was reported in the minutes of the next meeting of the County Police Authority, under the heading 'Accidental Discharge at the home of Tom King, Secretary of State for Northern Ireland'. This should have been the end of it, but it happened that there was a keen journalist who, in the midst of some fairly routine police authority matters, noticed this item and asked the police PR what my address was. This was very politely and promptly provided, and subsequently appeared not just in the local paper but in the *Daily Telegraph* and the *Belfast Telegraph* as well, which was hardly helpful.

Over more than thirty years of the Troubles, certain events have stuck in the public memory. One of those was undoubtedly the sequence of events that started with the shooting in Gibraltar of three unarmed terrorists by the SAS, commemorated in particular by one television programme, *Death on the Rock*. Intelligence sources had discovered that there was a plan to blow up an army band that would be playing for the Changing of the Guard at the Governor's Residence, a popular event for visitors to Gibraltar. It was thought that the terrorists had already parked their car, loaded with explosives, close to where the guard-changing would take place, and although they were walking away, they could be about to detonate the bomb by remote control, a technique often used in Northern Ireland. It then transpired that the car had not yet been parked at that site. It was subsequently discovered in a garage over the border in Spain, loaded with 64 lbs of Semtex. It was the largest bomb ever found in Spain, and would have caused a terrifying number of casualties, not merely to the soldiers involved in the Changing of the Guard, but to all the visitors watching the ceremony.

The Northern Ireland Office and I had not been party to these events, which involved the Ministry of Defence and the Foreign Office. We did get involved subsequently, very directly. First were the arrangements for the return of the three bodies from Gibraltar. They were flown to Dublin, then under tight escort by the Garda to the border, and from there by the RUC to Belfast. Arrangements were made for their burial in the republican Milltown Cemetery. There was a heavy police presence around the funeral, and also tight Sinn Féin/IRA security. A loyalist gunman, Michael Stone, took the opportunity to try to kill Gerry Adams and Martin McGuinness. He was armed with pistols and grenades, and although he failed in that objective, he did kill one Provisional IRA volunteer and two civilians, and wounded some sixty other people. He was chased by Sinn Féin's security people right down the cemetery but was captured by the RUC. This whole incident was subsequently shown on television, having been filmed by the news crews covering the main funeral.

The next step in this terrible saga came three days later, with the funeral of the people killed by Stone. There had been some criticism of what was alleged to be excessive policing of the previous funeral, and it was therefore agreed to adopt a less intrusive police presence. The security of the funeral procession was undertaken by Sinn Féin, who searched all the cars parked along the road that the procession would take. All seemed to be proceeding smoothly, when suddenly one of the parked cars pulled out and tried to escape. It was blocked by a black taxi, and a driver and passenger were dragged out of the car and searched. It transpired that they were two British Army corporals, although not in uniform, and the papers of one showed that he had previously served at Herford, the British army base in Germany. There was subsequently speculation that the PIRA may have mistaken that for Hereford, the base of the SAS, for whom they had a particular hatred. The two were badly beaten up and, while a local priest rushed to give them the last rites, they were killed. Once again another horrific incident came to be shown on TV, with film from the police helicopter covering the funeral from a distance. The initial report I had was that two people had been killed at the funeral, but that they were not British soldiers. It later became clear that they were, and the reason for the confusion was that they should never have been there in the first place. They were two signaller corporals, one handing over to the other, who was new to Northern Ireland. They had come from Lisburn to an army post in the centre of Belfast and were returning to Lisburn. It was believed that, instead of following the correct and safe route, the one who was handing over offered to show his colleague a little of West Belfast on the way back. Clearly they had no idea that they would be caught in the middle of the funeral, and had pulled into the side to let the procession pass. When they saw the Sinn Féin security team coming down the road checking every car, against the risk of another loyalist attack as at the previous funeral, they tried desperately to pull out and get away, but, tragically, without success.

One person I enjoyed meeting was Charles Haughey, when he was Taoiseach. He had damaged relations with Margaret Thatcher by supporting Argentina in the Falklands campaign, and had tried to establish a better rapport later with the famous gift of a silver teapot. In spite of his behaviour over the Falklands, it was said that Margaret Thatcher found him easier to talk to because she knew 'where he was coming from', which his Fianna Fail background so clearly demonstrated. He did initially, when in opposition, denounce the Anglo-Irish Agreement, but when he became Taoiseach he accepted it, and his deputy, Brian Lenihan, was an excellent co-chairman with me of the intergovernmental conference. On a visit to Dublin to meet Brian Lenihan, I paid a courtesy call on Charles Haughey, and I noticed a massive picture on the wall of the Ward Union Hunt. I was interested to see that it was a stag-hunt, as I had the Devon & Somerset and the Quantock Staghounds in my constituency. He told me that they hunted carted stags, which were not killed but were put back into trailers at the end of the hunt. I do not remember exactly what his own riding activities were, but I believe his son was in the Irish three-day event team together with the son of Robert Lowry, the Lord Chief Justice of Northern Ireland, a doughty unionist, which illustrated well that in sporting matters Ireland is often a united team!

I had a most interesting meeting with him lasting just under an hour, but I was amused to see that the press release from his office stated that he had received me for a quarter of an hour – this was presumably to avoid the impression with his supporters that he was being too friendly with the British Secretary of State!

On another occasion I visited Dublin as the guest of Brian Lenihan, to watch the England–Ireland rugby match. I went down there on the evening before and was a guest on the Gay Byrne show on RTE, the Irish television channel. This was an extremely popular programme and Gay Byrne was a very charming and interesting host.

The value of my appearance on the show was apparent on the following Monday, when I went to Newry to open a new industrial development. This was an area with a considerable nationalist element and the chairman, in his opening remarks, said quite bluntly that when he had been told that the Secretary of State would be coming, he was not sure how welcome I would be. He then added, 'But now we have all seen and heard him on the Gay Byrne show, I would like to say how pleased we are to see him here today!' What that brought home very clearly was the importance of RTE in communicating with the nationalist community, many of whom would watch only that and never the BBC.

While terrorist incidents continued in 1988 and 1989, it became clear that there were signs of a possible change of attitude by Sinn Féin/IRA. Having moved towards the twin track of the ArmaLite and the ballot box, I believe they realised that if they were to maximise the ballot box, the ArmaLite would work against them. In addition their leaders were getting older, the pressures on them were relentless and showed no signs of lifting, and if nothing changed their children would be committed to the same difficult life that they had faced. They were concerned about their own security, although it was also said that, in considering moves that might end the terrorist campaign, they were haunted by the fate of Michael Collins, who moved from terrorism to peace and was assassinated by his own people.

The first signals came via religious intermediaries, who said that Sinn Féin/ IRA did not believe that we would honour Clause 1 of the Agreement, the key principle of consent, that if the people of Northern Ireland voted to join the Republic the British government would agree to it. Apparently part of their reasoning was that they believed Northern Ireland was strategically essential for the defence of the United Kingdom, and that it was a vital element in the British economy. The strategic argument appeared to have originated from the two World Wars, when Northern Ireland did indeed play a key role in the war against the German U-boats. The economic argument appeared to be connected to the importance of Harland & Wolff and Shorts to the British economy. In fact, of course, the strategic argument was no longer so relevant in a world of intercontinental missiles, and, so far from being pillars of the economy, Harland & Wolff and Shorts were surviving only through substantial contributions from the British Exchequer. I answered this concern in a speech I made to the Northern Ireland Institute of Directors late in 1988, when I said that the United Kingdom had no strategic or economic interest in Northern Ireland that could override the democratic wishes of its people, and this theme lived on in all the exchanges up to the Good Friday Agreement.

Although it took another twenty years before the real fruit of an end to the IRA's major terrorist campaign was achieved, I have always believed that the Anglo-Irish Agreement was the vital start to the fundamental changes that followed. David Trimble and John Hume took the first steps towards a genuine partnership in devolved government, which subsequently led on to what would have been inconceivable in earlier years: the DUP and Sinn Féin working together, in the persons of Paisley and McGuinness.

One interesting feature when the changes were made in respect of Articles 2 and 3 in the Irish Constitution was that the principle of consent was to be governed not just by referendum in Northern Ireland, which was the original provision in the Anglo-Irish Agreement, but that the Irish government also insisted on a referendum in the Republic to determine whether its people actually wanted to be joined up with Northern Ireland. I was interested to see this requirement as I always wondered whether, in the final analysis, the Republic really would wish to embrace the sectarian pressures that could so easily arise in the North.

In July 2007 Operation Banner was ended. This was the name given to the operation for the deployment of the army in Northern Ireland. It had started in August 1969, and those thirty-eight years represented its longest deployment ever. Certainly at times mistakes were made and republicans took every opportunity to present the army as a vicious occupying force. The truth was that in general they and the RUC played an outstanding role in safeguarding the people of Northern Ireland. In spite of, tragically, suffering a substantial number of casualties, they carried out their work with a professionalism and good humour that I do not believe could have been matched by any other army in the world. Their achievement in helping to ensure that terrorism would not prevail made possible the progress to the more peaceful and sensible world of the Good Friday Agreement. But they were not alone in this endeavour, with so many playing their part, not least the people I had the privilege of working with in the Northern Ireland Office and the Northern Ireland Civil Service. They shared those challenging and often dangerous times, illustrated all too clearly when the well-respected head of the Northern Ireland Civil Service, Sir Kenneth Bloomfield, and Lady Bloomfield were bombed out of their house.

In these memories of those years in Northern Ireland, I am very conscious that they are dominated by a number of individual events, and do not do justice to the wide range of our efforts to help improve the life of the Province. The success in reducing unemployment with significant new industrial investment, the legislation to eliminate religious and political discrimination in employment, the rejuvenation of Belfast city centre and the urban and industrial development in Derry, the growth of a community relations policy, were all energetically pursued by the excellent team of ministers that served with me.

What made all our efforts so worthwhile was the knowledge that we were backed by the overwhelming majority of people of both the unionist and nationalist communities, who longed for a safer and more peaceful Province, and this was reflected in the excellent team spirit these challenges and dangers produced. I hope I contributed to this, and I was particularly cheered by a message I received from one of my constituents, Vivian Ellis, the well-known composer of many popular songs from the 1920s through to the 1960s. He took a keen interest in my career, and having just heard Paddy Ashdown on *Panorama* saying some kind things about my time in Northern Ireland, he added a verse from his 1929 hit musical, *Mr Cinders*, more recently revived by Sting:

> '*Even when the darkest clouds are in the sky,*
> *You mustn't sigh and you mustn't cry,*
> *Just spread a little happiness as you go by*', and you do!

By the summer of 1989, after four years as Secretary of State for Northern Ireland, I thought it was time for a move. I learnt that George Younger was going to stand down as Defence Secretary to become the chairman of the

Royal Bank of Scotland. Ian Stewart, who was then with me as Minister of State in Northern Ireland, had previously been a Defence minister and suggested that I should indicate to the Prime Minister that I would be very interested in taking over as Defence Secretary. In the subsequent reshuffle, I was delighted to be given that post. My time in Northern Ireland had been an ideal preparation for Defence, as I had been working closely with all three services for the previous four years. I was particularly pleased, as well, that I was succeeded by Peter Brooke, who had close family connections both north and south of the border and had an excellent understanding of the issues involved.

8 DEFENCE AND THE GULF WAR

When I became Secretary of State for Defence I had little idea what a momentous period it was going to be, with the ending of the Cold War after forty-five years, a total change of the position in Europe, and quite soon thereafter the biggest deployment of British troops and armour on active service since World War II, following Saddam Hussein's invasion of Kuwait.

Things had certainly already changed, with the better relations between the UK and the Soviet Union, marked particularly by meetings between Margaret Thatcher and President Gorbachev, but nobody anticipated the speed of the collapse of the Soviet Union and the ending of the Warsaw Pact, where all the countries in Eastern Europe had been locked together in a tight military alliance. The confirmation of that better relationship with the Soviet Union was marked in my very first week by an official visit to the UK by the Soviet Defence Minister, Marshal Yazov, which was to lead to a return visit by me the following year.

His visit so early on did have one very helpful consequence. George Younger, my predecessor, had been fully involved in all the arrangements for the visit. It made obvious sense for him to continue to act as host and to escort Marshal Yazov round the programme of defence activities arranged for him, while I settled into my new office. As a result we had something most useful that I think had never happened before: a joint hand-over for a week between outgoing and incoming secretaries of state.

During that time we did have one particularly important meeting. This was to discuss the new Merlin helicopter that Westland was producing. It had been subject to considerable change in the course of its design, and a number of voices, not least from Number 10, were suggesting that the order should be cancelled. George and I listened to the presentation, at which it was explained that the proposed changes would mean that the helicopter no longer met the original brief, the major change being the addition of a third engine. The helicopter was intended to operate from a frigate in an anti-submarine role, in which it could travel some 150–200 miles from its ship and remain for four or five hours in a submarine search area. The weight of the extra engine significantly curtailed the length of its stay in the search area. While it was clear that it could not now meet the original brief, it was also clear that it was an impressive new machine, with its additional engine providing extra safety and reliability. There had been a number of helicopter accidents recently, among them to those servicing the oilfields in the North Sea, with some significant loss of life. I thought there was a powerful argument that, as well as its military capabilities, which were the prime interest of the Ministry of Defence, it could well have major potential for civilian use, with its extra safety features opening new opportunities in export markets. George agreed and the order for the Merlin went ahead. I was pleased to see its success, with sales to a number of other countries, culminating in the ultimate endorsement when it was selected as the official helicopter for the President of the United States, a decision subsequently taken by other governments as well.

Early in September 1989 I visited our forces in West Germany and the British Sector in Berlin. General Sir Peter Inge was the Commander-in-Chief and he gave a dinner for me to which he invited a senior German NATO colleague. From my visit I had already formed the impression that things were changing, and I asked him, 'What do you think about the possibility of Germany being united again?' He answered me very directly: 'It's what every German longs to see but I know it's never going to happen.' Two months later the Berlin Wall came down and suddenly the whole world changed. Within a short period, Germany did indeed become united.

The German general's opinion was widely shared, not least in London. On my return from Germany I happened to be sitting outside the Cabinet room in Number 10 with John Major, who for that brief period was Foreign Secretary. In the light of my recent visit, I asked him what our policy was on a united Germany. John, having only just taken up his new post, very understandably said, 'I don't know, but I'll find out.' When I saw him the next day before a Cabinet meeting, he said, 'I asked my officials what our policy was on a united Germany. We don't have one!' It wasn't a surprising answer, since the situation had been unchanged for more than forty years.

One person who was caught out by this totally unexpected development was Margaret Thatcher, when she expressed her instinctive hostility to the idea of a united Germany. When it became a reality, she found she was still dealing with Helmut Kohl, who had been Chancellor of West Germany but was now Chancellor of a united Germany, and she had to restrain her views.

From the start of my time at Defence, it was clear that the Soviet Union was in real trouble. One system that helped to hold it together was conscription, in which young men from the various different republics were obliged to serve in the Soviet army. This caused growing resentment, which came to a head following the Soviet invasion of Afghanistan. The consequence was increasing disaffection in the various republics at having to supply their young men as conscripts to fight for the Soviet Union in what they saw as very much a Russian enterprise. I watched with interest the report of continuing and growing dissent, which reached a climax in Lithuania: the young men due for conscription refused to serve and disappeared, and the Lithuanian government and parliament in Vilnius refused to make any attempt to apprehend them. At the same time reports came in from East Germany of Russian soldiers on railway stations trying to sell their rifles for any cash they could get, to alleviate their miserable conditions.

A year later, when Germany was united, I saw for myself how miserable those conditions were when Gerhard Stoltenberg, the German Defence Minister, took me to an East German barracks, and I was appalled to see how run-down and slum-like they were. In one respect they were exactly like the cookhouses we had had in Africa for the askaris in the KAR forty years before, where they simply used to light a fire on the floor and hang a pot over it.

It was clear that this was symptomatic of the whole East German infrastructure, much inferior to that of the prosperous West Germany. This was further confirmed by Gerhard Stoltenberg, who told me that a friend of his, responsible for the very successful West German Deutsche Bahn railway system, was now responsible for the East German railways as well. One of the first things he had discovered was that a vast number of new concrete sleepers had been made with sand from the Baltic; full of salt, they were all crumbling away, and the railway was faced with a huge task to replace them.

At the end of September 1989 the troubles of Northern Ireland hit the headlines again when the IRA detonated a bomb at the Royal Marines School of Music in Deal. It was one of the worst terrorist outrages on the mainland, with ten young bandsmen killed and a number of others badly injured. It was said that the IRA had been trying to mount a campaign on the mainland for eighteen months to boost their morale, which had been severely dented by a string of setbacks in Northern Ireland and an apparent weakening of the IRA's status among Republican sympathisers. It was clear that whatever little status it had left was further massively damaged by the killing of these young bandsmen. Having visited the School of Music immediately after the bomb and seen some of the injured in hospital, I was particularly appalled that, at the time of the Labour conference in Brighton barely two weeks later, 500 yards from the Grand Hotel, the scene of the 1984 bomb, Gerry Adams had been invited to speak at a meeting, and had received a standing ovation.

One interesting visit in my first year was to Hungary, a former member of the Warsaw Pact, one of that group of nations previously corralled by the Soviet Union behind the Iron Curtain ever since World War II. My visit coincided with the arrival of a large number of East Germans in Budapest. Their opportunities for holidays at that time were pretty limited, but Hungary was one place they could visit, and a number had decided to see if its new situation would provide the opportunity at last to escape to the West. They camped in Budapest and refused to return to East Germany. The stand-off lasted for some time, but in the end the Hungarian government, faced with this vast influx and finding no other way to deal with the situation, allowed them to leave; they travelled on to Austria through the old Iron Curtain and so reached the West. At this time Erich Honecker was the head of East Germany, and the cars they travelled in were the smoky, noisy Trabants – the living symbol of East German inadequacy in the car industry. As this huge convoy of cars escaped to the West, one witty commentator described it as 'winning for the Trabant Car Company the Erich Honecker award for export achievement'!

At the end of my visit, which had coincided with this extraordinary exodus and the collapse of the Iron Curtain, they gave me a piece of the barbed wire from it. This happened to be just before the Conservative party conference in Blackpool, and I decided to use the wire as a prop in my speech. I was wondering how best to use it and Jeffrey Archer gave me some excellent advice: to hold it up high and keep turning it very slowly so that the audience in that huge hall and the television cameras had time to focus on it. In my speech I said that I had just come back from Hungary, the first NATO defence minister to pay a visit to a former Warsaw Pact country, 'and they gave me this – just a piece of wire, but it's not just a piece of wire – it is part of the 200 miles of the Iron Curtain and it is all coming down, and no one has done more to help make that happen than the leader of our party, our Prime Minister Margaret Thatcher.' The whole conference erupted with applause at this tribute to her, which she certainly deserved for the leadership she had given in helping to end the Cold War, and I was very lucky to have such a wonderful prop to include in my speech.

As it happened, that wasn't my only trophy, as in the following March I was in Berlin again, visiting our forces, when they kindly presented me with a piece of the Berlin Wall, which everybody in the city had been so pleased to knock down.

When it was still standing as the prison wall that prevented East Germans from escaping to the West, it had been covered in graffiti on the West Berlin side, with a host of expressions of outrage at this negation of freedom. One visiting British MP was looking at all the messages in every possible language, when he suddenly noticed one in English: 'Geoff Boycott, we love you!' Back in England, describing his visit to Berlin at a constituency meeting, he mentioned this unexpected message of support for the famous Yorkshire and England cricketer, when somebody in the audience, clearly not a Yorkshire supporter, shouted, 'Which side of the Wall was it written on?'

In April 1990 I went to see our garrison on the Falkland Islands, landing on the new airstrip at Mount Pleasant which had been built to replace the much more limited facility at Port Stanley. I was interested to see the airstrip as, when I was Secretary of State for the Environment with certain planning responsibilities for the Falklands, it had fallen to me to give permission for it. Moreover, when I was Secretary of State for Transport, I was inspecting transport facilities in East London, among them the port of Tilbury, where a small passenger ship was moored. A number of men going aboard told me that they were going to the Falklands to build the airstrip.

The trip involved an eight-hour flight to Ascension Island, a break for refuelling, and then another ten hours on to the Falklands. The flight went very smoothly to Ascension Island, where I was welcomed by the station commander and made a brief inspection of the facilities for this staging post for the Falklands. We took off again and our journey continued uneventfully for the next five hours, but then the captain came back to tell me that there was a strong cross-wind on the single airstrip at Mount Pleasant and we would not be able to land there. We could divert to South America, either to Montevideo or a Brazilian airport. By then the crew would be out of time, there wouldn't be another crew there, and we would have to sit and wait for twenty-four hours before we could resume the journey. The alternative would be to return to Ascension Island, where a further crew would be available; we could spend the night there and start again the following morning. The weather forecast was that the winds would abate and there should be no problem completing the journey. It was clear that the sensible thing to do was to go back to Ascension, so we turned round for the five-hour flight back, and ten hours after we left we were back where we started.

This delay did have one redeeming feature, when the station commander and his wife kindly put me up for the night, and in the evening took me down to a steep shingle beach where we saw turtles coming out of the sea and laying their eggs. It was a fascinating sight and something I had never seen before. The next morning we took off again and ten hours later arrived in the Falklands. I was greeted by the general officer commanding, who said it was exceptionally bad luck to have had to turn round the day before. However, I discovered when I got back to the ministry that, so far from being rare, it had been a fairly frequent experience, given the weather the Falklands often faced.

One new style of diplomatic engagement developed recently was the organising of Anglo-French summits, in which the French president and a British prime minister met together with a small number of senior colleagues in some appropriate location for informal talks. President Mitterrand had organised one such gathering in some style, and Margaret Thatcher was very concerned to find an interesting location for the next year's summit, to be held in Britain. It was proposed to pick Waddesdon, the Rothschilds' French-style château in Buckinghamshire, which proved an inspired choice.

The occasion got off to a slightly confused start because I had an important previous engagement and had to rush there in a helicopter from the Ministry of Defence. The pilot was not quite clear where he was supposed to land; finally he chose the wide drive in front of the house. He landed, unfortunately, slightly too close to it, where the red carpet had already been rolled out for the arrival by car of President Mitterrand. The down-draughts from the helicopter had the effect of picking up the red carpet that had just been rolled out and rolling it right back into the house again, so my arrival was not universally appreciated by the staff at Waddesdon.

The subsequent gathering was extremely enjoyable, with an excellent after-lunch guide in Jacob Rothschild, whose family house it was. Unlike so many famous French châteaux, which are rather empty, Waddesdon was full of fascinating French furniture, including one piece I remember, the famous French writer Guy de Maupassant's desk. In addition it had a magnificent library of old French books and Mitterrand was fascinated by them. This all contributed to an ideal location in which to entertain an extremely erudite French president, and was an excellent example of the care that Margaret Thatcher took in arrangements for visits of foreign leaders.

❋ ❋ ❋

Following the visit of Marshal Yazov to the UK the previous year, in May 1990 I paid a return visit to the Soviet Union, the first ever by a NATO defence minister. Relations were much improved since the depths of the Cold War, particularly after the meetings between Margaret Thatcher and President Gorbachev, with the Warsaw Pact crumbling, and the Berlin Wall and the Iron Curtain gone.

Jane came with me and we had a very friendly welcome from Marshal Yazov and his wife. They had taken a lot of trouble over both my programme and Jane's. Mine started with meetings with Yazov and his senior team, a speech to a large gathering of senior military, and then most interesting demonstrations of Soviet military capabilities. The first was an air display with the latest Soviet fighters, followed by a full armoured regiment being dropped in front of me and my party. The Soviet system for airdrops seemed to involve smaller parachutes for faster descent, but with retro rockets fitted on the underside of the platform on which the armour was strapped, with a trailing line that touched the ground first and fired the retro rockets to slow the rate of fall. It appeared to work, although some fell behind a wood and were never seen again. Nonetheless, a large number did survive and were lined up in review order after this impressive display. It was then followed by a low-level drop by Soviet special forces, jumping from low-flying aircraft and showing their skills by landing only a few yards in front of me. They peeled off their parachutes, marched forward, and then whipped off their berets, out of which tumbled a wonderful assortment of auburn and fair hair. A *Daily Express* photographer in the press team captured the moment, and the picture was captioned 'Tom King meets the 007 girls, licensed to kill'!

Quite separately I had been briefed to raise with Yazov our concern about a Soviet biological weapons programme. We were aware that they had been producing substantial quantities of anthrax bacteria, and smallpox and plague viruses, which could be quickly mounted on intercontinental missiles. Margaret Thatcher was briefed to raise the same issue with President Gorbachev and we each received clear denials of such a programme. Having received these denials, we were interested to learn later that President Gorbachev had then cancelled the programme, but without any apparent effect, as it was cancelled again by President Yeltsin in 1992. Yeltsin would certainly have known something about it because there was an accidental release of anthrax at a Soviet weapons plant in Sverdlovsk when he was the local Communist Party head, and there had been a number of deaths. When I raised the existence of the programme with Marshal Yazov, he dismissed it completely, saying it was a silly rumour arising out of the death of a few diseased rabbits on the Chinese border.

For our stay in Moscow the original plan had been for us to stay at the British Embassy, but our hosts were most insistent that we should receive hospitality in the state guest-house. We were shown into our extremely comfortable suite and Jane had a quick look round. She came out of the bathroom saying that she couldn't find any towels. In less than a minute there was a knock at the door and a maid stood there with a pile of towels. We realised that our conversations would travel far and, while careless talk had to be avoided, we did have the best room service ever, with no need to press the bell!

After Moscow, we visited the Soviet Black Sea Fleet in Sevastopol, starting with an inspection of a Soviet frigate, then a meeting with the Admiral commanding this vital Soviet base. The serving officers in my party noted the poor fighting condition of the vessels we saw, which suggested that they were not given any priority, as NATO had dominated their only outlet into the Mediterranean. Finally we visited the amazing war memorial that commemorates the Battle of Sevastopol, one of the Hero Cities of the Soviet Union for its feats in World War II. The Admiral was my host at an excellent dinner, during which we were serenaded by the Black Sea Fleet Orchestra. After the traditional testing round of vodka toasts, the dinner finished on a memorable note. My party included Air Chief Marshal Sir Peter Harding, the Chief of Air Staff, who happened to be an excellent jazz pianist. The evening ended with Peter on a white piano accompanied in a rousing number by the Black Sea Fleet Orchestra, making an unforgettable moment in Anglo-Soviet relations!

From Sevastopol it was on to Leningrad/St Petersburg, with a Soviet general as my escort. During the flight we happened to be talking about how frontiers had been established in earlier years in different colonies, with lines just being drawn on a map, with no regard for tribal or other local, traditional boundaries. I told him about the border between British East Africa and German East Africa, now Kenya and Tanzania, where a line had been drawn straight up from the coast to Lake Victoria. Queen Victoria had been shown the proposed line on the map, and remarked, in reference to her cousin Kaiser Wilhelm, that cousin Willie had not got a mountain, as Mount Kilimanjaro and Mount Kenya were both in British East Africa. Changes were made and the border between Tanzania and Kenya now has the kink in it that puts Kilimanjaro into Tanzania, and Queen and Kaiser each had a mountain!

The general then told me the story about the building of the railway line from Moscow to St Petersburg. The Tsar had demanded to see what the proposed line would be. The engineers responsible were ushered into his august presence and with detailed maps showed how the line would accommodate the various geological challenges on the route. The Tsar was unimpressed by this complicated plan and asked to be given a ruler. He then drew a straight line from Moscow to St Petersburg and told the engineers that this would be the line. Nobody thought it prudent to argue and so, bowing low, they withdrew, thanking their supreme ruler for his outstanding advice. Once outside they looked at his plan and were seriously puzzled, but nobody was going to go back into the room to argue about it. When the line was built, it did go straight from Moscow to St Petersburg, save only for one significant loop in the middle. It is believed that the loop is there because the Tsar had his finger on the ruler!

In Leningrad (now St Petersburg again) I was the guest of the general commanding Leningrad district, where my first commitment was to lay a wreath in a very moving ceremony at the burial ground for the people of the city who had died in the siege in World War II. Two million people lost their lives in that brave resistance, and Leningrad certainly earned its title as another Hero City of the Soviet Union. As we processed the 150 yards from the entrance to the memorial, we passed on either side raised squares of ground, and I later learnt that each one contained 25,000 bodies.

There was no state guest-house in Leningrad, and my party and I stayed in a hotel specially reserved for important visitors. We had an instant illustration of how rigidly controlled so much of the Soviet Union was at that time, when I needed to speak to the office in London. My private secretary went to arrange it but got the shock reply that to put a call through to London would take three days, presumably requiring all sorts of official approvals before it could be done. Fortunately, as the guest of the general, a quick call to his office did the trick and our call came straight through, though I suspect we were not the only people on the line!

Recently there have been rumours that attempts would have been made to compromise President Trump during his earlier business visits to Moscow. I am certain that Soviet, and now Russian, intelligence regularly tried to do this with important visitors. In my own case, while we were in Leningrad, when I was at an outside meeting, and Jane was alone in our bedroom, the door quietly opened and a very attractive lady walked in, but withdrew hurriedly when she found Jane there and not me.

It was certainly fascinating to visit the Soviet Union at a time of enormous change, in which my host, Marshal Yazov, was deeply involved. His military career had started as a sergeant at Stalingrad, that devastating struggle that finally turned the tide of the German advance in World War II. He was a long-serving general, became minister of defence and then persuaded President Gorbachev to promote him to marshal. However, at this time there was increasing pressure for more democratic control of the armed forces, and it was felt that the minister of defence should be a member of the Duma. He had been found a safe constituency somewhere north of Vladivostok, and he told me that immediately after my visit he would be travelling to it. It was going to take him three days to get there, and he would be away a week. All apparently went to plan and Mr Yazov, member of the Duma, returned and continued his duties as minister of defence!

I didn't see him again before he was caught up in the coup against Gorbachev. This happened because Gorbachev was trying to address the growing pressure for independence from the individual republics. He was sympathetic to the proposal that the Soviet Union could become a much looser collaboration of separate states, but this was strongly opposed by hardline members of the Communist Party, prominent among whom were the head of the KGB and Yazov. Gorbachev was proposing a new union agreement but indicated in private conversations that he would need to get rid of the hardliners, including these two. He did not realise that his conversations were being intercepted by the KGB, who then decided to act and launch a coup when he was on holiday in the Crimea. The coup leaders isolated him, cut off his communications, and demanded that he rescind his proposed actions. He resisted these approaches, but was clearly in an extremely difficult position until he was saved by Yeltsin, who supported him, and provided the leadership from the Russian Parliament that led in the end to the defeat of the coup. Both Yazov and the KGB head were arrested and imprisoned in the Lubyanka, the notorious Moscow prison. Yazov remained there for the next eighteen months on a charge of treason against the Soviet Union. However, he was then released, on the grounds that the charge was against a country that no longer existed. It was of course why he took part in the coup, because he believed Gorbachev was destroying the Soviet Union that he was trying to save.

❋ ❋ ❋

In June 1990 I paid an official visit to France as the guest of Jean-Pierre

Chevènement, my French opposite number, with the excellent hospitality and guidance of our ambassador, my old school rugger scrum companion, Ewen Fergusson, and his wife Sara. We had an excellent programme but of particular interest was that Ewen had arranged for me to appear before the Defence Committee of the *Assemblée Nationale*. I was apparently the first minister for a foreign country ever to appear before this committee, which I sought to do in French, without too many disasters! What was particularly friendly was that they had noticed that it was my birthday and at the lunch afterwards a handsome birthday cake appeared.

When I became Defence Secretary in July 1989 there was growing pressure for a major review of our defence capabilities and expenditure. The world seemed a more peaceful place, and the Cold War a lot less chilly. There were increasing questions about the scale of our deployment in Germany, where we had more than 100,000 troops, as for the past forty years.

We therefore set up a review of our total defence resources and manpower. The very wording of the title *Defence Review* had an unhappy history, since it was regularly seen as simply a Treasury exercise to cut some more money from the defence budget. An alternative title was conceived, *Options for Change*, which went forward under General Sir Richard Vincent, the Vice Chief of Defence Staff, a very seasoned Whitehall warrior and future Chief of Defence Staff, and Richard Mottram, a deputy secretary and future permanent secretary. The study covered all the services and involved some significant reductions among them, reducing the overall number in uniform from some 320,000 to around 250,000 over a period of years: to an army of 120,000, navy and marines of 60,000, and RAF of 75,000. The number of frigates/destroyers was to fall from forty-eight to forty, there was a reduction in the number of squadrons in the RAF, but by far the biggest argument arose over the reduction in the number of infantry battalions, from fifty-two to thirty-eight. In fact, the reduction in numbers in fighting strength was less than it appeared, because some of the battalions were significantly under-recruited. It did however involve the amalgamation of a number of old regiments with long traditions and great loyalties. This was particularly true of Scottish regiments, and a petition of more than 800,000 signatures was raised objecting to the proposals. As I was walking into the Chamber in the House of Commons in July 1990 to make the announcement about the outcome of the Options review, I was handed a telegram from a Captain McCubbin of the Gordon Highlanders, a regiment that was being merged with the Queen's Own Highlanders. We had given the affected regiments advance notice of the proposals, and Captain McCubbin's message was admirably military and concise: 'To Secretary of State Tom King, Whitehall, London – To hell with you – abusive letter follows!' The same dislike of our proposals for other infantry regiments, while conveyed in a rather different tone, dominated the response from many MPs, with hardly a comment on the changes for the other parts of the army, or the navy or RAF.

The overall reduction of some 18% left us spending some 4% of GDP on defence, about double the present scale. While Conservative MPs were concerned about the reduction, from the Labour benches the criticism was that it did not go nearly far enough. Tony Benn and Ken Livingstone complained that defence expenditure was still far too high, and Tony Banks took the opportunity to criticise the level of homelessness and unemployment by saying that we now would have the best protected cardboard cities and dole queues in Europe. I was very struck by the number of commentators who wondered why we had not made much greater reductions. One BBC interviewer challenged me as to why we could possibly need so many armed forces, and asked what possible threat there was, to which I, luckily, replied, 'The threat of the unexpected'. On the night of 2 August Saddam Hussein invaded Kuwait, and the unexpected had indeed happened, leading to our biggest deployment of troops and armour overseas since World War II; the Options implementation was then suspended during what became the first Gulf War.

Saddam's invasion of Kuwait took everybody by surprise. He had made accusations that over-production of oil by Kuwait represented 'economic warfare' against Iraq, and that Kuwait had stolen $2.4 billion-worth of oil from the oilfields along the Iraq/Kuwait border, but no one expected that his retaliation would be to invade Kuwait. He moved his troops down to the border but assured his other neighbours that he simply wanted to frighten the Kuwaitis. Both Jordan and Saudi Arabia hosted peace talks, but Iraq walked out and on the night of 2 August invaded Kuwait. Within a day its forces had not only captured Kuwait City but had reached the Saudi border. Saddam initially claimed that there had been a coup in Kuwait and that the Iraqis had been invited in by the new government. This pretence was quickly exposed and it was clear that he had underestimated the loyalty of the Kuwaitis to the Al Sabah ruling family. King Fahd felt betrayed by Saddam's false pledges and there was no doubt that Saudi Arabia felt threatened. The military view was that he could have reached Riyadh within three days, and as one Saudi prince said, 'He who has Kuwait for breakfast is likely to ask for something more for lunch!'

The question was often asked whether, if there had been no great reaction from the West, Saddam would have continued his advance to capture the valuable oilfields in Saudi Arabia's Eastern Province. I heard a story that Saddam's plan was indeed to continue and carve up Saudi Arabia completely, and expel the Al Sauds, the ruling family. His intention was that, while he took the oilfields in the Eastern Province, he would seek the support of the Yemenis by offering them the Southern Highlands of Saudi Arabia. Even more significantly, to enlist the support of Jordan he was planning to offer it the Hejaz, with the holiest sites of Mecca and Medina, from which the Jordanians had been driven out by the Al Sauds after World War I. The restoration of the old Hashemite kingdom would clearly have been an enticing offer, but I do not know if it was ever made to King Hussein of Jordan. There was one further person that Saddam wished to keep onside: President Mubarak of Egypt. Apparently Saddam did not intend to offer any share of Saudi land to Egypt, but proposed that it should receive $40 billion in compensation. As it happened, President Mubarak felt deceived by Saddam, who had assured him that he had no plans to invade Kuwait, so he joined our coalition and sent thousands of Egyptian soldiers to augment our forces.

One key misjudgement Saddam made was his belief that, while the United States and Britain would be fiercely critical of his action, they would not physically intervene in time. Here he was extremely unlucky. His choice of the night of 2 August to invade Kuwait should have been a clever one for him, as in both the United States and Europe most governments and parliaments would have gone on holiday, and would probably be very slow to respond. What he was not to know was that, at that very point, Margaret Thatcher was at a high-level conference in Aspen, Colorado, in the United States, to be joined the following morning by President George Bush. As a result the two people most likely among all the world leaders to have the concern and capacity to address this grave situation were together when the news came of the invasion, and they immediately agreed to take action. Very quickly, Dick Cheney, the US Defense Secretary, went to Saudi Arabia to offer military support for its defence. There was initially some concern in Riyadh about the idea of inviting non-Islamic forces into the kingdom, the home of the most holy sites of Islam, but King Fahd courageously issued the invitation.

The American forces quickly arrived and within a week thereafter we also had the first deployment of British forces, with Tornado and Jaguar aircraft arriving in Saudi Arabia and Oman, initially under the command of Air Vice Marshal Sandy Wilson, and extra ships reinforcing the Royal Navy Armilla Patrol in the Gulf. Once that happened the Republican Guard and armoured units that Saddam had advanced to the Saudi border quickly moved back, as the US and UK forces began to grow.

When I reflect now on the speed with which we responded and the scale of response that grew and grew, as the coalition of many countries came together to overturn this flagrant aggression, I have often wondered whether, if Saddam had invaded only as far as the Mutla Ridge, north of Kuwait City – thereby seizing the oilfields straddling the border which were the source of the friction between them – there would have been anything like the same level of support to evict him. The unanimity of response under clear United Nations resolutions also reflected the change in superpower relations at just that time. Previously Saddam might have expected some support from the Soviet Union, with its regular posture of opposition to the United States, but the totally different climate under President Gorbachev meant that this did not happen. The Soviet Union in fact supported the UN resolutions condemning the invasion.

Recently, in looking through the archives relating to the first days after Saddam Hussein's invasion of Kuwait, I came across an interesting note of something that I had quite forgotten. Following his capture of Kuwait, and with his Republican Guard divisions poised on the border between Kuwait and Saudi Arabia, the immediate worry was that he might decide to advance and take over the eastern oilfields of Saudi Arabia and possibly go even further, with Qatar, Bahrain and even the UAE potentially in his line of advance. The note I found was dated some days after the invasion of Kuwait, when the fear of this happening was extremely acute. The note reported that the UK Met Office had had a request from its Iraqi counterpart for a ten-day weather forecast for the Gulf region, including the eastern coast of Saudi Arabia. Under the normal arrangements of the World Meteorological Organisation, to which both the UK and Iraq belonged, the Met Office had been happy to oblige. They were quite unaware of the acute sensitivity of this information and the likely use to which it would be put. The note continued that this now had been a matter of further discussion between the Ministry of Defence and the Foreign Office, and it had been agreed that advice would immediately be given to the Met Office not to provide any more weather forecasts to the Iraqis. Thankfully the early arrival of American forces, followed quickly by us, halted the threat and the forecast was never used.

Following the initial despatch of aircraft and ships to give immediate support to Desert Shield, we decided to send an armoured brigade as well. I knew there had been concerns about the reliability of the Challenger tank engines, particularly when operating in a much hotter climate and in desert conditions. The brigade was in Germany at the time, and urgent work was done to ensure that the existing engines were in good order and that there were plenty of spare engines as well. This unfortunately resulted in the removal of a lot of engines from the remaining tanks in Germany, leaving very few fit for service there. It was clear that we would need substantial back-up engineering support as well, so I held a meeting of the Defence Industrial Council, which included the heads of all the main defence contractors. My message to them was quite simple. They were in the business of selling their equipment not just to us in the Ministry of Defence but to many other countries as well. That equipment was about to be put to a real test and in very public view. This would be their showcase, and they had a crucial interest in seeing that it performed well for us. They got the point completely and the result was the largest ever deployment of technicians in support of the operation of their equipment in active service conditions. As far as I'm aware they had no difficulty in getting volunteers to go to the Gulf, and they played a vital part.

The unexpected and rapid deployment to the desert of the 7th Armoured

Brigade, some 7,000 strong, posed a number of challenges. I was concerned that our troops should be properly equipped and well turned out, and I had heard some worrying rumours about desert uniforms. It transpired that, a couple of years earlier, it had been decided that we would never need desert uniforms again and that a lot of them had been sold to, of all people, the Iraqis! I asked to see the lists of what uniforms were actually available. The general responsible came and showed the list to me, but I had a little difficulty in understanding it. I said to him, 'It looks to me as though we have 7,000 tops but no trousers, is that really right?' What I did then was certainly in no ministerial handbook. We could not wait for the problem to be handled through some lengthy procurement process, with the brigade just about to go to the Gulf. It happened that during my time in Northern Ireland, Marks & Spencer had been extremely helpful in supporting businesses there. I knew the chairman, Richard Greenbury. I told him the problem and asked him who he thought could help us. He immediately said to try Andrew Baird, an important supplier to M & S, and we contacted them straight away. If my memory is right, they produced 7,000 pairs of camouflage desert trousers in not much more than a week, and our troops were able to leave on this urgent deployment in the proper uniform. I believe that Baird's had actually had a lot of them made in Morocco!

Once it had been decided to send major ground forces to recover Kuwait, the next question was who should now command the whole operation in the Gulf. The first proposal that came to me through the Ministry of Defence was a lieutenant general with mainly European experience, but Margaret Thatcher, who often had her own separate sources of advice, was determined that Major-General Peter de la Billière should be appointed. As soon as I met him and learned of his background, it was clear that he was eminently qualified for this new responsibility. As it happened, nearly forty years before, we had both been junior officers in the Light Infantry, although we had never met. However, the important points were that he had a fine reputation as a soldier; he had considerable experience with special forces, had had tri-service command in the Falklands and, most importantly, was very familiar with the Arab world. It proved to be an excellent appointment. He immediately established good relations with General Norman Schwarzkopf, the American commander-in-chief, and with HRH Prince Khalid, the Saudi joint commander. With the obvious risk of serious trouble in this complicated scenario, these good relations were a key factor in the ultimate success of the operation.

One particular feature of Peter's leadership was knowing the importance of mutual understanding and respect in the Gulf countries in which we found ourselves. From his own knowledge of the local cultures, he ensured that our troops were educated and respectful of these. He produced a pamphlet explaining Arab culture, how to behave in an Arab country, and some basic Arabic. In this way he undoubtedly helped reduce the tensions and difficulties that could otherwise have arisen for those serving for the first time in a very different culture.

Part of my responsibility was to ensure that we maintained maximum public support in the UK for our forces in the Gulf as they undertook this unexpected major commitment. To do this, and to meet the huge demand for news and information about everything that was happening, I was regularly in touch with Peter, always pressing for any information that he could give me. Initially he found this difficult, and was worried that I was trying to interfere with his legitimate responsibilities of command, but he came quickly to appreciate the extraordinary scale of public interest. One particular event showed this very well. As the months went by during which we tried to get Saddam to leave Kuwait peaceably, it was clear that our troops would still be stuck in the desert at Christmas. Some newspapers ran a campaign for people to bake cakes as Christmas presents for them, and we had undertaken to ensure delivery. Peter told me afterwards that the absolute deluge of wonderful cakes pouring out of the RAF transport planes made clearer than anything the scale of that public interest. In his book *Storm Command*, he kindly paid a very generous tribute to our work together, while not omitting the difficulties that had occurred in the early stages. It is so generous that I cannot resist repeating it, including his honest and fair criticisms of me:

By now, at the end of the war, Tom King was greatly respected all round the Gulf. He proved brilliant at dealing with the rulers and putting over the British point of view with firmness, but also with tact and fine political judgement. By giving me his full support in-theatre, he had built up my standing as the senior British commander, to my own substantial benefit. His determination to work in hands-on fashion undoubtedly caused problems at all command levels, because he became too much involved in the detail of operations, and his obsession with the press was another diversionary factor. Nevertheless, he was an immensely loyal supporter of the Armed Forces and did his able best to fight our corner in the war. In my one-to-one dealings with him, I could appreciate his need for detailed information, to answer questions in the House of Commons and keep abreast or ahead of the media at their own game. Besides, I believe the personal knowledge gained from our frequent talks gave him an understanding which he could never have acquired if he had not visited and kept in touch so keenly. As a result he spoke about the war with exceptional authority at home and that in itself was a great help to us. It was a measure of how well he grasped in-theatre problems that he backed me wholeheartedly at one of the cardinal moments of the deployment when I asked for our ground forces to be increased to divisional strength. Without this generosity of support my own task would have been much harder.

Why there was such pressure for ever more information and reports on events was because this was, in a real sense, the first TV war. CNN had just launched the first-ever global TV twenty-four-hour news service, and this was combined with massive press presence in the Gulf, embedded with our forces. General Schwarzkopf told me one day that there had been some casualties in a training exercise, and that a press photo had arrived in Washington before the incident had even been reported to him. A further difficulty came from the different time zones, so that we could have a Schwarzkopf press briefing from Riyadh, a few hours later one from me in London, and a few hours after that another from Dick Cheney in Washington as well, with the vital requirement that we all sang the same song!

One key challenge we had always to bear in mind was the serious religious issue about the acceptability or otherwise of Christian troops at the very centre of Islam. The King's special title, to which he attached the highest importance, was Custodian of the Two Holy Mosques, Mecca and Medina. Saddam sought to stir up hostility to King Fahd by saying that he had permitted infidel forces to be based in Islam's holy sites.

Fortunately there were remarkably few major incidents in spite of the serious difference in cultures, notwithstanding that Christmas came while we were there. Once when I was returning from visiting King Fahd in Jeddah and taking off to fly back to Riyadh, I looked down and noticed the massive new pilgrim terminal that had just been built to accommodate the millions of Muslims making their pilgrimage to Mecca and Medina. I then noticed the fleet of US tanker planes parked just behind the terminal, who were providing in-flight refuelling for the massive airlift of men and materials from the USA going to their base in the Eastern Province. I subsequently discovered that these planes were from the US National Guard and that half the pilots were women, flying these massive planes over a country where at that time women were not even allowed to drive a car!

There was one early complaint when USAF servicewomen were unloading cargo at Dhahran, and in the heat they had stripped down to the bare essentials, leading to immediate complaints from the Eastern Province Governor who was responsible for ensuring that women had to be totally covered at all times in public. I remember on another occasion a morning meeting with Schwarzkopf. He was looking rather tired, and it turned out that he had had to get up in the middle of the night to fly down to Jeddah to see King Fahd. Apparently some of the wives of Americans working for Saudi Aramco, the vast oil company, ran a theatre group and had decided to provide some entertainment for the American troops who had just arrived. Their choice was a musical, *The Greatest Little Whorehouse in Texas*! Unfortunately CNN included a clip of the show in their news broadcast, quite unaware that in their late-night audience was none other than His Majesty King Fahd, obviously anxious to keep in touch with all the latest news at this dangerous time. The discovery that this raunchy show was actually happening in the kingdom resulted in the immediate summons to Schwarzkopf and the rather bleary-eyed general that I saw the next morning.

As the steady build-up of forces for Desert Shield continued, the pressure on Saddam to withdraw or face the certainty of painful defeat was steadily increasing. It was clear that we could not stay for ever, with our forces sitting in the desert as the summer came and it was becoming too hot. We were moving towards a deadline when we would have to launch our attack if Saddam did not withdraw, which he was showing no sign of doing.

At this critical moment in late 1990, I suddenly faced upheaval at home with the challenge to Margaret Thatcher and her subsequent resignation. It could not have come at a worse time for me in my efforts to support the morale of our forces in the Gulf. I was a regular visitor there, and my consistent message to them was that the whole country was behind them, led by a Prime Minister that they all knew, from her leadership in the Falklands campaign, would back them to the hilt. That it was a critical point was clear, since at the very Cabinet meeting at which Margaret announced that she was resigning, I had the next item on the agenda: seeking Cabinet endorsement to send a further 16,000 troops to the Gulf, to build us up to divisional strength.

With the change of prime minister, I was suddenly faced with continuing the message of the Prime Minister's support, but with a prime minister that most soldiers had never heard of, so rapid had been his promotion in government. It was said by a colleague that none of us knew what we were getting, and that John Major couldn't quite believe his elevation to his new role! Nonetheless, he soon came out to meet King Fahd, and then went into the desert and, notwithstanding his lack of previous defence experience, spoke very well to a number of gatherings of our troops, confirming his full support for them.

The change of prime minister had unfortunately coincided exactly with a major meeting in London to commemorate the fortieth anniversary of the first meeting there of the North Atlantic Assembly, the parliamentary arm of NATO. This was to start with a meeting in Westminster Hall where some 2,000 senators, congressmen, *deputés* and other representatives of the NATO countries, plus visiting delegations from the Soviet Union, Poland, Bulgaria and Czechoslovakia, would receive a welcoming address from the Prime Minister. The difficulty was that on the morning of 28 November we did not have a prime minister. Margaret Thatcher was on her way to tender her resignation to the Queen, while John Major waited to be called to the Palace to be appointed. The alarm was raised the day before when the coming problem was recognised, and since Douglas Hurd, the Foreign Secretary, was abroad I was asked to stand in. It was certainly a daunting assignment, with such a huge audience of senior parliamentarians and in that magnificent hall, and I did commiserate with the audience on their bad luck in meeting on the only morning in the last ten years when we did not have a prime minister. As I explained, 'You invited the Prime Minister to address you, she readily accepted, but he can't come'! Helped by the sympathy that I think is often extended to last-minute understudies, I enjoyed it, and I like to think the audience did too.

I subsequently had the pleasure of listening to President Obama addressing a joint meeting of both Houses in Westminster Hall. He opened his remarks by saying that it was a very special privilege to be invited to speak in the Hall, a privilege, he said, previously enjoyed only by Nelson Mandela and the Pope. It was not the time to say that others had had that privilege as well!

In the build-up to the decision to launch the attack against Saddam Hussein and to evict him from Kuwait, Air Chief Marshal Sir Paddy Hine, our top joint commander with Norman Schwarzkopf, gave a top-secret presentation in a secure room at the Ministry of Defence to John Major, me, and other senior ministers and chiefs of staff. The briefing covered the special battle plan that Norman Schwarzkopf had made. The core of it was that, after an effective air campaign, the land campaign would involve the appearance of a full-frontal assault while actually moving the major land forces far out to the left, driving through where the Iraqi defences were weaker and then swinging round in a large left hook and trapping the main bulk of the Iraqi army.

At the end of the meeting, as I discovered later, Paddy had had other engagements in Whitehall, and asked his staff officer to take the laptop with the top-secret battle plan back to his Northwood HQ. This officer set off with his driver in his official car but, on his way back, he happened to notice in a garage forecourt a pick-up van which seemed very much the kind that he had been looking to buy. He stopped to look at it and got his driver to take a look as well. To their horror, when they got back to their car, they found the laptop had gone and with it the top-secret plan for the coming attack. This could not have been more embarrassing. There was an extremely nervous period in which we tried to establish whether this was a brilliant Iraqi theft, or simply a smart bit of work by some local thief, and whether the whole plan had or had not been compromised. The *Mail on Sunday* got hold of the story, and a few days later we got a message to say that the laptop could be recovered from a car park in St John's Wood. This was duly done, and with the laptop was a note: 'I may be a thief, but I am a patriot too'! He certainly was, and we were extremely lucky that the matter didn't turn out to be a great deal worse.

Throughout December the massive build-up continued of the coalition forces and equipment; by far the largest were those of the United States, with our own contribution not only in numbers but of key capabilities that filled some useful gaps in the Americans' own strengths. The deployment of these was complemented by the planning of a brilliant air campaign.

While this build-up was continuing, final diplomatic efforts were being made to try to persuade Saddam to withdraw, but without success. With no adequate response to the final warning, the air campaign was launched in mid-January, with British Tornados making daring low-level attacks to drop our specialist weapon, the JP233, which was designed to crater Iraqi airfields and prevent their air force from flying. This very challenging assignment did, sadly, lead to some initial casualties, but after that the air campaign proceeded with superb efficiency over the next six weeks, severely damaging the Iraqi positions and disrupting their communications.

That was exactly what Schwarzkopf wanted, to give the land attack the best chance of breaking through the Iraqi lines, minimising the casualties in so doing. His plan succeeded brilliantly. After this extremely powerful six-week air campaign the land attack went exactly as planned, with his left hook breaking through and advancing virtually non-stop to its objective, and indeed with minimum casualties. Within four days the Iraqi army was fleeing from Kuwait City and across the border back to Iraq, leaving vast quantities of equipment as it fled.

As the news of this stunning success came back to London and Washington, far more quickly than anyone had expected and the objective of expelling Saddam from Kuwait having been achieved, the question was what should happen next. At our regular morning meeting of the War Cabinet, as the news came in, we agreed to adjourn and each speak to our opposite numbers in Washington to get their views on the next step. I went back to the Ministry of Defence and put through a call to Dick Cheney, the US Defense Secretary. The response I got, as did all the others with their opposite numbers, was that he was in the White House with the President and would ring me back. We later learned that at that meeting General Colin Powell, the Chairman of the Joint Chiefs of Staff, showed pictures of the massive destruction of Iraqi weapons and transport on the Mutla Ridge as the Iraqis were fleeing. Powell's well-known quote, 'It's just a turkey shoot, Mr President', summed up the total Iraqi collapse. It was then that the decision was taken to announce a ceasefire, and we agreed with that.

It was many years later that I learned that the question of continuing the pursuit all the way to Baghdad was raised at that White House meeting and George Bush had invited views from his senior colleagues. The first responses were that it could certainly be done, but there were a number of caveats, one being that the plan might not have the same UN support if we were invading another sovereign country. On the military side there was the prospect of higher casualties, as they would then be facing the much tougher units of the Republican Guard, who had largely withdrawn previously from Kuwait. The final key contribution came from one wise adviser, who simply asked two questions: 'If you get rid of Saddam, who will you put in his place, and secondly, how long are you prepared to stay?' The challenges in answering those two shrewd questions appeared to settle the matter, and it was decided to stop. What a pity those same questions were not put twelve years later, when the same issue of invading Iraq and removing Saddam arose again.

When the ceasefire was announced, I decided to go, together with David Craig, the CDS, to see our forces and congratulate them on their achievement. With such a successful outcome I wanted to ensure that they got the best possible coverage for their victory, and I invited four leading figures from the media world to come with us: John Birt, the head of the BBC, Stewart Purvis, the head of ITN, and Max Hastings and David English, the editors respectively of the *Daily Telegraph* and the *Daily Mail*. My office rang theirs with my invitation to come to the Gulf, but in each case an understandably protective PA said that unfortunately they had other commitments. I asked my office to check that the principals concerned had actually been told what the invitation was. At this, each one of them decided it was too good to miss, and a day later we were on our way.

The only plane available was a BAe 146 of the Queen's Flight, which was perfectly good but had a rather short range, involving a refuelling stop at the

British base at Akrotiri in Cyprus. This was a very active twenty-four-hour supply and staging post for the Gulf, which meant that at midnight, when we arrived, I was able to do a tour of inspection with the base commander while my guests were sensibly trying to get some sleep. After a brief stop in Riyadh to collect Peter de la Billière, it was on to Bahrain and up to Kuwait. The last part of the flight was like a journey through hell, as we flew through huge pillars of smoke from the burning oil wells that Saddam had set alight. I was greeted by the Crown Prince of Kuwait, who, I learnt, had just arrived himself from Taif, where the Kuwaiti ruling family had been given refuge by King Fahd. We transferred to a Sea King helicopter and flew north beyond Kuwait City and the Mutla Ridge, the scene of total destruction of which we had seen the pictures. We landed further north where our armoured division had halted and were greeted by General Rupert Smith, who was commanding the division. Another person to greet us was Kate Adie, the BBC reporter, who, with her TV crew, had been with the armoured division throughout the attack, and was intrigued to see her boss, John Birt, getting out of the helicopter as well. I then did an immediate interview with Kate which, with the advantage of the time difference, went out live on the BBC 7am news.

Not only was Schwarzkopf's left-hook land offensive wonderfully quick in liberating Kuwait and expelling the Iraqi forces, but it did so with a fraction of the casualties we had feared. I had been briefed that they might be as many as 10% of our force of 45,000, but in the event it was a fraction of 1%. I was particularly touched afterwards by a postcard I received from Peter Brooke, my successor as Secretary of State for Northern Ireland. Peter had a wonderful memory for history and his card, with three ancient knights in armour, quoted from Shakespeare's *Henry V* after the battle of Agincourt: the king asked, 'Where is the number of the English dead?' and the herald replied, 'Edward, Duke of York, the Earl of Suffolk, Sir Richard Ketley, Davy Gam Esquire, none else of note, and of all other men but five and twenty.' Peter went on to say that until now, when we had published our figures, he had never really believed the Agincourt casualty list!

It was certainly an enormous relief after Saddam's threats of 'the mother and father of all battles' – battles in which he might have used chemical weapons. That great relief undoubtedly encouraged the early calling of the ceasefire by a president who had received warnings of much higher potential casualty figures.

My own view on calling the ceasefire when we did was that it was in fact twenty-four hours too early. If we had completed the left hook we would have trapped a Republican guard division and the loss of that would have significantly weakened Saddam and put a far greater limitation on his capacity for mischief later.

After the ceasefire was established, the next task was to gather up the vast range of Iraqi military equipment that we had captured. It was assembled on a huge parade ground in Dhahran. As I went round I suddenly remembered the visit that Douglas Hurd and I had made to Paris for a meeting of the Western European Union just after Saddam's invasion of Kuwait. Ewen Fergusson, our ambassador, warned us that there was a real problem over whether the French would support Desert Shield. It transpired that Iraq was France's best customer for defence equipment and that my opposite number, Jean-Pierre Chevènement, was president of the Franco-Iraqi Friendship Society! There had apparently been a serious hiatus in determining the French government's position until President Mitterrand firmly intervened and ensured that France joined the alliance. The scale of French arms sales had become increasingly apparent when Desert Storm began and the air campaign started. France had sent its Mirage jets to support the coalition, but these initially had to be grounded, since the same planes had been sold to the Iraqis and there was a serious danger of misidentification. At the parade ground in Dhahran I was reminded of our visit to Paris, as we inspected a wide range of Iraqi French-built equipment – this included in particular some Roland anti-aircraft guns and a number of large, gleaming white tubes, marked Aerospatiale AM 38, which was the first time that I'd seen Exocet missiles of the kind that had done such damage to our ships during the Falklands War. Some time after Desert Storm there was an enquiry under Lord Justice Scott as to whether the UK had not properly observed its export rules about selling arms to Iraq, and I did recall that in walking round this park in Dhahran, the only piece of British equipment that I found was one Land Rover!

Having been so closely involved in Gulf War I, I was an interested observer of Gulf War II in 2003. The first has been described as a war of necessity and the second as a war of choice. Certainly Gulf War I was very necessary after Saddam's flagrant aggression against Kuwait, and the threat he represented to Saudi Arabia as well. This was clearly recognised by successive UN resolutions, with the formation of a huge coalition which in the end comprised no fewer than thirty-two countries, and a force strength of 750,000. Gulf War II, twelve years later, the war of choice, took on the tougher task of invading Iraq and tried to do it without that same UN backing and coalition and with a far smaller force, numbering barely 130,000. It was of particular interest to me because of the familiar faces on the American side: a Bush again as president, but this time his son, somebody with much less experience in foreign affairs; my old opposite number, Dick Cheney, now Vice President; and Colin Powell, the former Chairman of the Joint Chiefs of Staff, now Secretary of State. The person I didn't know was Donald Rumsfeld, Defense Secretary, who had been a very close colleague of Dick Cheney for many years – both of them had for a long time regarded Saddam as unfinished business.

Prior to Afghanistan and Iraq the US was effectively the sole superpower in the world and had the opportunity to be a real force for good. The tragedy of Gulf War II was that it demonstrated all too clearly America's limitations. It has been described as a win-win for Iran, in that the Americans successfully removed Saddam Hussein, a long-term ambition of the Iranians, and at the same time clearly revealed the limits of their power, since they would never be likely to undertake an operation on that scale again, something that had previously been a significant Iranian concern. The defeat of Saddam and his Sunni supporters led to the increase of Iranian influence in Iraq with their fellow Shias, as has continued to this day, and the further most unwelcome consequence was the reappearance of former members of Saddam's army as the core of ISIS.

The particular moral I draw from Gulf War I is the importance of a clear objective, for that to be achieved in the shortest time, and then to withdraw without being caught up in local political and tribal conflicts and running the risk of being seen as an occupying army. The problem of Gulf War II was the existing complication of Afghanistan. The attacks on the Twin Towers of September 11, 2001 and the huge loss of life made firm retaliation inevitable. Having made a very effective attack on Al Qaeda and removed the

Taliban government which had been accommodating them, the Americans switched their attention to Iraq before their Afghan task was complete. I compare the initial attack on Al Qaeda and the Taliban as like using a stun grenade. It does not kill people, but temporarily immobilises them so that they can be quickly captured before they recover. What effectively happened in Afghanistan was that a stun grenade was thrown, paving the way for a successful outcome, but attention then switched to Iraq, giving the Taliban the chance to recover and regroup, which is why, nineteen years later, success has still not been achieved and in both Afghanistan and Iraq the struggles go on.

During my time as Secretary of State, it fell to me to recommend who should succeed Sir David Craig as Chief of Defence Staff. The advice I got was that the proposal was my responsibility and that there was really only one clear rule: it had to be one of the existing chiefs of staff. I received some internal advice but also consulted Lord Bramall and Lord Lewin. Although they made an effort to see the broader picture, there was an inevitable tendency to recommend somebody from their own service. However, the interesting thing they said was that, if you didn't have to appoint one of the existing chiefs of staff, Dick Vincent, who was then the Vice Chief of Defence Staff, would be very good. Michael Quinlan, an outstanding permanent secretary, agreed, noting that Dick had thought deeply about Russia. I was impressed by the amount of support he had elsewhere as well, and I felt that, if we had a really strong alternative candidate, the previously binding rule could lapse. I therefore recommended to Margaret Thatcher that we should appoint Dick Vincent; she supported this, and his name was submitted to the Queen for approval. When we were able to announce Dick Vincent's appointment, it happened to coincide with the day on which Admiral Sir John Fieldhouse, a former chief of defence staff, was taking his seat in the Lords. His two supporters were Lord Bramall and Lord Lewin, two other former defence chiefs. I went to the House of Lords and sat on the steps of the throne while the new Lord Fieldhouse was introduced in the traditional ceremony with his two robed supporters. As they processed out of the Lords Chamber I went with them and said, 'Having you three former chiefs of defence staff together, I thought you'd like to know that I am today announcing Dick Vincent will be the next CDS.' Terry Lewin said to me, 'That's excellent news and I congratulate you most warmly.' I asked him if he knew Dick well but he said he didn't, and for him the important thing was that I had not been hidebound by the old rule that it had to be an existing chief of staff. Dick was subsequently elected by his NATO counterparts to be the Chairman of the Military Committee of the Alliance.

I have been interested to see that this different approach has since been followed on more than one occasion.

Soon after the liberation of Kuwait and Saddam's defeat in the south, the Kurds rose up in revolt in the north, with disastrous consequences for them. They had assumed that Saddam would be too weak to attack them, but in fact, while he had sustained substantial losses over Kuwait, he still had significant forces. In particular, while the Kurdish *peshmerga* forces could reasonably cope with Iraqi infantry, the air power of his gunship helicopters was hugely damaging for them.

What had happened in the ceasefire talks conducted by General Schwarzkopf was that the Iraqis were required to ground their aircraft, but were given permission to fly their helicopters. They had pleaded to be able to do this for humanitarian relief and evacuation of casualties. In the event this concession was immediately abused and the Iraqis continued to operate gunship helicopters, giving them a critical advantage against both the Shia uprising in the south and the Kurds in the north. Attacks by these helicopters led to thousands of Kurds fleeing their homes and taking refuge in the mountains. Graphic pictures appeared of their plight, and John Major played a leading part in organising Operation Provide Comfort, an international coalition to protect them. The Americans, ourselves, and the French all provided troops and got Turkish agreement for support as well. We provided a full Marine Commando and a squadron of RAF Tornados. The Marines went into Northern Iraq, and the Tornados were based in Turkey, from where they enforced a no-fly zone against Iraqi helicopters in Northern Iraq.

As it happened I was due to make an official visit to Turkey as the guest of the Turkish Defence Minister, a colleague in NATO. After a first day of formal meetings in Ankara, I flew up to Diyarbakir in eastern Turkey. There the Turkish Air force had a substantial base, which had become the forward supply base for our Marine Commando in northern Iraq. I found that when the Commando had first arrived there had been real problems with the attitude of the Turkish military, who were very unenthusiastic about the arrival of British forces at their base. This was at a time when, although there was political agreement to our being based there and our involvement in northern Iraq, the military had great power in Turkey and they were certainly not happy with the situation. Initially they had made our position extremely difficult, and the only place they were willing to let our forces camp was right beside the runway, on which Turkish jets were regularly taking off and landing with considerable noise and disturbance. This could have become extremely difficult but we had one stroke of luck. Air Marshal Bill Wratten, who was responsible for the air operations, came out to Diyarbakir and paid a courtesy call on the regional commander of the Turkish forces. As he walked into the commander's office, the Turkish general suddenly looked up and shouted out, 'Bill, how are you?' It then transpired that he had been a colleague on the Royal College of Defence Studies annual course in London and they had become good friends. After that the problems were rapidly resolved, and the international value of RCDS became apparent.

After inspecting the base, we got into a Chinook helicopter for what proved to be a most fascinating flight. We flew low all the way down the Tigris River to Zavko in Iraq, with the rear tailgate, open to the floor, providing a wonderful view of the scene below. You could see children herding sheep and goats, and the ancient caves where people still lived along the route of the river, a sight that cannot have changed much since biblical times.

We landed at Zavko and I was given a presentation on the work of our Commando in establishing themselves there. There had been trouble with some Iraqi troops in the town, which the American troops had less experience in tackling. The Marine Commando were able to demonstrate the lessons they had learnt in West Belfast on how to patrol in urban areas, and had soon dealt with the Iraqi troops. From there we flew to the small fortified hilltop town of Al Amadiyah where I met the local Kurdish leaders together with the colonel in charge of our Commando. It was good to see what an excellent relationship there was, and to receive their gratitude for the work we had done to save them. What was good to see also was the work of Médecins Sans Frontières, who had come in under our umbrella, and were tackling the many serious medical problems of the people who'd been living high on the mountains at great risk, in nothing but flimsy tents. I also remember well that, as I was talking to the Kurds, there was suddenly a roaring noise overhead and I saw RAF Tornados enforcing the no-fly zone, the clearest possible confirmation of the effectiveness of Operation Provide Comfort.

As Gulf War I drew to a close, it was right to recognise Peter de la Billière's achievements during this challenging time. Before he was appointed to take command of British forces in the Gulf, he had been about to retire as a major general. On the appointment he was promoted to lieutenant general, and subsequently, in recognition of his outstanding leadership throughout the Gulf War campaign, to full general. Rather than letting him retire, I asked him to stay on as my Middle East Adviser in view of the wide respect in which he was held in all the Gulf states, and I was keen to see the UK gain maximum benefit for what we had done.

One significant development during my time at Defence was an attempt to develop a much closer relationship with the French in the nuclear field, as the only two European NATO countries with a nuclear capability. An official visit I made to France had included a visit to their nuclear submarine dockyard in St-Nazaire. When Jean-Pierre Chevènement, the French Defence Minister, paid a return visit to the United Kingdom I took him to Faslane and we went aboard a Polaris submarine returning from its regular patrol. We were shown around the submarine, including the equipment that dealt with echo-sounding for depth identification. I was talking to the sailors and asked how well all the impressive-looking equipment had actually worked. One of them immediately replied, 'It all works extremely well except for this one machine over here.' I was wondering what the problem was and Jean-Pierre, beside me, was interested too. We saw that the machine in question was made by Thomson, a French company. However we noticed that it had a number of labels stuck on it, '*café au lait*', '*café noir*', '*café latte*', and the sailor said, 'This machine is hopeless – we can't find where to put the money in!' Jean-Pierre, who was a very charming man, loved this wonderful bit of sailor humour, and it all contributed to a very successful visit to Faslane.

❁ ❁ ❁

In the late summer of 1991 I visited Zimbabwe and Namibia to see the training teams that we were operating in each country. In Harare we were training the Zimbabwean army, as well as soldiers from Mozambique who were fighting the rebels in their country.

The visit to Namibia was particularly interesting. This vast, thinly populated country had been German South-West Africa until World War I, when it was taken over by South Africa. Later on the United Nations became involved and tried to remove it from South African administration. As the struggle for an end to apartheid in the neighbouring South Africa progressed, so independence for Namibia was achieved. During the struggle, there had been a civil war between the South-West African People's Organisation (SWAPO) and the South African-backed South-West African Territorial Force (SWATF). SWAPO had been backed by the Soviet Union, and many of its leaders trained in Moscow. When elections were held, SWAPO won a majority, but great efforts were made to unify the country, and part of that was creating a Namibian army including both SWAPO and SWATF. I visited them undergoing training with their British instructors, and as I walked down the line of soldiers drawn up for my inspection, I asked each one who he had been with before. It was very impressive that they alternated completely between SWAPO and SWATF.

When I later visited President Nujoma, the new president, he had one particular request. He had recently been on an official visit to Zimbabwe and had been very impressed by the drill of the guard of honour that welcomed him. A return visit by President Mugabe was due, and he was very anxious that his new country should put on an equally impressive welcoming ceremony. We immediately agreed to send out a Guards sergeant major to sharpen up their drill. I heard later that the ceremony had gone extremely well and that we had a very grateful president, a classic illustration of what might be called British soft power!

Namibia is a very large and arid country, and to be successful the farms needed enormous acreage – I understood 10,000 acres was the minimum viable size. Although it had not been part of the German Empire since 1919, there was still a substantial German element in the population, and indeed the only flight from the capital, Windhoek, to Europe went to Frankfurt. There were suggestions that at the end of World War II a number of leading Nazis might have escaped there to hide in the plentiful supply of very remote farms. Part of my team stayed in the Kalahari Sands hotel in Windhoek, which was famous for its long bar. It was mischievously suggested that a prize should be given if one of the team would walk into the bar, click his heels, raise his right arm in salute, and see how many stood up!

After Windhoek we went north to another training camp near Grootvontein, not far from the Angolan border. The Namibians showed me round a very impressive parade of armour, artillery and other military equipment. The British colonel commanding our training team told me that he had never seen any of this equipment before. He had been very anxious that my visit went well, and so a couple of nights before he had sat down with the senior Namibian officers, and they had shared a few bottles of vodka together, a drink that the Namibians had got a taste for from their time in Moscow. He told them that it was important that they made a good impression during my visit, and the sudden appearance of all this equipment was the Namibian response – they had brought it over by night from Angola where they had been hiding it.

❈ ❈ ❈

Not long after he became President of the Russian Federation in 1991, Boris Yeltsin stopped in London on his way to a summit meeting in Washington with President Bush. He had his senior ministers with him and it was arranged that his team would meet John Major, Douglas Hurd, me, and Norman Lamont, who was then Chancellor. The arrangement was that each of us would have an initial meeting at 8.30 in our ministries with our opposite numbers and then at 9.30 we would meet up in Number 10 for a round-table session. My opposite number was Marshal Shaposhnikov, effectively the Minister of Defence in the new Russian Federation. I had never met him before, as my previous dealings had been with Marshal Yazov when the Soviet Union still existed, and I was anxious to establish a good relationship to take advantage of the new climate following the end of the Cold War.

It so happened that a great friend of my son's was involved with Sotheby's wine department and I knew that they were having a sale of old Russian wine that had come from the cellars of the Grand Duke Vorontsov in the Crimea. I thought it would be a nice touch at the end of our meeting in the Ministry of Defence if we were able to share a glass of this fine old wine. I mentioned it to Simon Webb, my excellent principal private secretary, but I had no idea whether in the short time available they would be able to get hold of any bottles. However, towards the end of our meeting, after a good cup of Ministry of Defence coffee, the door opened and in came a tray of glasses and bottles of this wine. The Russian team didn't initially focus at all on what the bottles were and then suddenly Shaposhnikov's number two turned to him and said, 'Look at that bottle.' It was 1933 Crimean wine and tasted rather like Madeira. After a couple of suitable toasts we then, in much more friendly mode, marched across Whitehall from the Ministry straight into Number 10. We went into the Cabinet room, where a rather glum Yeltsin was facing John Major, each with a cup of Number 10 coffee in front of them. As we were taking our places round the table, Shaposhnikov said something to Yeltsin. It so happened that our interpreter overheard what he said: 'You will never guess what Mr King has just given us to drink in the Ministry of Defence,' and told him what the wine was, to which he got a very unamused reply from President Yeltsin, 'God, I thought Khrushchev had drunk all that years ago!'

Any alcohol deficit that Yeltsin had suffered that morning had an interesting sequel. He flew on to Washington for his summit with President Bush, but on the way back the Aeroflot plane could not manage the whole distance from Washington to Moscow and had to refuel at Shannon in Ireland. Albert Reynolds, the Taoiseach, decided that this was an important occasion which should be properly recognised. He therefore took senior members of his Cabinet down to Shannon to meet President Yeltsin and his colleagues. The Aeroflot plane duly landed, the red carpet was rolled out, and the Taoiseach and his colleagues stood expectantly at the bottom of the steps to receive their distinguished guest. They stood there, and stood there, but nobody emerged, until eventually a rather embarrassed aide appeared and said that unfortunately President Yeltsin was not well and would not be able to leave the plane. Although there was no proof, I don't think anybody was in much doubt that Yeltsin's well-known enjoyment of refreshment had been amply satisfied on his return flight and he was quite incapable of descending the steps. And so, the plane having been refuelled, it took off to return to Moscow and, sadly, the Irish ministers returned unrequited to Dublin.

Nothing illustrated more clearly the extraordinary change in relationships after the collapse of the Soviet Union than an item on the agenda in our meeting with President Yeltsin in Number 10. Suddenly the Russians were facing the situation that some of their nuclear weapons were no longer under their own control. A considerable number were based in Kazakhstan, now an independent country, and Russia lacked adequate capability for their safe transfer back to the Russian Federation. We knew they were looking for help, and it was clearly in the interests of the whole world that these weapons were kept as safe and secure as possible. At our meeting with Yeltsin I was able to propose that we would provide suitable additional vehicles for the secure transport of their nuclear weapons back into Russian territory. After some further discussion our proposal was accepted and a treaty was subsequently signed for UK technicians to help dismantle the Soviet nuclear weapons and assist their transfer back to Russia.

❀ ❀ ❀

Early in 1992 the problems of the break-up of the old Yugoslavia and the conflicts between Serbia, Croatia and Bosnia were becoming more and more apparent. The issue arose of possible NATO intervention. If that were to happen, the UK and France were likely to get involved, and I invited Pierre Joxe, the new French Defence Minister, to come to London to discuss the situation.

We had a very helpful meeting, at the end of which I hosted a lunch for him and his team in Admiralty House, on the edge of St James's Park. It was a lovely spring day, and at the end of lunch I suggested to Pierre that we had a brief walk round the park while we continued to discuss the possible approaches that we might take together over these problems. During our walk we were starting to cross the bridge over the lake when I suddenly stopped him: 'In a few moments I'm going to introduce you to somebody who knows more about Yugoslavia than you or I will ever know.' I had just noticed that, quite by chance, on the other end of the bridge was a famous fellow MP, Sir Fitzroy Maclean. He was the man who, during World War II, on Churchill's orders, had parachuted into Yugoslavia to make contact with Tito. At that time no one knew much about Tito except that he was known to be leading a staunch Yugoslav resistance against the German occupation. Fitzroy did indeed make contact and it was the start of a close interest for him in Yugoslavia, becoming a personal friend of Marshal Tito and a regular visitor after the war. I introduced Pierre, who was fascinated to meet him, and I subsequently sent Pierre a copy of Fitzroy's great book, *Eastern Approaches*, which tells the whole story of his remarkable activities.

My last international engagement as Secretary of State occurred during the 1992 election. This was a conference in Paris of the Defence Ministers not just of NATO, but also a number of members of the old Warsaw Pact. Round a long table sat no fewer than thirty-three ministers, seated in alphabetical order of their countries. Two away on my left was Uzbekistan, then Dick Cheney of the USA, myself for the UK, on my right the Ukraine, next Turkey, Spain, and then Russia (no longer the Soviet Union). Nothing could have marked more clearly the final end of the Cold War, and three remarkable years of my time at Defence.

9 THE INTELLIGENCE AND SECURITY COMMITTEE

Early in 1992 John Major asked me if I would be interested in becoming the Governor of Hong Kong, seeing it through its final five years of British rule before the hand-over to China. After four years as Secretary of State for Northern Ireland and then three years at Defence, both of which involved a good deal of time away from home and family, I did not want to embark on an even greater separation, the condition of which was that I would agree to do it for the whole five years. Nor did I think it would appeal to Jane, which she confirmed.

Having declined the offer, I subsequently talked with John about the future. We were coming up to an election, and John was keen to know, in advance of forming a new government afterwards, what my own thoughts were. I had had the privilege of being Secretary of State for Defence during a quite remarkable period of success for the United Kingdom, starting with the sudden end of the Cold War, the collapse of the Soviet Union and the reunification of Germany. I then had responsibility for the largest deployment of UK forces and armour since World War II following Saddam Hussein's invasion of Kuwait, which led to a spectacularly successful coalition campaign to liberate that country. During the seven months of the build-up and the launch of the air and then the land campaign, the Ministry of Defence had really come alive, moving on to a twenty-four-hour, seven-day-a-week work pattern as we coped with the manifold challenges of logistics, coalition procedures, rules of engagement, media commitments and much more. Morale was high, relations with our key allies were excellent, and the successful outcome was achieved in barely seven months, with the minimum of casualties. After such a remarkable period, as we moved back to our previous peacetime level of activity there was inevitably some sense of anti-climax, and I told John that I thought it might be time to take a break after thirteen years of continuous ministerial responsibilities. I had no desire to be Home Secretary, the department most exposed to unexpected shocks and PR disasters, as has continued to be the case. The only position I would have sought was that of Foreign Secretary, but I recognised that Douglas Hurd was excellent and that there was no vacancy. I discovered only a short time ago from the recently published third volume of Charles Moore's Thatcher biography that Margaret had originally wanted to make me Foreign Secretary ahead of Douglas Hurd, but he was definitely the right choice.

As I stood down from government, I reflected on how, over the years, we were the lucky recipients of a wide range of presents that were kindly given to us by our hosts in various countries, some more useful than others! We have a pile of photograph albums of these various visits and some glassware, not least some excellent Tyrone crystal from my time in Northern Ireland.

Three particular gifts I remember well. The first occurred during my visit to Indonesia. This started with an official welcome in Jakarta and a meeting with President Suharto. The next day we flew to Surabaya for a meeting with the military. We discovered that Surabaya had a particular reputation for delicious dishes of snake meat. As we were leaving in our RAF VC 10 the next morning to fly to Kuala Lumpur, I was told that our host, the general, had kindly sent us large containers of a particular delicacy, python and cobra stew. I didn't want anyone in my large team to miss this fascinating opportunity, and I walked down the plane offering some to everyone, but I am afraid there was a disappointing lack of takers. Actually, while I thought the python was pretty tough, cobra seemed more like chicken and was quite good.

While most presents were modest enough and could be retained, there was one that I certainly could not keep. As we flew back from my visit to the Soviet Union, I was told that Marshal Yazov had sent to the plane a leaving present for me. It turned out that it was a Kalashnikov automatic, a kind fraternal thought from one Defence Minister to another in case of trouble. Predictably, I did not see that again!

There was another very generous present that I was not able to accept, and that was in Bahrain. I had been kindly invited to a farewell tour of all the Gulf countries when I stood down from government, in appreciation of the role that the UK played in their defence in the Gulf War. After a very pleasant meeting with the Emir, the Crown Prince took us to the ranch where they kept their spectacular herd of Arab horses. As we sat on cushions in the yard a wonderful parade of horses was galloped past us. We adjourned to the house for some refreshment, and when we came to leave there were two magnificent Arab horses drawn up ready for us to choose. The ambassador had already warned us that this might happen, as he had had exactly the same challenge some months before. The RAF, who had been based in Bahrain during the Gulf War, had also been given a horse, and there had been concerns as to how this should be handled and who could look after it in the UK. I think it was finally solved with the assistance of the Queen Mother in finding a trainer to take it over. It was a very kind thought to offer one to me, but having been forewarned, we were able to decline without, I hope, any offence being given.

I said that some of the presents were more useful than others, and high on the useful list was one that the Bridgwater Conservative Association gave me on my twenty-fifth anniversary as MP. They sensibly asked Jane what she thought I would like, and she said, 'Why not give him an apple press?' We had previously hired one for a couple of years to make use of the fruit from our small number of apple trees. With the new equipment it has become a regular habit to make apple juice and some cider as well. Cider was much more difficult to start with and I remember giving a bottle to a friend of mine who kindly told me that he thought the second prize would be two bottles! I am getting a little better at cider but where I have had real success is with apple juice. I make only about a hundred bottles, half of which come from an apple variety called Discovery. This has a very red skin and produces delicious pink juice. The Royal Bath and West Show has an annual apple juice and cider competition with one class for single-variety juice at which I have been lucky enough to win some prizes. The cider hasn't quite made that standard yet!

Another reflection on my earlier career concerned my occasional attempts at speaking a foreign language. I would certainly not claim to be a great linguist, but I had learnt enough French at school to speak it on a few occasions, and I had had to learn Swahili when serving in the King's African Rifles during my National Service (see Chapter 2). After my army service I never expected to speak it again, until I found myself, as a minister, in Nairobi representing the United Kingdom at the tenth anniversary meeting of the United Nations Environment Programme (UNEP), whose headquarters were there. As successive ministers spoke in their various languages through interpreters, I took the opportunity to open in Swahili, to the astonishment of some bored Kenyan attendants standing around the conference hall, and to the amusement of the Kenyan ministers, our hosts.

My Swahili stood me in good stead the next day when I flew with our High Commissioner to open a new road from Embu to Meru around the foothills of Mount Kenya. Funded by UK overseas aid, the project, with new cuttings and viaducts, had converted an extremely winding uphill-downhill, 100-mile road to a much more level road of barely fifty miles. In the opening ceremony I gave the whole of my speech in Swahili to the large African audience. I don't know whether they understood it or not but they seemed to enjoy the novelty of a visiting British minister speaking in their own language.

I remember that flight for another good reason. Our route took us very close to where I had served in the Mau Mau campaign. I was looking to see if I could identify the farm, but without success. I then realised that I was looking for a farm surrounded by forest in the foothills of Mount Kenya, but that, very sadly, the forest had all been cut down. That became a major issue in Kenya and President Moi launched a major tree-planting programme to combat this serious crisis.

I have referred elsewhere to the visit to Canada and my speech in French to the annual dinner of the Québec Chambre de Commerce; and to my giving evidence in French before the Defence Committee of the *Assemblée Nationale* in Paris, at the end of the Gulf War.

These earlier efforts in foreign languages passed off safely, but I did get caught out early in my time as Secretary of State for Northern Ireland. I was at a lunch in Belgium promoting inward investment into the Province, and I spoke half in French and half in English, translating as I went along. It was suggested to me that I should say something about the Anglo-Irish Agreement, which we had signed just a few weeks before. I didn't think the Belgian audience would be too interested in the nicer details of it, so I gave a fairly shortened version. My truncation unfortunately gave the impression that the Irish Taoiseach, Garret Fitzgerald, in signing the Agreement had effectively accepted that Northern Ireland would remain part of the United Kingdom in perpetuity, and not become part of a United Ireland. In my truncation, I failed to include the vital caveat that this would be the position 'provided that that is what a majority of people in Northern Ireland wanted'. A journalist, either British or Irish, in the audience immediately reported my remarks, which were then picked up in Parliament by my Labour shadow, and I had to quickly apologise and correct the record to prevent serious friction with the Irish government.

Having stood down from the Cabinet after the election, I returned to the back-benches and subsequently John Major asked me to become the first Chairman of the newly created Intelligence and Security Committee, being set up to provide democratic oversight of the Secret Intelligence Service MI6, the Security Service MI5, and GCHQ. The existence of these intelligence agencies had never previously been acknowledged, but once the decision was taken for them to become legally established, they had to be publicly declared. Not until 1989, when the Security Services Act was passed, had the existence of MI5 ever been admitted. Not until 1994, with the Intelligence Services Act, was there public admission of the existence of MI6 and GCHQ, and contained in that Act was the establishment of the Intelligence and Security Committee to oversee them. The challenge was to give these agencies confidence that sensitive information provided to this new committee was really secure. As I had had regular dealings with all the agencies, both during my time in Northern Ireland and in Defence, and with other ex-ministers, as well as senior opposition members, on this first committee they knew they were not dealing with a bunch of unknown back-benchers and this helped build their confidence in the early stages.

This was the right way to start and I think it drew on lessons from other countries. When a similar committee was to be set up in Australia, the first one did not last very long, as apparently the government had merely asked for anyone interested in intelligence matters to apply to join it. A number of people volunteered, but it then became clear that they were interested because they were all strong critics of the intelligence and security agencies, and so that didn't work. I believe something similar happened in Germany as well, but certainly not in Russia, where it appeared that the intelligence oversight committee of the Duma was entirely manned by senior ex-KGB officers: this certainly established a friendly relationship with the agencies, but hardly adequate independent oversight. It seems the position was quite different in France, where the head of the DGSE, the SIS equivalent, answered only to the President and not even to the Prime Minister. On the other hand, perhaps the most substantial illustration of democratic oversight was in the United States. I went with my committee to meet our opposite numbers on Capitol Hill and the US agencies who were such a critical part of our intelligence alliance. When we met the Senate intelligence committee, in addition to the senators in their secure committee room there were no fewer than twenty-nine staffers. The head of the CIA was said to have complained that there was hardly a day in his period of office when he did not spend some time on Capitol Hill in front of one committee or another.

As confidence grew that our Committee could be trusted, so the range of oversight increased well beyond the scope of the original legislation. It started with covering just the administration, policy and expenditure of the agencies, but now covers their work as a whole, including, retrospectively, specific operations. What I believe the agencies now accept, after their initial nervousness, is the real value of the Committee in maintaining public confidence in their work. When there is a serious threat level, people recognise their importance, but at other times, if there are press stories of some bungled operation or a security breach, they can quickly be subjected to much criticism, often unfairly, and when the need to maintain security prevents them being able to defend themselves properly. That is when the Committee, operating inside the 'ring of secrecy', can fully investigate, and the public can have confidence that there is independent scrutiny and democratic accountability for the actions taken.

The most obvious example came a little while after Labour came into government, following the remarkable defection from Russia of Vasily Mitrokhin, who had been the chief archivist of the KGB and who for twelve years had been making secret notes from KGB files on every year from 1917 to 1984. When it was learnt that he had decided to leave Russia, the SIS organised a brilliant exfiltration for him and his family, and the files that he brought proved a treasure trove of intelligence, including in particular details of Soviet spy activity in the UK. One particular item that came to light was the name of the longest-serving British Russian agent, an eighty-seven-year-old ex-secretary who had been passing on atomic secrets to her KGB controllers, but who, when she had been identified, had never been interviewed or prosecuted by MI5. The great-grandmother, labelled by *The Times* as 'the Spy who came in from the Co-op', became a media sensation, and MI5 and Jack Straw, the Labour Home Secretary, came under heavy fire for what looked like negligence on their part. The difficulty was that her case was part of a whole dossier of other top-secret items, which could not be publicly revealed.

I was speaking at a political supper in Cheltenham when I was told that the Home Secretary needed to speak to me urgently. Jack Straw asked me if the Committee would undertake an enquiry into the whole handling of the Mitrokhin affair and, in particular, of Melita Norwood, the lady in question. I said that, provided we had access to all the relevant secret files, I thought the Committee would certainly be willing to carry that out. We did so, and in the process demonstrated very clearly the value of an independent committee of responsible parliamentarians examining top-secret intelligence and coming to a properly independent view. I was particularly pleased with the *Times* leader when we produced our report:

> The devastating Parliamentary criticism of the failure by Britain's security service to tell the government of its coup in obtaining a vast archive of KGB secrets is unprecedented. Never before has a Parliamentary committee been given such access to documents detailing MI5's operations; never has the service been so publicly reprimanded; and never has Britain's failure to catch a long-standing Soviet spy been so embarrassingly underlined as it was in the Intelligence and Security Committee's report on last year's revelations in the Mitrokhin archive. Yet the report can do nothing but good for Britain's security and intelligence services. For the Parliamentary committee has made abundantly clear that not only can it be trusted with some of the most sensitive information in British intelligence, but that it can produce a report that is thorough, focused, rigorous in identifying individual failings and yet in no way compromising Britain's security. This in the end can only solidify the basis on which the security services operate, and bolster public confidence in the way they are policed. MI5 is rightly

smarting at the lapses exposed yesterday; but in the long term it should welcome this strikingly successful example of public accountability.

I had always believed that this was a crucial role for the Committee, and was very pleased that, when this major challenge came, it discharged it so well. I would add, in relation to the early concern that parliamentarians could not be trusted with secrets, that I do not believe that there was a single leak during the seven years in which I chaired the Committee. Sadly, there were leaks during that period but they came from the agencies' staffs themselves, in particular David Shayler and Richard Tomlinson.

My seven years as chairman had started in 1994 with my appointment by John Major, the Conservative Prime Minister. In 1997 there was a change of government, with Tony Blair as the new Labour Prime Minister. Since Labour had been out of office for eighteen years, they had hardly anybody in their ranks with any ministerial experience, and they found it difficult to make all the necessary appointments. It was then suggested to Tony Blair that he should invite me to continue as Chairman of the ISC, albeit with a changed membership involving, now, a majority of Labour members. I was happy to continue and I believe that there was a real advantage for the credibility of the Committee to be chaired by a member of the opposition. If an issue came up involving criticism of the Foreign Secretary or Home Secretary, with their responsibilities for the agencies, and the Committee were to find that the criticisms were unjustified, the accusation could not be made that the judgement was influenced by party loyalty.

The issue of ministerial responsibility did arise later, when the Labour government came into office. Although the SIS and GCHQ came under the Foreign Secretary and MI5 came under the Home Secretary, it was also said that they answered directly to the Prime Minister. It was clear that he, with more than enough problems on his plate, was not always able to take as close an interest as might be desirable in the working of the agencies. We discovered that in Germany Chancellor Kohl had appointed a minister of state with particular responsibility for all the German intelligence and security agencies. We made some enquiries about this arrangement and it soon became apparent that with the excitement of these responsibilities, and the fascination with the issues that crossed his desk, this minister had in some way become, in the James Bond tradition, a sort of super M. One of his more recent adventures had been to hire a private Gulfstream jet to go to Tehran to supervise personally the liberation of some German hostages.

This was obviously a risk with such an appointment, but we raised the matter in our annual report to John Major as worth considering. He, however, was clearly advised that such a responsibility should not become too far divorced from his office and he did not pursue it.

I thought no more about it at the time, but I subsequently learned what happened following the change of government in 1997 when Tony Blair marched triumphantly down Downing Street and into Number 10. After the customary warm welcome from the staff, he went into the Cabinet room with Sir Robin Butler, the Cabinet Secretary, who welcomed him to his new responsibilities and asked if he could give some advance guidance as to which ministers would be doing what in the new government, so that appropriate arrangements could be made in the different departments. He also asked whether there were to be any changes in the remits of the various departments. Tony Blair set out the main appointments of Gordon Brown as Chancellor, Robin Cook as Foreign Secretary and Jack Straw as Home Secretary; then he added that he had now decided it would be sensible for there to be a minister with special responsibility for the intelligence and security agencies, as had been raised by the ISC. Stories differ as to whether it took thirty seconds or longer for Robin Butler to persuade Tony Blair that this was an extremely bad idea! He reminded him that Harold Wilson had himself thought that he was being undermined by MI5, and that it was very important that the Prime Minister continued to take direct personal interest and responsibility for the agencies.

I discovered afterwards how this had started. John Gilbert MP, a former Labour minister, had been a member of my committee, and much attracted by the German arrangement. As I understood it, Labour wanted him to stand down from his own safe Labour seat to allow for a new member that they wished to bring into the government, and promised him a seat in the House of Lords. He agreed to do this but only on condition that he would be appointed the minister of state responsible for the intelligence agencies. Once Robin Butler had persuaded Tony Blair not to create this position, that condition could clearly not be honoured. Instead he was made a minister of state, not in the intelligence role, but back doing the same job he'd done eighteen years before as Minister of Defence Procurement in the Ministry of Defence.

The setting up of the Intelligence and Security Committee in the UK attracted considerable international interest, not least from the newly liberated republics of the former Soviet Union, in particular the Baltic states. The first of these was Estonia, and I was invited to go and speak to the Estonian government and Parliament about the new arrangements we had for overseeing our intelligence and security agencies. Having lived for too long under the harsh regime of the Soviet agencies, with no proper democratic oversight, the Estonians were very keen for their own intelligence and security arrangements to have such oversight.

Jane came with me for a most interesting visit to Tallinn, the charming and beautiful capital. I had a very good welcome from Estonian ministers and MPs, who were very keen to learn of our arrangements. During our visit there happened to be a free period one afternoon and our ambassador asked me if I would like to go and visit the closed city of Paldiski, where the Soviet nuclear submarine crews had been trained and from which Estonians had been barred. It was the most depressing sight, with a bunch of run-down tower blocks of flats where Russian naval families had been abandoned when the Soviet Union collapsed. Many of them had been there for a good number of years and had no home to go to in Russia, and Russia clearly had neither money nor housing to offer to get them to return. They had become part of the 25% Russian proportion of the population of Estonia, which later formed the element, as in Latvia and Lithuania, which President Putin was to seek to exploit.

10 THE EXCEL STORY

At the same time that I became chairman of the ISC, Andrew Mackay, my former Parliamentary Private Secretary, told me about a new enterprise in which a friend of his was involved. This was a proposal to build a new exhibition and conference centre for London. His friend was Iain Shearer, a person with considerable property and development experience, who was the chief executive for a consortium bidding to be the developer of this new centre, planned to be on the Royal Victoria Dock in East London. They were seeking a non-executive chairman for this consortium, and Andrew thought, because of my previous experience in Docklands as local government minister, that it could be of interest to me. Some ten years before I had taken through the legislation that had set up the London Docklands Development Corporation, which had then been responsible for the spectacular transformation of a vast area of derelict docks into Canary Wharf and the other massive new buildings around it. Iain approached me and I agreed to be chairman of this consortium: and so my involvement with what became Excel London was born!

The origin of Excel lay in the desire of the Association of Exhibition Organisers (AEO) to have a new exhibition centre in the London area. There was a shortage of exhibition space in London, with only Earls Court and Olympia as significant centres. Olympia was pretty elderly, and Earls Court lacked many of the features that more modern centres elsewhere in the world could offer. The Association therefore invited Iain to find a suitable location within the M25, and to design a modern exhibition centre. Initial investigations included somewhere near Heathrow, Ashford in Kent, and near Rainham in Essex. It was clearly a very demanding task to meet the extensive requirements of an exhibition centre fit for the twenty-first century, and I understand that none of the possible sites fully met what was needed. He had had good contacts with the London Docklands Development Corporation, and the suggestion came in 1990 of the Royal Victoria Dock, a hundred acres of derelict land, sandwiched between Canary Wharf and London City Airport, one of the last vacant pieces in the jigsaw of the massive redevelopment of London Docklands. The LDDC agreed that it would be a suitable site and invited bids for the construction and operation of a new exhibition centre.

As far as I'm aware there were three bids. One I believe was from an Italian company, the second from Earls Court and Olympia, and the third from our consortium. We were chosen to be the developer, and a battle then started to raise the necessary funds for its construction. This proved significantly more difficult than we had hoped, the City of London showing a real lack of interest in funding a start-up. There was certainly considerable interest in funding the required bond issue, provided that we could get the business, and Iain succeeded in persuading some fifty-three shows to commit to relocate from Earls Court, Olympia, and the NEC in Birmingham. However, there was real difficulty in getting an equity partner. We then had a great stroke of luck when it turned out that Stephen Brooks, an exhibition organiser and Chairman of the AEO, had an exhibition running in Kuala Lumpur in the Mines exhibition centre recently built by a company called Country Heights. This company was led by a young entrepreneur, Tan Sri Lee Kim Yew. Stephen Brooks told him of our interest in finding a new investor, and he immediately expressed an interest. It so happened that at that time the Malaysian economy was running rather hot and Dr Mahathir, the Prime Minister, was encouraging Malaysian companies to invest overseas. Lee Kim Yew saw the opportunity to invest in an industry of which he already had experience, with the additional satisfaction of meeting Dr Mahathir's request. Together with an award-winning new-style property bond from Barclays, his funding of the equity triggered the start in 1998 and Sir Robert McAlpine's won the contract to build it. I remember well the ground-breaking ceremony at the very start. John Prescott was then Deputy Prime Minister and Secretary of State for the Environment and he came down to do the ground-breaking. When I greeted him, he told me how interested he was to come to the Royal Docks, as the last time he had been there was forty years before, when he was a young ship's steward on a liner about to sail to New Zealand. He told me that just before the ship sailed they had had a surprise late passenger, none other than Sir Anthony Eden, recuperating from the serious illness that had caused him to resign as Prime Minister.

After that interesting start construction went ahead, although not without its challenges, one of which was the discovery of a number of unexploded bombs. The London Docks had been a prime target for German bombers in the Blitz, and a couple had fallen on the Royal Victoria Dock. Unexpectedly, we also found a number of British bombs in a huge pile of rubble by the dock, and it transpired that some smart contractor who was clearing spoil from a British bombing range, possibly at Foulness, had found the deserted dock a convenient dumping ground. The army came, and very early one morning the bombs were safely detonated. In spite of this and other significant challenges, on time and on budget Excel was built, and very good it has proved to be.

The involvement of the AEO and the consultation with its members about the whole layout of the site produced an exhibition centre well designed to accommodate the demanding requirements of their industry. Easy lorry access right on to the exhibition floor is a particular feature, recognising that for every three- or four-day exhibition there may be a week or more of build-up, and then the speediest possible access is required to dismantle it all before the next show arrives. Keeping this dead time as short as possible also makes a difference for all the catering outlets that are so busy during events but have little income during the build and dismantle times. Another important feature are the moveable partitions that enable the long halls down either side of the main boulevard to be divided into separate halls, thus maximising the number of events that can take place simultaneously. This feature was used most noticeably in the London Olympics in 2012, when Excel earned the distinction of being the most intensively used venue ever in the history of the Olympics, with seven Olympic sports running concurrently.

While we had provided a wonderful new facility for London, and achieved everything that we wished in terms of its quality and operational effectiveness, one major customer, who had previously committed, delayed bringing their shows till year two, and we then lacked adequate working capital to see us through this initial period in 2000/2001. By that time part of Country Heights' equity share had been acquired by another Malaysian entrepreneur, Ananda Krishnan, and when it was clear that we needed additional equity funds he stepped forward and led the restructuring that enabled Excel to continue. With this change of ownership, Iain Shearer stood down, and Jamie Buchan was appointed as the new CEO. Iain had done an outstanding job in the construction and launch of Excel, but the challenge now was the successful commercial exploitation of this great facility, and Jamie Buchan's previous career had fitted him very well for the role.

Once the restructuring had been achieved, Excel made excellent progress and it soon became clear that we needed additional exhibition space together with a purpose-built international conference centre. We approached our banks, Barclays and RBS, who were initially ready to supply the necessary funds. Unfortunately our application coincided with the start of the banking crisis and both of them indicated that they might not be able to offer as much as they had previously suggested. This reached its climax with a visit from the London office of RBS, who had the unhappy task of telling us they had now received new instructions from the head office in Edinburgh not to offer any new funds to anybody without the express agreement of Sir Fred Goodwin, then in charge of the bank. This was the sad confirmation that the wheels had finally come off RBS, and it went into public ownership. Ananda Krishnan was faced with a new challenge: did he take on additional financial commitment or take his profit? In the end he decided to take the significant profit that his brave investment had earned, and to sell his shares to Abu Dhabi. To his credit, Ananda did this only on condition that Abu Dhabi undertook to make the further investment in the extension of Excel, including the new large convention centre, which by that time had received planning permission and was ready to go ahead. Abu Dhabi's proposal came via their own exhibition centre ADNEC, and after appropriate due diligence, they confirmed their desire to proceed. When we asked how they proposed to fund it, they very simply said, 'Go to the National Bank of Abu Dhabi, 1 Knightsbridge.' They did indeed provide the funds without any of the difficulties then affecting all the British and American banks, and Excel's second phase was built.

When ADNEC took over, I stood down as chairman, but they asked if I would remain on the board, which I continue to do. Their first years coincided with the difficult market situation but subsequently the improvement in the overall market and the successful introduction of the excellent new facilities have presented a much more attractive picture. From the British viewpoint, while there is enormous investment by overseas buyers in property in London and elsewhere in the UK, the difference with Abu Dhabi's investment in Excel is the benefit it brings for London and indeed the whole UK economy. Our average annual attendance is close to four million, of which over one million are from overseas. These visitors make a significant contribution to the government's target for business tourism, and bring substantial business both for London hotels and for the wider economy as well. It is worth remembering also that while most convention and exhibition centres in the world are funded by cities and governments, Excel has achieved it all without calling on public funds. I recently came across a press release of 2007 from Ken Livingstone, then the Mayor of London, who stated that there was no prospect of an international convention centre going ahead. He said, 'The problem with the convention centre is it never actually breaks even. You have to have a subsidy via a bed tax from the 4*and 5* hotels but now that the government has ruled out the recommendation of a bed tax there is no prospect of a convention centre going ahead.' It was barely a year later that we decided to go ahead on our own and very successful it has been for Excel, for ADNEC, and for London.

When the Convention Centre was built in 2010, I invited Boris Johnson, Ken's successor as Mayor of London, to come and open it in front of an audience of some 500 special guests. He did this in his own inimitable style, beginning with a paean of praise for London, claiming more restaurants than Paris, more museums and art galleries than New York, but then adding his own invention, 'Until Tom King told me, I had no idea that there was nowhere in London where the International Society of Gastroenterologists could have their annual convention and dinner.' He then added that, with so many people visiting every corner of the world and eating lots of foreign food, there was a huge demand for gastroenterologists, and lots of them would come to a convention, many bringing their wives with them as well. He couldn't resist adding, 'or those who were, for the period of the convention, their wives!'

He was certainly right about the numbers that do attend conventions, medical or otherwise, and they often bring a partner and take the opportunity to see more of the attractions of London or of other parts of the country. That is why conventions are so valuable to every major city and country and there is great competition for them. Before we opened our International Convention Centre, London hardly touched this valuable market, our share being about twentieth in the world, but I'm pleased to say that London now is probably fifth and climbing.

Today Excel London is a world-class exhibition and convention venue. It is an amazing story that started for me in 1994 and which continues today. The Royal Docks have been the home and workplace for generations of East Enders for a hundred years and are in a real sense hallowed ground for them. As the trade moved away, the docks all became derelict, and the first time I visited the hundred acres of the Royal Victoria Dock, the only living things I saw were two foxes! Now the old cranes are the one reminder of that past glory, and they look down once again on a bustling, busy dock full of life. It is a story in which a wonderful team of Excel people have played their full part, and I'm very proud to have been involved with them.

Postscript

It is a wonderful story, and I had just finished writing it when the coronavirus struck, and suddenly everything stopped. Now Excel has been converted, almost overnight, into what could potentially be the largest intensive-care hospital in the world, under its new title of the Nightingale Hospital. This was done against the fear that the existing London hospitals would be overwhelmed by too many seriously ill patients, and the vital need then for an additional resource, but thankfully that has not happened so far.

11 LATER LIFE AND THE HOUSE OF LORDS

When I stood down from the Commons in 2001, I received the honour of a peerage and joined the House of Lords.

For my introduction into the Lords I had two excellent supporters, George Younger, my predecessor at Defence, and Patrick Mayhew, my successor but one in Northern Ireland, with of course good family support in the gallery.

In October I made my maiden speech in a debate on Afghanistan. After the September attack on the Twin Towers in New York, masterminded by Osama bin Laden, British troops had gone to Afghanistan to support the American pursuit of bin Laden and his Al Qaeda followers. During my speech, I carried in my pocket the cap badge of my old regiment, the Somerset Light Infantry. This badge proudly displayed the name of the Somersets' battle honour of 1842, Jellalabad, which it had earned in the first Afghan War. In 1840 the British had launched a punitive expedition into Afghanistan, which was successfully achieved, but then things became more difficult and it was decided to withdraw into India. 14,000 set out on that return journey but only one single person safely reached Jellalabad, which was garrisoned by the Somerset Light Infantry. The Afghan forces that had massacred the retreating column from Kabul then besieged Jellalabad, but it was successfully defended by the Somersets, and the Afghans were forced to retreat.

After the massacre of the returning force, a disaster coming so early in the new Queen Victoria's reign, she was keen to recognise the Somersets' achievement and awarded them the battle honour of Jellalabad and the special title of Prince Albert's Own. I made the point in my speech about the lesson of that war: it was easy to get into Afghanistan but much harder to get out, as the Russians had so recently found out for themselves. Now, nineteen years on since that maiden speech, with the Americans and us still involved, my warning was surely right.

What I remember about that speech was the daunting quality of an audience of the fellow contributors that you can have in the Lords. The range of past experience included among others one foreign secretary, three chiefs of defence staff, our ambassador to the United Nations, a chancellor of the exchequer, a speaker, a cabinet secretary, a senior judge, a bishop, the chairman of a major bank, and two of my predecessors as defence secretary, a quality of audience unequalled in any other legislature in the world. It is that range of experience and knowledge – whether they otherwise be judges, professors, scientists, educationalists, or business leaders, the list goes on and on – that bears out the claim that on any subject arising in the House of Lords there will be a couple of people who will know as much about it as anybody in the world.

Where this is often most evident is not in the main proceedings in the chamber but in the various Lords committees that take evidence and report on important current issues. I well remember, during my visits to Brussels as a minister, European officials telling me that the quality of these reports from the Lords committees was the best they received from any country.

I have served on various committees during my time in the Lords. One particularly interesting committee addressed the issue of 'Who owns the news', which looked at the role of proprietors of major newspapers, but also at the significant changes particularly in young people's sources of news. At that time I had no idea of how many people there were for whom the traditional sources of news from television, radio and newspapers no longer applied, and social media was then their only source, with the increasing risks of fake news and foreign government manipulation. This committee was chaired, very suitably, by Lord Fowler, now Lord Speaker, who prior to his distinguished career in the Commons and government had been a well-respected journalist. Much more recently I have been serving on the Joint Committee on National Security Strategy. It is called 'Joint' because it includes members from both the Commons and the Lords, the Commons members being the Chairs of all the key Commons Select Committees, and from the Lords, a good range of experience as well.

More recently the House of Lords has come under increasing criticism that it should be completely changed, that the membership should be subject to some form of election, and that in any case there are far too many members. I agree about the numbers, and efforts are in hand to seek to reduce them. If, however, we did move to some form of election, it could possibly just produce a clone of the House of Commons, and we would certainly lose most of the knowledge and experience from the present House of Lords. There would then need to be some procedure for resolving disputes between the two houses, if they were both elected, as has to happen in the United States between the Senate and the House of Representatives. The common criticism of the Lords is from people who say it's wrong to be ruled by people who are not elected, but this misunderstands the present arrangement: the House of Lords does not rule. It amends and revises legislation, but the Commons always has the final say. When bills are brought from the Commons, it is the job of the Lords to scrutinise them, amend them if it is thought necessary, and then return them to the Commons for further consideration. Often the Lords make a substantial number of amendments, which can reflect the fact that the time allocated for the bill's consideration in the Commons was too short, or that the particular subject of the bill was not one with which MPs were particularly familiar. So far from the Lords being guilty of deliberately interfering with no good reason, it is always interesting to note how many of the Lords' amendments are accepted by the Commons as necessary improvements to that particular legislation, without any disagreement.

My own view is that, provided the present slimming process continues to tackle the problem of numbers and that there is strict control over the appointment of new members, I would not go for major changes to the Lords. While nobody else has a system quite like ours, I believe that, properly operated, it has real merits in retaining a wide spread of experience in the legislature, without overriding the people's democratic rights.

In 2010 I was approached to become the Prime Minister's Personal Trade Envoy to Saudi Arabia. This was part of a new initiative by the Department of Trade to enlist senior figures from Parliament to help support British companies in vital export markets, and I was approached because of my previous close involvement with the Kingdom during my time in Defence, particularly during the First Gulf War. This then led to a series of visits helping British companies win orders for the various ambitious programmes in the country. I remember in particular one gathering in Riyadh in connection with the huge railway and metro programme that was just being launched, another in Jeddah for their major new hospital programme, and jointly opening the Saudi British Energy Week in Al Khobar with the giant company Saudi Aramco.

I did wonder, when I took on the role of envoy, whether people in Saudi would still remember me, as it had been some years since I had been there, but I was quickly reassured about that, at an early meeting with a couple of ministers and princes, when one of them greeted me with 'You used to have bigger glasses!' That was indeed true, and it was the clearest possible confirmation that they did indeed remember me. If they had simply said, 'Yes, of course we remember you,' I would have thought they were simply being polite. I then remembered that my earlier visits to Saudi, at a time of great tension and fear of attack by Saddam Hussein, had coincided with the launch of CNN's twenty-four-hour news, on which I had often featured, and when everybody from King Fahd downwards had been watching the news very keenly, my large glasses had made a lasting impression!

While I have now stood down as an envoy, the programme of envoys continues to provide senior political leadership in our trading efforts in a number of selected countries in support of the small team of fully stretched ministers.

In May 2016, I had the great privilege of being invited to move the motion of thanks to Her Majesty for the Queen's Speech at the start of the new session of Parliament. As well as addressing the important issues contained in the Speech, it is traditional for the mover and seconder to include some light-hearted moments. My invitation had come from the Leader of the House, Baroness Tina Stowell, and I congratulated her on her courage in inviting me without having any idea of what I might say. I couldn't resist opening with part of a song from the well-known musical *South Pacific*:

> *A hundred and one pounds of fun*
> *That's my little honey bun!*
> *Get a load of honey bun tonight*
> *I'm speaking of my sweetie pie,*

Only sixty inches high,
Every inch is packed with dynamite.

In Tina's excellent speech at the end of the debate she took up the challenge: 'I wish that I were 101 pounds, and I should like to put on record that I am not sixty inches. I am sixty-one inches!'

In my speech I referred to the recent election of Sadiq Khan as the new Mayor of London and my respect for the fact that, as the first Muslim Mayor, his signing-in ceremony had been held in Southwark Cathedral in the presence of the Dean, and the very next day he had attended the Holocaust memorial ceremony in the presence of the Chief Rabbi. Nothing could have shown more clearly the importance of tolerance and respect for other faiths in a world beset by sectarian hate and division. I also paid tribute to Ruth Davidson, the Scottish Conservative leader. Having been born in Glasgow of an English father and a Welsh mother, and with my affection for the Province from my time in Northern Ireland, I saw myself as a 'walking United Kingdom', and I admired her stout defence of the Union.

I then drew attention to a single sentence in the Speech, 'My government will hold a referendum on the membership of the European Union', which did indeed take place some five weeks later. I said that I thought there was a growing cry across the country for more information and facts with which to make this vital judgement, and whether any fact could be generally accepted by all sides. I thought one fact was that every one of the twenty-seven other countries wanted us to stay and that hardly any of them thought that there was any risk that we might vote to leave, which had not helped David Cameron's efforts for some necessary changes in our European arrangements. I also said that the Commonwealth might be sorry to lose a friendly face at the EU table, and that particular problems could arise for Gibraltar and for Northern Ireland with the border issue. I also quoted a very recent letter in *The Times*, signed by thirteen United States Defense Secretaries and National Security Advisors, whom many of us knew: 'Should the UK choose to leave the European Union, the UK's place and influence in the world would be diminished and Europe would be dangerously weakened.' I said that my own view was that we should remain but that we should immediately employ what I thought would be a very large Brexit vote to play a leading role in promoting the much more fundamental reforms that were clearly needed in the EU.

As we know all too well, the vote for Brexit proved even bigger than expected, and the challenge now is to try and ensure that the dangers foreseen are overcome, and the UK continues to play its full part in the world, an increasingly troubled world with the massive challenges of a global pandemic adding to climate change and population explosions leading to failed states and mass migration of people.

❋ ❋ ❋

During most of my time in government Margaret Thatcher was Prime Minister, and the enormous impact of her leadership on the fortunes of our country was very clear to me. In March 1979, shortly before she became Prime Minister, the *Economist* magazine published Sir Nicholas Henderson's valedictory despatch before leaving office. He had been our ambassador in Paris, and an old tradition of the Foreign Office was that ambassadors in their final despatch could let their hair down and say what they really thought without fear or favour. Somehow the *Economist* had got hold of it and printed it under the title 'Britain's decline: its causes and consequences'. As a young man Henderson had been at the Potsdam conference and saw Churchill and then Attlee dealing on equal terms with Stalin and Truman, with no German or Frenchman present. While he accepted it was inevitable that we would not quite maintain that position, nonetheless in the mid-1950s we were still the strongest European power militarily and economically. 'It is our decline since then in relation to our European partners that has been so marked so that today we are not only no longer a world power but we are not in the first rank even as a European one. We talk of ourselves without shame as being one of the less prosperous countries of Europe.' He also drew attention to how much our role as Washington's European partner had declined in relation to that of Germany or France.

Before her I doubt then whether many people in other countries would have known the name of the British Prime Minister, but when she resigned eleven years later the shock went round the world. In many countries people who might not have known the name of their own Prime Minister

The Royal Marines at Poole, Dorset, in 1990
demonstrating very convincingly to me a
submersible Land Rover!

The First Sea Lord, Admiral Sir Julian Oswald,
and I with the new Merlin helicopter, 1990.

— and bring back the symbol of a new beginning

MR King's final day in Hungary was marked by the gift of a piece of the "Iron Curtain" from the border between Hungary and Austria.

After receiving the framed and authenticated strip of barbed wire from the Hungarian Defence Minister, Colonel General Ferenc Karpati, Mr King commented:

"This is a small piece of barbed wire — but its significance is enormous. At this very moment Hungarian troops are dismantling 200 miles of the Iron Curtain that for so many years has defaced the frontier between Hungary and Austria. At last the Iron Curtain starts to fray — and the sooner it is totally removed, the better."

● The inscription above the piece of wire reads: "This piece of barbed wire is a part of the 'Iron Curtain' alongside the Hungarian-Austro border, that palpably represented the division of the European continent into two halves. Its dismantling was made possible by the will of the Hungarian people and the recognition of peaceful co-existence and mutual interdependence. We believe that the artificial, physical and spiritual walls still existing in the world some day shall collapse everywhere."

Bringing back a piece of the 'Iron Curtain', a strip of barbed wire, a gift from the Hungarian Defence Minister, October 1989.

Meeting the '007 Girls' (licensed to kill!), Soviet special forces after their demonstration low-level parachute drop, 1990.

Marshal Yazov and his wife, together with British Ambassador Roderick Braithwaite, welcoming Jane and me to Moscow in 1990.

As a guest of the Admiral (on my left)
commanding the Soviet Black Sea Fleet
at Sevastopol, 1990.

The French Defence Minister, Jean-Pierre
Chevènement, with Jane and me, 1990.

After my appearance before the Defence
Committee of the Assemblée Nationale
in Paris in 1992, a birthday cake was put
before me!

The tents of all the Kurds who fled to the
mountains to escape Saddam's helicopter
gunships, 1991.

Meeting the Sultan of Oman, Qaboos
bin Said, in 1991.

With Sheikh Zayed of Abu Dhabi, Founder
President of the United Arab Emirates, 1991.

Singing the National Anthem at the
seventy-fifth anniversary at Gallipoli,
May 1990: Margaret Thatcher; behind
her Charles Powell; TK; the First Sea
Lord, Sir Julian Oswald, and the Chief of
General Staff, Sir John Chapple.

Addressing the crew of one of the ships in the
naval deployment in the Gulf War, 1990.

With General Peter de la Billière on his
appointment as commander-in-chief
of British forces in Operation Desert
Shield, 1990.

The special Post Box
number for Christmas
gifts to our forces stuck in
the desert in Saudi Arabia
during Operation Desert
Shield, 1990.

US Secretary of Defense Dick Cheney escorts me into the Pentagon, 17 September 1990, six weeks after Saddam invaded Kuwait. *Official Apartment of Defense Photo*

Meeting President George H.W. Bush at the White House, September 1990, with (l. to r.) Simon Webb, my private secretary; Anthony Acland, UK Ambassador; Brent Scowcroft, US National Security Advisor. *Official White House Photo*

Kate Adie and the BBC television team greeting me at the end of Stormin' Norman's victorious 'left hook' by the 1st Armoured Division, 1991.

General Rupert Smith debriefs on Desert Storm to me, David Craig, Peter de la Billière, Max Hastings, John Birt, and a clutch of brigadiers, 1991.

Some of the French Exocet missiles that had been sold to the Iraqis, photographed in 1991.

With General 'Stormin' Norman' Schwarzkopf, commander-in-chief of Operation Desert Shield, 1991.
Ministry of Defence. Crown Copyright

Speaking to a Royal Marine
detachment in Northern Iraq on
Operation Provide Comfort, 1991.

Jane launching HMS *Iron Duke* at
Yarrow's yard in Glasgow, the day
after the victory in the Gulf on
28 February 1991.

Cartoon by Gerald
Scarfe *Sunday
Times*, 3 March
1991, of me with
John Major and
Douglas Hurd.
© *Sunday Times
& Scarfe*

Outside Number 10: President Yeltsin and senior Russian ministers, with John Major, 1992. Norman Lamont at left; I am in the middle.
© *The Guardian*

Three Very Important People! Margaret Thatcher gave a dinner at Number 10 in 1989 for former President Ronald Reagan. Jane was given the seat of honour.
© *The Press Association*

After hosting The Queen Mother's ninetieth birthday parade on Horseguards, 1990.
Crown Copyright

I had the honour of 'rolling out' Vanguard, the first Trident nuclear submarine, 1992.

The Nolan Committee meeting at Leeds Castle, Kent, to finalise their report on Standards of Conduct in Public life, 1994.

Campaigning in a Bridgwater election in 1997, with some loyal friends.

After the '97 election, Jane and I in front of the statue of Robert Blake, Cromwell's Admiral and General at Sea, and Bridgwater MP.

The only photograph taken with my sister, Stella (Tess) Clarke, when we were both on parade. Here, as Chairman of Knightstone Housing Association, she is opening their new houses in the old Coal Yard in Bridgwater, 1998.

As Chairman of the Intelligence and Security Committee, making our annual report to the Prime Minister, Tony Blair, 1998.

I enter the House of Lords, with two excellent supporters, George Younger (left) and Paddy Mayhew, 2001.
© *Universal Pictorial Press & Agency Ltd.*

As President of the Royal Bath and West Society in 2004, presenting a prize at the Dairy Show.

With my old friend Baroness Jean Trumpington, who made us both famous again with her notorious 'two-finger' salute!

Modelling a sweater for the Brora fashion catalogue, staying at the home of a friend who had launched the brand.

The unveiling of the statue of Margaret Thatcher in the Members' Lobby of the House of Commons, with most of the old team, 21 February 2007.

The clearing of the site for Excel, 1999.

Excel: the ground-breaking ceremony performed by John Prescott, 1998.

The Squibbing Climax of the Bridgwater Carnival, 2010, the oldest in the country, celebrating the failure of Guy Fawkes to blow up Parliament: 150 good men and true line the street and squib!

all knew of Mrs Thatcher, the Iron Lady. A succession of presidents and prime ministers used to think it essential to visit her in Number 10 to have a suitable photograph taken to include in their election address, and so demonstrate their international standing!

Among the qualities that she brought to her position was first and foremost her ability to work hard. She was nearly always very well briefed, and often drew on outside contacts and experience as well as the government briefs. That she often worked late into the night could occasionally be visible in a cabinet meeting with a discreet yawn, and she admitted that she got used to only four hours' sleep a night, sometimes less. That was confirmed for me by one occasion at a reception in Number 10 when she was welcoming her guests. Just in front of me was a director of the BBC World Service and she told him how much she appreciated their news broadcasts. She said she listened to Radio 4 news at midnight and 1am and then she switched in later hours to the World Service.

She didn't have an easy time when she first became leader of the party, with the shadow cabinet divided between the wets and the dries. Taking over as Prime Minister, after the disastrous last period of the Labour government with the winter of discontent and all the union strife, the first years of government were difficult for her. What of course saved her was the Falklands war, with her courageous leadership culminating in a successful election and a much strengthened position as Prime Minister, which she needed to meet the inevitable and massive challenge of the miners' strike.

Her robust support for NATO and for the freedom movements in the Soviet bloc, particularly Poland, earned great admiration in the United States and excellent relations with President Ronald Reagan. The scale of that admiration was very well illustrated in an interview on American television with the well-known broadcaster Walter Cronkite, who at the end of the interview said, 'Mrs Thatcher, will you accept my nomination for President of the United States!' I saw for myself, in my meetings with the Gulf rulers, that as well as the contributions we were making to their security, they appreciated very much how Margaret Thatcher's key relationship with President George Bush had helped ensure such a positive US response to Saddam Hussein's invasion of Kuwait.

After fifteen outstanding years, initially as Leader of the Opposition and then for much longer as Prime Minister, the manner of her departure was a tragedy. Just as we were about to go to war to defeat Saddam Hussein, where her leadership in the world response had been outstanding, I had hoped that she would see it through, and that then would have been the time to decide to retire.

One final memory was her very kind concern for families. I have already mentioned that she would not let me accept the challenging and potentially dangerous office of Secretary of State for Northern Ireland without first checking with Jane that she would be willing for me to do it. I remembered also that when I first joined the Cabinet as Secretary of State for the Environment, it was a few days before my mother's death; Margaret asked me whether my mother had known this before she died, and was very pleased to know that she had.

❋ ❋ ❋

Could I have been Prime Minister? The answer clearly is yes, if circumstances had been a little different. I remember David Owen saying that after he had been Foreign Secretary for about a year and a half he realised it was really a fluke whether or not you became Prime Minister, and that it was too accidental to be obsessed with. Kenneth Clarke, who stood three times for the leadership, said that in his experience of leadership elections they were always won by some candidate that nobody had thought of until the last three or four weeks and that he didn't remember anybody who started campaigning for the leadership in the year or two before the vacancy getting anywhere near it. The truth of this was borne out with the unexpected failure of Margaret Thatcher, although winning the ballot but not by a sufficient majority to prevent a second round, leading to the victory for John Major, and much more recently, after the Brexit referendum, the overnight departure of David Cameron and the sudden promotion of Theresa May.

Margaret's departure at a critical moment for me, with my responsibilities in the First Gulf War, had prevented the possibility of any sort of leadership campaign. When I was approached by Andrew Mackay, my excellent Parliamentary Private Secretary, and Alan Clark, I said I would not put my name forward unless I was sure of at least thirty votes to start with, and it was quickly apparent that the other campaigns were too far advanced in signing up support to make that possible. Alan Clark describes in his *Diaries* his support for me, and claims that I was Willie Whitelaw's choice, which, if true, would have been a powerful endorsement, but he was no longer in government. Alan's support was in marked contrast to many other earlier references in his diaries, when he sought often to undermine me to get my job, and I did wonder if this new support was based on his hope of becoming Secretary of State, having created the vacancy by my promotion!

Alan often drew historical analogies in his diaries, and one of the thoughts he had in suggesting me as PM was that after the dramas and excitement of the Thatcher years, what was needed was a period of calm and less controversial leadership. He said that he saw in me some echo of the Baldwin style, provincial, with an industrial background and good at communicating with people at all levels. I think he took this last point from a visit that we made together to a Remploy factory whose employees were all disabled ex-servicemen. It came under Alan's area of responsibility as Minister of State in Defence, but it was clear that he didn't particularly enjoy having a friendly chat with everybody as we went round. For me, after my years in charge of the Bristol factory, it was very familiar and I enjoyed meeting a wonderful group of people both on the shop floor and in the management.

It was not a happy period for the party, with some real confusion over the most suitable successor. Margaret Thatcher had originally thought that Michael Heseltine would be her successor, but subsequently decided to promote John Major and encouraged people to vote for him. John had had a remarkable rise in government from junior minister to Foreign Secretary and then Chancellor in barely five years. He was a man of considerable ability and charm, but I did not feel at that time that he was ready as a leader and so, when asked, I agreed to nominate Douglas Hurd, which Chris Patten seconded. However, it soon became apparent that John's campaign was well advanced, and, with Margaret's active support, he was a clear winner.

Some years later *Prospect* ran a series of articles under the heading 'What if', which considered different outcomes that could have occurred in famous historical events, starting with 'What if the crowd had urged Pontius Pilate to pardon Jesus instead of Barabbas?' A later one in the series, written by an old friend, Philip Goodhart, was 'What if' Nigel Lawson had not refused to attend yet another Chequers Sunday lunch to discuss the introduction of the poll tax. Nigel was strongly opposed to it, but in his absence the tax went forward, with the disastrous consequences that it brought for Margaret Thatcher. Philip's scenario was that if the poll tax had not happened, Margaret would have continued longer in office, and I would have subsequently become Prime Minister!

There is no shortage of 'what if's'. If Margaret Thatcher had decided to contest the second ballot, and if Michael Heseltine had then withdrawn, as he admits with hindsight could well have been the best option for him, she could have continued in office until the successful completion of the Gulf War and then retired in an orderly fashion without the damaging split in the party that had ensued. His withdrawal would then have earned him a lot of credit in the party and significantly enhanced his chances in the subsequent leadership election.

I was disappointed not to have been able to support Michael, with whom I had worked closely, first as his deputy in opposition to the Aircraft and Shipbuilding Bill, and subsequently as Minister of State with him at the Department of the Environment. What I knew was that behind the Tarzan image, and the celebrated rousing speeches, he was a very effective minister, delegating well and getting results. I would pick out in particular his role as Minister for Merseyside after the Toxteth riots as an outstanding example of executive ministerial leadership, for which he is well remembered on Merseyside. Unfortunately, he had then become far too divisive a figure in opposition to Margaret, and it was not possible to support him at that time.

There was no question that John Major was lucky, after such a brief time in Parliament, to get to Number 10. He was much helped by the backing of Margaret, even if she later did have doubts about her choice and talked about becoming a back-seat driver. Her original preference was for Cecil Parkinson, whom she was about to make Foreign Secretary until the details of his affair became known, but another 'what if' was if the details of John Major's private life had surfaced rather earlier than actually happened.

All of which bears out David Owen's accurate comment about how much luck is involved in winning the prize.

❋ ❋ ❋

The more I recall the extraordinary events of my roller-coaster life, the more I recognise how incredibly lucky I have been to have Jane as my wife. Throughout this book, I've made various references to her, and I make no apology for remembering them again now. I don't know if she would have taken me on if she had known all the myriad activities in which we were to be involved. Being plucked out of Swinging London and set down in unknown territory in Scotland was challenging enough for a new bride to set up home and to have our first child, our daughter Elisa. After two years there, including the near-disaster when I almost drowned a heavily pregnant Jane, we moved down to the West Country and a completely new environment, a second child, our son Rupert, and a new home to create. Six years later came politics and all the pressures of a candidate's and then MP's wife. In those days there was no talk of family-friendly hours, and Parliament regularly sat till 10 or even 11.30pm. She put up with an awful lot during this early time in Parliament, but she really did complain on one occasion. She had come to London to spend some time with me, and the House was debating and voting on the Industrial Relations Bill. This was a highly contentious measure in which, with my industrial background, I was quite involved. The Labour opposition insisted on voting every single amendment that they had tabled, which meant voting every quarter of an hour all through the night on two separate nights, without my being able to go to bed at all, or see anything of Jane.

Bridgwater was some fifty miles from our home near Bath and the constituency stretched a further forty miles to the county boundary with Devon. As the children were then quite young we decided to keep our home but to have a base in Bridgwater for work in the constituency. With a flat in London as well, Jane coped wonderfully with three homes on the go all the time. That was difficult enough but when I later became Secretary of State for Northern Ireland, she faced an even greater challenge. First of all, it involved regular visits to Northern Ireland, getting to know it, hosting dinners and parties, including royal garden parties, at Hillsborough, my official residence, as well as making many good friends in the Province. But, secondly, the whole paraphernalia of security embraced us, to protect us against the serious terrorist threat that existed at that time. A police post was established at our home and was manned round the clock, and for the next twenty years she had to live side-by-side with police. In London we had to move out of our flat and into secure accommodation.

In general, the constant presence of police security caused few problems, and it certainly lowered the crime rate in our village and the surrounding area. There was one unfortunate incident when a small parcel arrived in the post. In checking it, the police found it was ticking, so it was immediately put far away in a field by our house, and subsequently blown up. It had been addressed to our daughter, Elisa, and when the police examined the remains of the parcel, they found a small carriage clock and a birthday card with best wishes from her godfather, my old jazz trumpeting friend, Tom Lane!

Jane did make one particularly valuable contribution over Hillsborough. This fine building with its excellent gardens was much valued by many people in Northern Ireland, but its upkeep and decoration had been left to a government department that was not ideally suited to the task. She discovered that Chequers, the prime ministerial home, had had a similar problem, and a small committee of well-qualified people had been appointed to care for it, and to provide more continuity than a series of prime ministers and their partners could do. She learnt that Chequers had in fact got the idea from the White House where apparently Jackie Kennedy had set up just such a committee. Jane suggested that we should do the same for Hillsborough and we were able to recruit an excellent committee, which soon had a good impact on the furnishing and decoration of the house, and the enhancement of the gardens.

When after four years I became Secretary of State for Defence, while she still had to endure the same tight security, she was able to support me in a whole range of fascinating visits to other countries. This was the time when suddenly the Iron Curtain was disappearing, and I was the first NATO Defence Minister to visit both Hungary and what was still then the Soviet Union. She was a huge asset in helping to establish friendly relations with other Defence Ministers and their wives. Another very special visit was to Washington, where we had a warm welcome from my opposite number, Dick Cheney, and his wife Lynn, and it was all the more enjoyable because her former flatmate, Jenny, had recently married Anthony Acland, our excellent Ambassador.

All this she did while still, in the early years, being an active farmer and shepherd – lambing a hundred ewes; being a superb mother and grandmother, and, despite all the pressures, looking wonderful, too. At my original selection meeting for the Bridgwater constituency there were some twenty candidates being interviewed and the selection committee had a secret code to remember who was who. I later discovered my code name. I conceitedly thought it might be something like 'the best speaker', but in fact it was 'the one with the beautiful wife', and perhaps not all the committee were paying full attention to my words of wisdom! The view of Jane as a beauty was confirmed in a diary piece by the journalist Angela Huth, at the Conservative Conference at Blackpool, 'Mrs Tom King, much the prettiest of the Tory wives'. It is true that she may have been slightly biased, having been at school with Jane, where, in her article, she said Jane aged nine was much better than any of them at teaching rabbits to walk in harness!

All these years later it does indeed confirm how lucky I was that, in spite of all the pressures of such a busy life for us both, under her good hand the family flourished, and two happy marriages and five wonderful grandchildren carry the family on.

ACKNOWLEDGEMENTS

As this memoir has crept into print after all these years, I owe huge thanks to many people, some of whom are recognised in the various chapters. Sadly, there are too many more to mention them all, but I hope they will find some enjoyment in these shared memories of some interesting times.

First must come all our good friends in the constituency that helped me get to Parliament, and then stay there!

In Parliament Susie Ripley coped with my earliest days, Hilda Wood carried on from there, and Jane Monroe achieved the daunting challenge of helping to convert my Dragon dictation into legible sense.

For the more detailed chapters on Northern Ireland and Defence, I was much helped by two excellent former Private Secretaries, David Watkins and Simon Webb.

Ken Baker gave me the helpful introduction to Ian Strathcarron and the Unicorn Press; they in turn provided the admirable Elisabeth Ingles, who has guided me with great diligence and good humour to the finishing post, the whole suitably marshalled by Ryan Gearing.

The other acknowledgement must go to Paul Taylor, who for more than forty years has been the lynchpin of our home and, more than anyone, made possible the nomadic saga that these pages tell.

INDEX